BENDING

"Drawing on his experience as the first executive director of the Human Rights Campaign Fund, Vic Basile has written a valuable addition to the story of one of the most consequential movements in post-World War II America: the fight against homophobia. His readable narrative corrects a glaring omission in one widely accepted version of this record: the central role played by conventional political activity in our success." —Congressman Barney Frank

"This book will become the definitive record of the national movement for civil rights for LGBTQ people that has led to where we are today, not only in our country but in much of the Western world and beyond." —Winston Johnston, LGBTQ activist and confidant of Coretta Scott King

"The clout of the gay community on Capitol Hill and in American politics was transformed because of Vic's leadership. There's no way we would have survived the epidemic without an institution like the Human Rights Campaign Fund. Vic had the political experience, along with the intellect and skill, to know what needed to be done." —Gregory King, former communications director of the Human Rights Campaign

"Vic Basile was exactly the right person for Human Rights Campaign Fund at the time he was there because he was skilled at building the organization. It's very different to build something versus maintain something. Vic had a vision of what gay political involvement could look like—he had an optimism that was infectious, and he was able to engage people and persuade them to do things that that they probably never thought they would do.

Vic was the critical person for that time. He built the organization beyond what I think any of us could have ever guessed or envisioned." —Eric Rosenthal, MD, MPH, first political director for the Human Rights Campaign Fund

"Vic brought a group of people together that really wanted to do something. I can't say how difficult it is to find those people and convince them to do the work. I went on that board because Vic was persistent and eloquent about what was happening in the community. He showed me where I could make a difference and guided us through a vision of where we needed to be going."
—Ellen Malcolm, founder of EMILY'S List

"This necessary book describes the energy and focus of those who engaged in thoughtful, considered hard work to correct unjust wrongs suffered by the gay community. As such, it not only tells a story of what they accomplished but serves as a step-by-step model for others who see the need to change minds, attitudes, and law in order to work toward a society that serves all." —Kathryn Berenson, former TV news producer and journalist

"This is a story we can't have the luxury of forgetting. Those who no longer are here are the ones on whose shoulders this movement rests. Every LGBT American should read this book." —Joe Tom Easley, former president of the HRC Foundation and co-chair of Lambda Legal

BENDING TOWARD JUSTICE

BENDING TOWARD JUSTICE
A Memoir of Two Decades of LGBTQ Leadership and the Founding of the Human Rights Campaign

Vic Basile
with Donna Mosher

Querelle Books
New York, NY

Bending Toward Justice: A Memoir of Two Decades of LGBTQ Leadership and the Founding of the Human Rights Campaign.
Copyright © 2023 by Vic Basile.

All rights reserved, including the right of reproduction in whole or in part in any form.

Cover photograph by Patsy Lynch

Typeset by Raymond Luczak

Published by Querelle Press, LLC
2808 Broadway, #22
New York, NY 10025
www.querellepress.com

979-8-9850341-6-5, print edition
979-8-9850341-7-2, e-book edition

Distributed by Ingram Content Group
To order: Ingramcontent.com

Printed in the United States

First US Edition

To Jim Basile

I have had the honor of working in the administrations of two United States presidents, with union leaders, members of Congress, and political advocacy organizations. But no one has had a greater impact on my character and my career than my dad. No one inspired me to dedicate my life to making a difference for those who are in need or discriminated against like he did.

I credit my commitment to public service—whatever good I have done in the world and any difference I may have made in others' lives—to my dad's influence and inspiration. I dedicate this book with love to Jim Basile.

"The arc of the moral universe is long,
but it bends toward justice."
—*Martin Luther King, Jr.*

"We have been battered and marginalized, drained and neglected. We stood, nearly alone, against the worst medical epidemic of this century. In a stunning display of love and humanity, we built our own systems of care and support.

"Dr. Martin Luther King and his followers built a ministry of affirmation, not anger. Not long before his death, he said, 'The arc of the moral universe is long, but it bends toward justice.' We will let our adversaries take that as a threat, because we take it as a promise—a promise we intend to keep.

"AIDS has taught us all we need to know about profound pain and love and self-help. We have discovered that we have much to teach this nation. My friends, a new day dawns, when we join hands to finally realize the promise of America."

—Elizabeth Birch,
Human Rights Campaign National Dinner, November 8, 1997

Contents

Author's Note i
Foreword iii
Chapter 1: Of Historic Significance 1
Chapter 2: Quiet Activism from a Coat Closet 5
Chapter 3: The So-Called "Moral Majority" 11
Chapter 4: The Sleeping Giant Stirs 18
Chapter 5: "It Is a Phenomenon" 30
Chapter 6: People Were Dying 51
Chapter 7: Vic Basile Takes the Helm 60
Chapter 8: Sadness and Some Silver Linings 67
Chapter 9: Yellow Kitchen Gloves at 1600 Pennsylvania Avenue ... 73
Chapter 10: I Want to Live 81
Chapter 11: Dinners and Drinks 94
Chapter 12: Marvin Collins and the Federal Club 108
Chapter 13: Gays Speak Out 117
Chapter 14: To Know Us Is to Love Us 125
Chapter 15: Enlisting Champions 139
Chapter 16: Dan Bradley Again Aligns the Stars 159
Chapter 17: A Call to Come Out 164
Chapter 18: A Tipping Point 176
Chapter 19: Progress—A Lot of It, And, Still, AIDS 188
Chapter 20: So Much More than a Fund 205
Chapter 21: "In one night, everything seemed to change" 212
Epilogue 217
Acknowledgments 221
About the Author 223
Appendix 225
Index 231

Author's Note

When I came out in 1979, members of our community preferred the terms "gay" and "lesbian" rather than "homosexual." "Homosexual" wasn't overtly derogatory, but too often it was used by those in the majority, avoiding the terms we favored. Even *The New York Times* resisted the word "gay" until 1987, using "homosexual," as you will see in a few places where I include quotes from the newspaper. The acronym "LGBT" wasn't commonly used until the 1990s and LGBTQ came much later. The term "queer," which signifies inclusion today, was used pejoratively until recently—for many of us who are older, it can still sting. And, unfortunately, many activist organizations in the 1980s, including the Human Rights Campaign, were unaware of issues central to the transgender community then.

In this book, I use "LGBTQ" where I share a present-day perspective and "lesbian and gay" where it better reflects the milieu of the times.

The Human Rights Campaign today is the largest LGBTQ political organization in the country with an annual budget of almost seventy million dollars and a staff of more than two hundred. During its lifespan, the organization has had seven leaders. It originally was simply a political action committee with a mission of supporting candidates for Congress who were committed to equal rights for lesbians and gays. Later the mission expanded to include lobbying and field organizing. In 1995, HRC again expanded its mission to include a variety of programs that provide support to the larger LGBTQ community. However, this book is not meant to be a comprehensive history of the Human Rights Campaign up until today, but rather a memoir of my time at the organization as I experienced it first-hand.

As I wrote this book, we lost Joe Tom Easley. We also lost Winston Johnson and Jim Hormel. I hope I have honored them in commemorating their work in the movement, as well as all the others who, as Joe Tom noted, "on whose shoulders this movement rests."

Foreword
by Congressman Barney Frank

Drawing on his experience as the first executive director of the Human Rights Campaign Fund, Vic Basile has written a valuable addition to the story of one of the most consequential movements in post-World War II America: the fight against homophobia. His readable narrative corrects a glaring omission in one widely accepted version of this record: the central role played by conventional political activity in our success.

There are two parts to his presentation. First, he celebrates the pioneering work of one of our movement's unsung heroes. Steve Endean shared with other young men in the seventies both a fascination with political organizing and a talent for it. But unlike many of them, he was gay, and unlike almost all of that minority—including myself—he chose not to conceal his sexuality in the interest of a conventional political career, but to make it the focus of his political work.

Basile documents the importance of Endean's work in the establishment of a gay and lesbian presence in American politics at the national level. Electoral work had begun in New York, Los Angeles, and notably with the example of Harvey Milk in San Francisco. But their work had focused on their local concerns.

The transformative impact of Endean's work at the national level is best described by noting that the most prominent LGBTQ rights organization of the last half century began as the fundraising arm of the Endean-founded Gay Rights National Lobby. The graduation of the Human Rights Campaign Fund into the Human Rights Campaign is a happy example of the child overshadowing the parent.

Part two of Basile's exposition is the record of how that offspring played a leading role in showing that insistence on exercising our rights as citizens could close the gap between democratic ideals and imperfect reality. For a variety of reasons, the undramatic, unglamorous work of helping elect supportive officials and then lobbying them to do the right thing gets much less attention in the chronicles of our movement than marches, demonstrations, picketing, sit-ins, die-ins, and locking onto things.

But these exciting efforts have been much less a factor in our victories than the mundane conventional political activity at which Endean excelled and which Basile took a lead in institutionalizing.

With the imperative of minimizing intra-movement controversy he obeyed in his HRC leadership capacity, Basile marks this more by omission than explicitly. He does not denigrate performative politics, but the greater attention he gives to working to change the political landscape speaks for itself.

This preference for making controversial points in a straightforward, declarative manner applies also to another essential aspect of our fight for fairness. The issue of LGBTQ rights has become overwhelmingly partisan—not by our choice, but because of the rightward movement. He does correctly attribute this to the rightward movement of the Republican Party in general, and on LGBTQ issues especially. He is diplomatically silent on the failed efforts of some in our movement to make unrequited love for the GOP, but he is unequivocal in acknowledging that they have not brought good results.

The fight against bigotry based on sexuality and gender identification has made great progress but is incomplete. This book is a good guide for how best to continue that journey.

Chapter 1:
Of Historic Significance

It was a historic moment for the fifteen hundred elegantly dressed people in Washington, D.C.'s Grand Hyatt ballroom, just blocks from the White House.

"Ladies and gentlemen," announced Elizabeth Birch for the Human Rights Campaign, "it is now my deep honor to present to you the president of the United States."

The crowd rose to its feet in thunderous applause. Never before had a sitting president addressed an LGBTQ audience until that moment on November 8, 1997, when President Bill Clinton was the keynote speaker at the first Human Rights Campaign National Dinner.

Ellen DeGeneres and Anne Heche were in the audience with Betty DeGeneres, civil rights icon Dorothy Height, Wade Henderson who was president of the Leadership Conference on Civil and Human Rights, Ambassador James Hormel, and elected officials, labor and corporate executives, and countless LGBTQ leaders from across the country. C-SPAN cameras ran live coverage, enabling many thousands around the country to share the historic occasion.

Although impossible to document, it seemed as though there were more reporters and cameras in the room than had ever covered an LGBTQ event before.

The historic significance of the president's appearance that night was clear to everyone. No one could deny how far the movement had come since Stonewall. But everyone knew how much further we still had to go and how truly dangerous it could be for us just to live our lives. If those listening to the president that night had been lucky enough to avoid being gay bashed, a quick scan of the local gay papers too often told of others who hadn't been so fortunate. Just eleven months later, there would be no escaping the horrific description of Matthew Shepard tied to a fence and left to die in a Wyoming field.

Every person in that ballroom lived with this reality, but the older attendees knew firsthand how truly terrifying it could be to be gay during the McCarthy era's "lavender scare." They remembered the 1950 congressional hearings on the "Employment of Homosexuals and Other Sex Perverts" that categorized them as national security threats and described them as perverts and child molesters. They remembered when President Dwight Eisenhower issued an executive order that banned "homosexuals" from the military and civilian federal employment. They recalled the horrifying witch hunts that publicly exposed and humiliated many thousands of federal employees. Not only did many lose their careers, but many lost their families as well. Too many committed suicide.

Those older attendees likely saw the horrifying 1967 CBS documentary anchored by revered journalist Mike Wallace called *CBS Reports: The Homosexuals.*

> "Most Americans are repelled by the mere notion of homosexuality," Wallace reported. "The CBS news survey shows that two out of three Americans look upon homosexuals with disgust, discomfort, or fear. One out of ten says hatred. A vast majority believe that homosexuality is an illness; only 10 percent say it is a crime. And yet, and here's the paradox. The majority of Americans favor legal punishment, even for homosexual acts performed in private between consenting adults ...
>
> "The homosexual bitterly aware of his rejection responds by going underground. The average homosexual, if there be such is promiscuous—his sex life, his love life consists of a series of chance encounters at the clubs and bars he inhabits."

The animus and discrimination against gay people were not confined to the federal government. Many state and local governments did the same. Florida was especially aggressive, using its notoriously cruel Johns Committee to expose and drive gay teachers, professors, and students from their jobs and academic pursuits at the state's public universities.

During that time and well beyond it, police routinely raided gay bars, arresting patrons, and releasing their names to the media. During one of these raids at the Stonewall Inn in New York's Greenwich Village in June 1969, the patrons, some who were transgender, fought back in an uprising that would last for three days and mark the beginning of the modern-day LGBTQ rights movement.

That history, filled with richness and brutality, inspired the establishment of what is now the largest and most influential organization supporting LGBTQ rights in the country. I was the first executive director of that organization, taking it in six years from ambitious and almost viable to becoming the twenty-fourth largest of some five thousand political action committees in the United States. I led the organization's massive lobbying effort to pass legislation mandating federal policy for fighting AIDS, we gave to more than a hundred friendly campaigns and committees, and we initiated several high-pressure actions in response to anti-gay legislation. For better or worse, politics in this country responds to money, and politicians learned they needed to respond to our community and our legislative agenda.

HRC's growth and influence have multiplied with each succeeding leader. Today the Human Rights Campaign has some three and a half million members and supporters, some one hundred seventy-five people on staff, a building worth more than $50 million, and a budget of almost $70 million. Seven leaders have propelled the organization to its present stature.

HRC lobbies the federal, state, and municipal governments on LGBTQ legislative and regulatory matters, advocates before the courts, participates in judicial and executive branch nominations process, leads and actively works on national civil rights coalitions, educates the public, participates in elections, and works at the grassroots level on civil rights and political matters of national, state, and municipal importance.

But virtually no one remembers the handful of courageous individuals who started a small organization in 1980 to help bend that moral arc toward justice for their community. A few are still here. Many—too many—died of AIDS. All of them should be remembered, and no one more than Steve Endean, the young man who started what is now called the Human Rights Campaign with little money and a whole lot of grit.

Chapter 2:
Quiet Activism from a Coat Closet

In 1973, Steve Endean walked into Minnesota's capitol building for the opening of the legislative session. Without a shred of lobbying experience, the state's only gay-issues lobbyist harnessed a "ready-fire-aim" attitude and began wandering the halls and offices of the Minnesota State House in St. Paul. Raw and untested, he soon would understand precisely how politics worked, learning on the job over three legislative sessions as he made multiple, unsuccessful attempts to repeal the state's sodomy law and pass an anti-discrimination bill.

When he encountered the ire of individual legislators, he chalked it up to business as usual. But when he met men in the State House he recognized from Sutton Place, the Twin Cities' most popular gay bar, he did not shy away. He refused to out anyone, but he quietly let them know he knew their "secret."

Steve dared to privately confront one legislator he had met at Sutton's before a critical vote. He walked into the man's legislative office and closed the door. He needed just one more vote to get the anti-discrimination bill out of committee, and this man could deliver it.

"I just want to let you know that the gay civil rights bill is going to come up in your subcommittee tomorrow," he said. "I know you're going to do the right thing because I understand you have a special sensitivity to the issue. It may cause you a little grief from constituents, although it isn't going to cost you reelection, and I just wanted to thank you in advance for your support."

Steve's gentle but pointed approach worked.

Steve began his lifelong love affair with politics in the summer of 1970 as a full-time volunteer aide to Wendell Anderson's campaign for Minnesota governor. He was twenty-one and just becoming aware of his sexual orientation. He feared that if his secret were discovered, it would hurt his candidate. Reluctantly, he quietly left a job he loved without ever explaining his reason to the campaign.

Steve Endean was committed to taking the fight for gay rights off the streets. He insisted on propelling the movement out of the 1960s, eschewing "gay liberation" for a more concrete, quantifiable mainstream acceptance of lesbians and gay men. He wanted to get average nongay citizens to think of "gay rights" as nothing more than simple fairness for a segment of American citizens. This, in his opinion, could only come through the pursuit of gay civil rights and the necessary legislation that would deliver them. He believed passionately that mainstream political activism could and would achieve that goal by pursuing pragmatic political achievements—a quiet activism that would be less threatening and thus more acceptable to politicians and the public.

He rejected the loud, sometimes lewd street protests of gay men and lesbians trying to undermine mainstream conventional behavior. Take San Francisco's Gay Freedom Day parades in the 1970s, before they were called Pride parades. Men might sport skimpy leather outfits or drag. Women rode motorcycles topless. "It's a parade of homosexuals," as one announcer described the day. "Men hugging other men...cavorting with little boys... wearing dresses and makeup." Many carried signs demanding "Gay Liberation."

If this description seems exaggerated, consider that to the general public then, homosexuals were considered at worst an abomination in the eyes of God and at best criminals for whom sex was illegal.

A positive image of gay life and love in the mainstream media was inconceivable—and this was before a terrifying, deadly disease exiled us even more. No law protected us if we made love to—or even just loved—another of the same sex, even at home. Same-sex dancing was illegal. Women lost custody of their kids when they came out. Lesbians and gays were discriminated against at work, at school, and at church. Too many of us lived in secret and in shame.

"Our job as gay rights advocates was, and is, to create the right 'we/they' in the public mind," Steve wrote in his memoir. "As long as our opponents incorrectly try to portray our efforts as an attempt by the homosexual perverts to undermine traditional values, we have to continue to help demonstrate to nongay people in the heartland that our struggle is completely consistent with the traditional American value of fairness, as well as the now-well-established tradition of civil rights."

Steve believed that if the gay community were to convince legislators—and eventually average Americans—that lesbians and gays are no different than anyone else and equally entitled to the same fundamental rights, he needed to show up looking like "anyone else." Steve's quiet strategy to winning basic civil rights for the gay community might be considered counter-revolutionary for the times. Indeed, it was. So, he donned a coat and tie to hold respectful, professional, private talks with straight legislators who were in positions to enact laws.

He gathered a small group of like-minded friends and formed the Gay Rights Legislative Committee. It was never much more than a "paper" organization, and there was never any doubt about who was in charge. Proselyting from the coat closet of Sutton's in Minneapolis, where he checked men's coats for a quarter, he collected names, addresses, and small donations for his nascent gay political lobby group.

Steve's political interest quickly turned to two serious and ever-present threats to lesbians and gay men across the state. Like many other states at the time, Minnesota had a law on the books that made oral and anal sex between consenting adults a crime. When it was used—albeit not often—it was mostly to prosecute gay men. The second threat, common to every state at the time, was the lack of a law protecting gays from discrimination in jobs, housing, public accommodations, and public services. The combined effect of the two laws meant that victims could be arrested for having sex on a Saturday night and fired from their jobs when they got to work Monday morning. But employers needed no arrest or any other reason to fire gay or lesbian employees other than the fact that they did not want them on their payrolls. Minnesota had a human rights law; Steve wanted the legislature to add homosexuals to the groups protected in that law from discrimination.

When the liberal Democratic Farm Labor party (the Minnesota affiliate of the National Democratic Committee) in 1972 captured both houses of the Minnesota legislature, Steve knew he had a shot at pro-gay legislation when they convened in 1973. Sadly, the bill proposed failed. But Steve knew the fight would be long, and he was not deterred.

When the Minneapolis residents in 1973 elected a Democratic city council, Steve shepherded an ordinance in 1974 that made Minneapolis the third major American city to provide broad protections on the basis of sexual orientation for employment, housing, and other areas. Mayor Albert J. Hofstede acknowledged Steve's role for the bill's passage: "It never would have happened if it hadn't been for Stephen Endean."

St. Paul quickly followed with a similar ordinance. And in May, New York Congresswoman Bella Abzug introduced the first gay civil rights bill to amend Title VII of the 1964 Civil Rights Act to add sexual orientation to the existing list of protected classes (then defined as sex, race, color, national origin, and religion).

Finally, in early 1975, the future for a gay rights bill looked bright. Steve turned his attention again to the Minnesota House of Representatives. Public opinion polls showed broad support. The Democratic Farm Labor party held more than a hundred of the 134 seats. The senate majority leader supported the bill, as did the major newspapers in Minneapolis and St. Paul, many religious leaders, and various civic leaders.

Sadly, the Minnesota legislature, while liberal, wasn't quite ready to pass a bill they thought would provide protections for the full diversity of the community at the time, especially those who transcended gender expectations. It was 1975, but a national movement was coalescing.

Steve's activism earned him an invitation to Chicago to a small, exclusive conference of lesbian and gay leaders from across the country. David Goodstein, the wealthy owner of *The Advocate*, the country's only national gay newspaper, called the meeting. Attendance was by invitation only. For Steve, this intriguing restriction, plus the fact that the sole agenda item was a discussion about the need for a national political presence in Washington, left little doubt about whether he would accept the invitation. He didn't particularly like Goodstein because he felt he was pretentious and because Goodstein had made it clear that he thought Steve was too unpolished to be a good lobbyist. Nevertheless, Steve knew the man he would later dub the "Wicked Witch of the West" held enormous power because of his money and newspaper, so he was willing to put up with a bit of pompousness.

Goodstein, a former lawyer from New York City, pioneered using computers in financial analysis, co-founding CompuFund, a wildly profitable Wall Street mutual fund. Goodstein moved to San Francisco in 1971 to manage the portfolio of a bank, which fired him when one of the officers discovered he was gay, he claimed.

In addition to Steve and Goodstein, attendees at the Chicago gathering included the Reverend Troy Perry, founder and head of the Metropolitan Community Church (MCC); Jean O'Leary and Bruce Voeller from the National Gay Task Force (now called the National LGBTQ Task Force); Jack Campbell, co-owner of the Club Bath chain of bathhouses; Los Angeles attorney Ray Hartman; veteran gay activist and Democratic Party stalwart Jim Foster; and Oregon activist Jerry Weller. Goodstein hired security guards to keep the meeting private and uninvited guests out.

The result of the conference was a concept for a national gay political lobby called the Gay Rights National Lobby (GRNL), headquartered in Washington, D.C.

Although Steve was intrigued with what had just transpired in Chicago, much demanded his attention back home. He geared up for one more attempt to pass a gay civil rights bill in the 1977 Minnesota legislature. He was energized and more confident than ever that this time, victory was within his grasp. Polls showed 77 percent of citizens and every statewide elected official on record supporting the bill.

Steve was good at counting votes, and his tally among the Minnesota senators showed a very comfortable eleven-vote lead. However, shortly before the vote, a right-wing fundamentalist mobilization generated a barrage of constituent letters and phone calls to legislators from virtually every district in the state opposing his bill.

Steve, the ultimate organizer and vote-counter, never saw it coming. In the end, he watched the bill go down by two votes. The loss was devastating to him, so much so that he gave up on the idea of trying again, He believed that it would be years before a nondiscrimination bill would pass in Minnesota.

Chapter 3:
The So-Called "Moral Majority"

"What these people really want, hidden behind obscure legal phrases, is the legal right to propose to our children that theirs is an acceptable alternate way of life," Anita Bryant said one Sunday in March 1977 outside the church in Miami, Florida, where she taught Sunday school. "Before I yield to this insidious attack on God and his laws, and on parents and their rights to protect their children, I will lead such a crusade to stop it as this country has not seen before."

With that proclamation, Anita Bryant set back the gay rights movement that had been growing in the 1970s. At the same time, she awakened a sleeping giant.

Municipalities around the country had been enacting strong new ordinances protecting lesbians and gay men from discrimination in housing, employment, and public accommodations. Statements in support of gay rights were proposed for inclusion in the 1972 national convention platforms of both the Democratic and Republican parties. Also in 1972, a Democratic Party activist named Jim Foster addressed the Democratic convention in support of gay rights, the first openly gay person to do so.

Communities around the United States were challenging the discrimination against lesbians and gays. In Tucson, Arizona, four white teenagers found guilty of brutally murdering a gay man were given probation. The outraged community pushed for action, and in February 1977, the city council unanimously approved a comprehensive city nondiscrimination ordinance.

A year earlier, in Bryant's hometown of Tulsa, Oklahoma, a small group of gay activists asked the city to consider passing a gay rights bill. City commissioners authorized a study that demonstrated the need for a comprehensive ordinance opposing discrimination based on sexual orientation, which it expected to pass after a period of community education.

Even communities of faith were reconsidering their teachings on homosexuality. Liberal denominations took strong stands supporting gay rights, including the Unitarian Universalists and the United Church of Christ. The Presbyterian and Episcopal Churches began to reflect positions of tolerance. In 1976, the Episcopal Church ordained their first woman priest, who was also a lesbian.

The Metropolitan Community Church (MCC), founded in 1968 by ex-Pentecostal minister Troy Perry to serve gays and lesbians, had grown to more than eighty congregations by 1977, making it the largest national gay organization at the time.

A group of lesbian and gay Jewish congregations organized in the early 1970s, and the liberal Union of America Hebrew Congregations, began accepting the congregations as members.

Just one day before Bryant launched her so-called crusade, fourteen gay leaders from around the country had come together in a somewhat clandestine meeting in the White House with Midge Costanza, an assistant to President Jimmy Carter. Carter, a Southern Baptist moderate, had said he supported proposals to ban discrimination against homosexuals.

The lesbian and gay community finally was getting some traction in their fight for equal protection under the law.

Suddenly, a former beauty queen and a beloved icon of wholesomeness and so-called Christian values who had made a career selling orange juice brought the hard-earned legislative progress for human rights to a screeching halt. Anita Bryant issued a statement demanding to know why the White House was "dignifying these activists for special privilege with a serious discussion on their alleged 'human rights,'" and permitting them to "pressure President Carter into endorsement of a lifestyle that is an abomination under the laws of God and man."

Bryant easily harnessed conservative evangelicals and fundamentalists, including the Southern Baptist Convention, America's largest Protestant denomination, to claim that homosexuality was outside the boundaries of Christian-sanctioned behavior.

Evangelical religious organizations—soon to be called "the religious right"—incited anxieties over the cultural transformation sweeping the nation. And they began to act, calling for a more proactive involvement in political affairs.

While she was selling orange juice in the seventies, Bryant lived in Miami Beach and attended Miami's Northwest Baptist Church. When the Dade County Metro commissioners amended an anti-discrimination ordinance to include gays, she launched what she claimed was a divinely inspired campaign to repeal the ordinance, arguing that gays prey on children to convert them to homosexuality. "Homosexuals cannot reproduce, so they must recruit," she said. Supporters from the Roman Catholic Archdiocese of Miami and the Florida Conservative Union collected sixty-four thousand signatures demanding a county voter referendum to decide if the anti-discrimination ordinance should stand.

Her "Save Our Children" campaign drew 45 percent of Dade County voters to the polls, the highest turnout for a special election in the county's history. Nearly 70 percent of voters rejected the ordinance, expressing concern about homosexual teachers in the classroom.

"I voted against the fags," one voter said.

Leading the effort to fight the repeal was Jack Campbell, an openly gay businessman who owned a national chain of bathhouses, including one in Miami, that he operated legally as private clubs. To Campbell, the fight for gay rights was important to his business, and he supported it with time and money. Campbell also was active in local politics—he even ran for a seat on the Miami City Commission—and had earned a respect that benefited the local gay and lesbian community.

Celebrating the Save Our Children win with triumphant supporters, Bryant thanked the voters of Dade County for the victory for "God and decency."

Her husband, Bob Green, then addressed the media and kissed his wife before the crowd.

"This is what heterosexuals do, fella," he proclaimed.

The repeal of the civil rights ordinance shocked gays around the country and shattered their hopes for equal rights and protection. Indeed, they had good reason to be devastated. The growing acceptance for the lesbian and gay community had been crushed in a setback that would take decades and a deadly epidemic to rectify.

The tide of public opinion turned against gays with the force of a tsunami. The day after the vote in Dade County, several gays and lesbians were fired from their jobs, including a fifteen-year county employee. A month later, 65 percent of Americans said gays should be barred from holding jobs as teachers, and 54 percent thought they should not be allowed to be members of the clergy. Congress and state governments began passing new restrictive proposals. The Tulsa city government abandoned its efforts to pass a city gay rights law.

Invigorated by her success, Anita Bryant went on to mobilize fundamentalists, who successfully worked to repeal similar local ordinances in the liberal communities of Wichita, Kansas; Eugene, Oregon; and St. Paul, Minnesota.

St. Paul voters repealed their nondiscrimination ordinance by a two-to-one vote. Two weeks later, Wichita voters repealed theirs by a vote of five to one. The ordinance in Eugene was repealed by an almost two-to-one margin.

Leading the St. Paul campaign against repeal was a spirited trio of gay activists and Minnesota lobbyists: Steve Endean, Kerry Woodward, and Larry Bye. Another gay political activist and superb fundraiser named Terry Bean ran the Eugene campaign to fight the repeal. They reeled from those losses, taking them seriously and personally, but all would come back together to fight discrimination with a vengeance and on a much larger scale.

The successful repeals of local ordinances in the late seventies marked the beginning of organized opposition to gay rights that infected the nation, planting the seeds of intolerance in school boards, city councils, and local and state ballots across the country and energizing the religious right's bigotry and hate.

The *Washington Post* predicted the Save Our Children campaign had launched a "full-fledged extremist movement... with a particular appeal to bigotry."

The campaign catapulted the nascent crusade of Rev. Jerry Falwell who, just days before the vote, declared to supporters at a rally in Miami: "so-called gay folks would just as soon kill you as look at you."

Two years later, Falwell formed an alliance with a group of political operatives and founded a political action committee of evangelicals, conservative fundamentalist Jews, and conservative Catholics to, as one leader said, "elect like-minded people to public office and restore a sense patriotism and love for the country."

The anti-abortion, anti-Equal Rights Amendment, and anti-gay rights organization would exploit the power of television as Falwell turned his small Virginia church into a Christian communications empire. It harnessed the votes of like-minded church members, called a "moral majority" by one political operative, including many who had considered politics beneath them and weren't even registered to vote.

"We have a threefold primary responsibility," Falwell said. "Number one, get people saved. Number two, get them baptized. Number three, get them registered to vote."

The establishment of Falwell's "Moral Majority" marked the religious right's official entrance into interest-group politics and shaped a movement dedicated to opposing rapidly expanding social trends, including women's reproductive rights and equal rights for women and gays.

More conservative organizations and religious leaders joined in to hammer at the limited progress made by gay rights activists struggling to win legal assurances of their civil rights.

"I'm sick and tired of hearing about all of the radicals and the perverts and the liberals and leftists and the communists coming out of the closet. It's time for God's people to come out of the closet and change America," declared Southern Baptist televangelist Rev. James Robison at a gathering of a group called The Religious Roundtable. California governor Ronald Reagan attended the conference and asked for the group's support.

It worked. Jerry Falwell led the Moral Majority against President Jimmy Carter, who had demonstrated a modicum of support for gay rights but had to pull back in a futile effort to keep right-wing Christians from abandoning him in the 1980 election against Reagan. Perceiving incongruence between Carter's faith and public policy, the religious right abandoned the self-proclaimed born-again Christian for a twice-married, former Hollywood actor who signed a liberal abortion law as California governor.

Gary Jarmin's Christian Voice, Paul Weyrich's Free Congress Foundation, Republican Senator Jesse Helms of North Carolina, Phyllis Schlafly, Tim LaHaye, and others piled on to attack Carter's "lack of moral leadership."

Falwell continued to dehumanize gays and lesbians in a nationwide battle against the gay rights movement.

"The homosexuals are on the march in this country," Falwell wrote in August 1981 to supporters on his direct-mail list. "Please remember, homosexuals do not reproduce! They recruit! And many of them are after my children and your children."

Perhaps the most surreal opposition to gay civil rights legislation came from Terry Dolan, a closeted gay man who called himself a "constitutional libertarian" and founded the National Conservative Political Action Committee, or NCPAC. In the early 1980s, he also helped found a gay political group called Concerned Americans for Individual Rights, but he promised to abandon it if it officially endorsed gay civil rights legislation.

Dolan publicly denied he was gay, a hypocritical position considering he allied himself on issues with people who openly condemned homosexuality and used anti-homosexual rhetoric and a philosophy of hate for fundraising purposes. And despite his denial that his organization never engaged in gay-bashing, NCPAC sent one fundraising letter appearing over the signature of Rep. Phil Crane that included the sentence, "Our nation's moral fiber is being weakened by the growing homosexual movement and the fanatical ERA [Equal Rights Amendment] pushers (many of whom publicly brag they are lesbians)."

The "shriller you are," admitted Dolan in 1982, "the easier it is to raise money."

Dolan died of complications of AIDS at the age of thirty-six.

Sure enough, with little understanding or support, the emerging gay rights movement would make the perfect fodder for the right's fundraising endeavors. After Reagan's election in 1980, the successful movement in gay civil rights was on the verge of defeat.

But Anita Bryant's campaign of hate generated an important unintended consequence. The campaigns to repeal gay civil rights ordinances coalesced a community, awakening that "sleeping giant" and launching a nationwide movement. Many closeted gays and lesbians got involved in politics for the first time if only to boycott Florida orange juice, a boycott that ended Bryant's career pushing the product.

"Our campaign has mobilized gay people not only in Dade County," declared bathhouse chain owner Jack Campbell, "but in Florida, the United States, Europe, and around the world."

He was right. Campbell joined Steve Endean, Kerry Woodward, Larry Bye, Terry Bean, and others to lead efforts to change the discriminatory laws on a larger scale. No longer content to fight for their rights bit by bit, one municipality and state legislature at a time, they reconvened, marshaled resources, and made a few sketchy plans to establish an organization.

Chapter 4:
The Sleeping Giant Stirs

Having suffered heartbreaking losses in three successive legislative sessions and a devastating defeat at the hands of the fundamentalists in St. Paul in the repeal of the city's nondiscrimination ordinance, Steve reluctantly gave up his dream of passing lesbian and gay civil rights protections in Minnesota. Completely demoralized and convinced that it would be years before a statewide nondiscrimination bill could pass the Minnesota legislature, he decided it was time to abandon the effort. He was tired and ready for a change. Kerry Woodward and Larry Bye, equally heartbroken, moved to Oakland and San Francisco, respectively.

Steve licked his wounds from the string of losses and contemplated what his next move might be. A year had passed since the Chicago meeting with David Goodstein and the establishment of a Gay Rights National Lobby. He had heard little more about GRNL, but he thought if an opportunity existed to get it started, he might be up for a move to Washington, D.C.

Steve called Los Angeles attorney Ray Hartman, co-chair of GRNL's executive committee, to learn the status of the organization. When Hartman and board members Frank Kameny and Paul Kuntzler learned of Steve's interest, they convinced him to make the move, promising that he could function as a strong executive director with the freedom and authority he needed to build an influential national lobby. So, Steve packed up and headed to D.C. to become the executive director of the Gay Rights National Lobby. Little did he know before he left that Goodstein had abandoned the organization he initiated, leaving it with no financial base, no staff, most of the board seats vacant, and no presence on Capitol Hill.

Endean arrived in Washington to find the office telephone disconnected, months' worth of unopened mail piled on a desk, a nine-thousand-dollar tax debt, and nine dollars in the bank. But he had been promised twenty-five thousand dollars from a major Minnesota donor named Tom Weiser to use for his salary and organization expenses to help him get off the ground—or so he thought. In fact, Weiser reneged on all but a few thousand dollars.

So, Steve got to work to make himself and his cause known in the most political city in the world. The pale thirty-year-old, dressed in the lobbyist's uniform of a blue blazer, Brooks Brothers button-down shirt, and striped tie, set out to knock on the office doors of United States members of Congress. While there had been a gay rights movement in the country for years, Steve represented the first organization to attempt to earn gay rights through the established political process.

Rejecting the decades-long campaign for "gay liberation" in favor of "gay civil rights," he took the battle out of the streets, registered himself as a lobbyist, and marched into the marble halls of the United States Capitol in Washington D.C.

In 1978, when Steve Endean assumed leadership of the Gay Rights National Lobby (to become known as GRNL and pronounced as it sounds: *grr-null*), he found himself with no money or staff and facing a phalanx of opposition from the religious right. However, the defeats he experienced in Minnesota were not without benefit. Those battles may have left him scarred, but they had taught him much about politics, lobbying, and law-making, skills that would serve him well in his new and far more challenging role at GRNL.

Those of us who knew Steve described him as a visionary, a leader, a pragmatist, and an incrementalist. To be sure, he was all of these and more: smart, highly focused, goal oriented. His core conviction was that equality would be won only by working within the existing political structure. One need look no further than the original title of his memoir—*Into the Mainstream*—to understand that this conviction guided everything he did.

Steve implemented a strategy of pragmatic politics, and it would prove to be his legacy. He quietly committed GRNL, and later the Human Rights Campaign Fund (HRCF), to activities that candidates and legislators found non-threatening, could understand, learn from, and accept. It was a quiet activism that contrasted to that of the more vocal, even angry, groups that would dominate the news in the late 1980s. Steve's tactics included educating legislators and their staffs one-on-one, building coalitions, developing grassroots political pressure from our community, and establishing political clout that would enable him raise money and mobilize volunteers. In doing so, he initiated the three components that would enable us to influence Congress: lobbying, the political contributions, and constituent mobilization.

Pragmatic politics is a methodical practice that demands patience and a willingness to accept incremental victories, something most other organizations couldn't tolerate. Just as Steve encountered dissention in Minnesota from activists who wanted more than legislators were willing to give at the time, GRNL faced similar dissention.

Bruce Voeller, at Goodstein's initial GRNL planning meeting, promised the National Gay Task Force would relinquish any plans to lobby Congress. Steve's grace period didn't last long with Lucia Valeska, who led NGTF with a staff of eight and an annual budget of $350,000. She apparently considered GRNL a rival, publicly declaring it "a one-person operation with a board of directors that hasn't met for two years and has an annual budget of $50,000."

Their feud continued after Steve asked the moderate California Republican Congressman Pete McCloskey to introduce legislation to end the military's ban on homosexuals—in 1981. When Valeska learned of Steve's request, she asked McCloskey to abandon the legislation, claiming that the issue would anger the religious right. Now NGTF was lobbying against GRNL. It wouldn't be the last time organizations working for LGBTQ rights would find themselves at odds with each other. And it would be three decades before the United States military would allow us to serve openly.

Steve also confronted explicit prejudice from legislators who, by their liberal positions, should have lent at least some pretense of support for equal rights for everyone. He knew the challenge would be great and that a federal gay and lesbian civil rights bill could take a decade.

"I don't want people joining GRNL thinking we can get legislation passed in two, three, or four years," Endean said in an interview. "We can't. It's going to be a long, hard fight. I'm prepared to be here for as long as it takes."

No one was better cut out to carry the gay rights cause to Capitol Hill than Steve, who had been likened to a terrier for his dogged persistence. Nevertheless, I doubt he suspected the United States would take four decades to assure the LGBTQ community basic human rights. Only in June 2020 would those rights be guaranteed, when the U.S. Supreme Court ruled that the 1964 Civil Rights Act protects gay, lesbian, and transgender employees from job discrimination based on sexual orientation or gender identity.

Steve's chief goal at the time was to pass what became commonly known as the Gay Rights Bill introduced by Congresswoman Abzug. His strategy was to add cosponsors to the House bill and to eventually find at least one senator willing to introduce it in the upper chamber. When he had amassed enough cosponsors, the bills could move to hearings and eventually to votes in their respective chambers. It is the same mechanism that guides legislation to passage. But most other bills do not have as their sole purpose to provide equal rights to a very unpopular group, one which at the time was viewed as immoral, perverted, and sick by a large majority of the public.

Steve spent many hours of many days trudging up and down the ornate corridors of the imposing House and Senate office buildings, attempting to meet with members of Congress or at least with one of their staff members. Much to his disappointment, he was turned away from most offices, although he did succeed in meeting with some members or senior staff aides, and some of them actually signed on as cosponsors. The issue of gay rights was often uncomfortable, and the conversations were never easy. But the political process wasn't so polarized as it is today. Those congressional staff members who met with Steve and, later, with Human Rights Campaign Fund staff, would entertain a dialogue, at the very least.

Soon he realized that he was getting cosponsors only from the two coasts where there was a substantial recognized gay population. Other members would declare flatly, "I don't have any gay people in my district."

He worked to educate the legislators—or most likely their

staff—about the need for civil rights legislation. This was the first time many met with a gay man. In some cases, the most realistic goal was to secure a commitment that the congressperson would oppose antigay bills and amendments. That, Steve figured, was a victory.

Polls—and recent history—proved that most Americans did not object to civil rights for lesbians and gays. But Steve needed to prove to congressmen (and they were, for the most part then, men) that voters would not object to their support for gay rights. Fortunately, he met Joe Cantor, the specialist in politics and campaign financing with the Congressional Research Service at the Library of Congress.

"One night in 1979, I showed up to volunteer at Gay Rights National Lobby," Joe told me. "Steve was very intrigued that I worked for the Congressional Research Service and I that I knew something about money and politics. As we began to talk, I grew extraordinarily impressed with his down-to-earth pragmatism. His goal was to get us to be part of the political mainstream. "We're never going to be able to play in the big leagues," Steve told me, "unless we start getting more serious about being in American politics." That really impressed me about him.

"He told me he had a number of projects he needed my help on," Joe said. "One was to make the argument to politicians that supporting gay rights would not spell political suicide for them; that it was safer to be on the right side of this issue than a lot of politicians realized. At that time, it was still considered brave to do so. I took that project on. I'd say I put in three or four months of really hard work. I worked on it at the office, but on my lunchtime and after hours."

Joe researched news articles from around the country and interviewed several dozen gay activists. He found that politicians were discovering that support for lesbian and gay issues didn't hurt their election chances, and in some cases, it benefited them, depending on their districts. The resulting seventy-page study, titled "Does Support for Gay Rights Spell Political Suicide?" examined various city council, mayoral, state legislative, and congressional candidates who had supported lesbian and gay civil rights.

The report highlighted two 1976 congressional races where

opponents attacked the incumbent's sponsorship of the federal gay rights bill. In both cases, the sponsors—Reps. Gerry Studds of Massachusetts and Les AuCoin of Oregon—won handily. The evidence was even stronger at the local level, suggesting that support for gay rights could help candidates, particularly in races in San Francisco, Los Angeles, Houston, and Washington, D.C.

Joe Cantor's name was never attached to the report. He worked on his own time—it would have been inappropriate for him to have created the report as an employee of the Library of Congress.

Now Steve was finally getting meetings with some members of Congress or their senior staff. Some were agreeing to cosponsor or promised that they would, at the very least, vote for the bill. A few others told him privately that they were with him, but they were afraid to cosponsor—if they were attacked in the next election, who would have their backs?

As much as he hated to admit it, Steve realized these otherwise supportive members saw little or no visible gay constituency in their districts and no source of campaign volunteers or contributions.

Those two realities—the limiting power of the closet and the inability to support congressional friends at election time—frustrated him terribly. Nothing he could do or say would bring the people he needed out of the closet, at least not in the numbers necessary to change skittish congress members' minds. Missing from his arsenal were the two essential weapons successful lobbyists require: constituent pressure and money for campaign contributions. Steve had neither.

The gay community hadn't spoken as loudly as their opponents. They had been outorganized and outworked, particularly by the newly activated religious right. It was time for the community to get organized, get busy, get vocal, and be heard.

"When I arrived," Steve wrote in his memoir, "I discovered I had a more fundamental organizing task: to demonstrate to the community why they should care about national legislative efforts and a national bill that would clearly take a very long time to pass."

First, he assembled a board of directors with people he trusted. More than half were women. Steve knew the support of the lesbian community was critical to his efforts, and he made it a point to include them as much as possible.

Next, he took five hundred dollars from the meager sum in the GRNL bank account to buy a pass that allowed him to travel anywhere Eastern Airlines flew in a month. He visited lesbian and gay activists in fifteen cities over twenty-one days, drumming up enthusiasm for the nascent national gay lobby.

The 1979 March on Washington, drawing more than 120,000 people, proved the value of a national lobbying effort. Attendees participating in the Constituent Lobby Day visited fifty senators and one hundred fifty congressional offices to generate interest in gay civil rights.

That was the role of GRNL—to muster a community of lesbians and gays into a grassroots movement to speak out and demand the rights accorded to every other American. It became Steve's top priority.

Soon Steve realized he could not build a national grassroots movement alone. When a spate of one-hundred-hour weeks landed him in bed, he realized—for the time being—that he needed to hire help. He and the board raised substantial financial commitments to hire Kerry Woodward—and eventually three more women—to organize the gay-friendly West Coast states. Ultimately, the field team recruited a hundred and fifty volunteer field associates in forty states to develop local organizations to support GRNL.

It was 1980, and Steve was building two of the three essential components of a national political organization: lobbying and grassroots constituent influence. Now it was time for him to figure out how to grease Congressional palms with silver for their campaigns.

With the rise of the Moral Majority, by 1980, money became the common currency of legislative persuasion in Washington. The religious right was making its influence felt as it financed national political campaigns. The National Conservative Political Action Committee (NCPAC) and PACs connected to Jerry Falwell's Moral Majority and the Christian Voice were raising millions of dollars to defeat candidates who did not support their narrow view of morality.

After two years of walking the halls of the Capitol himself and developing the foundation of a solid grassroots organization with the help of his field directors, Steve realized he needed to tackle the third phase—making financial contributions to congressional campaigns.

The Federal Election Campaign Act of 1971 regulated the raising and spending of money in U.S. federal elections. It prohibited GRNL, registered as a lobbying organization, from contributing money to political campaigns. He needed a political action committee—the legal mechanism for which an organization can give money to candidates.

"When somebody agrees to cosponsor your bill," Steve said, "you can't let him or her sit out on a limb and let the Moral Majority cut it off. If they survive the fall, they are not going to support you again, and if they don't survive, not only have you lost a supporter, but you have also demonstrated you don't back up your people."

Steve turned to his Minnesota friend and founding GRNL board member Larry Bye, now a California political consultant, who had worked with him to fight the repeal of the anti-discrimination ordinances in Minnesota. Bye suggested a "prestigious advisory board composed of distinguished supporters of gay rights, all of whom would serve in a letterhead capacity only." And that was exactly what Steve proceeded to assemble.

Steve invited national leaders and organization heads to support GRNL by serving, literally, in name only. He asked them to join a "letterhead" advisory board. Initial members included Abzug, Joseph Rauh of the U.S. Conference on Civil Rights (now the Leadership Conference on Civil and Human Rights), authors Michael Harrington and Gloria Steinem, and folk singer Joan Baez. The mayors of San Francisco, Minneapolis, and Washington, D.C., agreed to serve on the committee, too. Eventually, the list grew so long it did not fit on the stationery.

Bye drew up a plan for a lesbian and gay political action committee, including a forecast of its fundraising potential from direct mail, major donors, and the now-iconic black-tie dinners. He presented it in July 1980 at a GRNL board meeting, held at the Holiday Inn on Thomas Circle in Washington, D.C.

"By rewarding our friends, 'punishing' our enemies, and

'tempting' those on the fence," Bye said, "we have learned how to impress nongay power brokers with our sophistication, seriousness of purpose, and sincerity. What we need to do is transfer some of the lessons we have learned at the state and local level to the federal level."

The GRNL board approved the concept of a new political action committee. Kerry Woodward and Jerry Berg agreed to co-chair the board. Steve was named treasurer of the PAC, while also serving as executive director of the Gay Rights National Lobby.

Steve needed seed money to get the organization off the ground. Three independent gay men contributed the legal limit of five thousand dollars each to the PAC—a significant and generous amount of money in 1980.

Jim Hormel from Minnesota was heir to the Hormel meat-packing empire. He had married, graduated from law school, had children, and served as dean of students at the University of Chicago Law School before coming out in the late 1960s and moving to San Francisco.

Dallas Coors, from the notably conservative Colorado beer family, lived in Washington, D.C. A banker, Coors was the lone Republican in the group of early donors and the original HRCF board of directors.

The third benefactor was David Goodstein of *The Advocate*, who, of course, had proposed the initial idea for the Gay Rights National Lobby.

With a dedicated board of directors and some money in the bank, Steve Endean registered the Human Rights Campaign Fund with the Federal Election Commission. The PAC was independent of GRNL so it could expand its fundraising scope. (A connected political action committee is restricted by law to raising money only from the organization's members.)

Purposely, "lesbian and gay" did not appear in the name—a topic of much deliberation. Steve believed it would allow him to run GRNL and the new PAC without any confusion about the distinct objectives. He also hoped that omitting the descriptor would overcome any candidates' reluctance to receive campaign money from the PAC without fear of judgment. Likewise, wealthy gay donors might feel more comfortable contributing to the PAC, which was required by law to report them on FEC documents.

To this day, critics still complain about the name. I believe Steve's decision not to use "lesbian and gay" in the name but to wrap the organization in the core belief Americans have in the importance of our "rights" as citizens was a stroke of genius. It wasn't uncommon in the eighties for candidates and even safe incumbents to refuse the money or return it after initially accepting it. Even the legendary progressive Barbara Mikulski of Maryland refused to accept HRCF's money when she first ran for the Senate in 1986. She was in a safe congressional seat and had been a cosponsor of the gay rights legislation Steve fought so hard for. And even though she was heavily favored in her Senate race, she was too afraid to take money from a lesbian and gay PAC. On election day, she vanquished the opponent who had "gay-baited" her by more than twenty points.

Steve and a friend brainstormed names for the PAC. They wanted to emphasize to legislators and their constituents that "gay and lesbian rights" wasn't some bizarre idea but a simple extension of the existing principles of civil and human rights and fundamental fairness. They focused on "justice," "civil rights," "human dignity," "equality," and "fairness" before settling on "human rights." Steve named the new political action committee the Human Rights Campaign Fund.

Now he needed some money to put behind his message.

Dallas Coors
By Vic Basile

Dallas Coors was a man with whom, on so many levels, I had so little in common. He was born to wealth; I was not. He was an ardent Republican; I am just as ardently a Democrat. He was the grandson of a great corporate baron; I once was a labor organizer. His name was Coors; I used to boycott his beer. Yet, despite all those differences, we connected from the moment we met in 1983. That moment is one I always will treasure.

I had just started as the first executive director of HRCF, and already there was a controversy. My labor background had become fodder for some who thought a more conservative person—a Republican, even—would have been a better choice to head the bipartisan PAC. Because Dallas was the lone Republican on the board, they appealed to him to intervene. He asked to sit down with me, and we talked for a bit. It was a casual conversation. I think he just wanted to get to know me, to see for himself how radical I was. Fortunately for me, he apparently liked what he saw. From that moment on, I had his unwavering support and, I'd like to believe, his lasting friendship.

Dallas Coors chaired the board finance committee, and that put us in regular contact. Occasionally we would get together for lunch, and he would use the opportunity to vent about whatever might have been troubling him about the movement, which often was plenty. He vented; I listened. In addition to being on my board and a generous donor, Dallas was extremely smart and extraordinarily committed to full civil rights for gays and lesbians. That commitment and his savvy, pragmatic approach to politics allowed him to rise above partisanship.

No doubt, his pragmatism came from his pedigree and his profession. He began his career as a Foreign Service officer in the 1940s in India. He later served in Saigon and wrote a study of the opium trade in Indochina. Dallas's grandfather was Adolph Coors, founder of the Coors brewery corporation, and of course, Dallas benefited from all that such a lineage would bestow on him. His generosity of time and money extended not only to the Human Rights Campaign Fund. He was a member of the Washington Opera Society, the Washington Performing Arts Society, the University Club, the F Street Club, the Annapolis Yacht Club, and the board of the Newport Music Festival.

When Dallas served on our board, HRCF was purely a political action committee that gave most of its money to liberal Democrats. But that fact never seemed to distress Dallas. What mattered was that we were supporting candidates who were good for gays and lesbians, no matter the party. He made generous financial contributions without being asked and wanting no recognition. It was how he operated, and unfortunately, why he never received his just due in the gay and lesbian community.

Dallas never retired from his activism. He could always be counted on to get involved, not only with his checkbook but with his presence as well. There was hardly an event in the community where I did not see him – frequently standing by himself, almost inconspicuous to the crowd around him.

So many gay people only think of a big bad beer company when they hear the name Coors. If only they could have known Dallas. If only they were aware of the enormous good done by this gentle man. But that was Dallas's style; that is what made him such an endearing, quiet champion.

Chapter 5:
"It Is a Phenomenon"

"Since I came out of the closet and resigned my position in Washington a few months ago, I spent the summer traveling north, east, south, and west on behalf of the Human Rights Campaign Fund and the Gay Rights National Lobby," Dan Bradley told Ted Koppel in a *Nightline* interview from the Waldorf Astoria in New York City.

"Gay and lesbian voters are participating in the political process more than they have ever done in the past. They have not come out of the closet publicly. But we are giving them a vehicle; we are giving them an opportunity to know that nationally, gay and lesbian people are organizing and participating in the political process. Those persons are going to the polls, and they're voting for the candidates that we can tell them support gay and lesbian rights. It is a phenomenon."

The movement's most significant event to date prompted the *Nightline* program on ABC on September 29, 1982. That night, former Vice President Walter Mondale gave the keynote speech at New York City's first HRCF black-tie dinner. Publicly, Mondale's spokesperson said Mondale's participation wasn't a political move, but it reflected his support for human rights and equal justice. However, privately, Mondale's aides cited the gay community's growing influence in electoral politics as an important new fundraising constituency.

"There was a dinner tonight—a big one—at the Waldorf Astoria in New York," declared Koppel as he opened the show, "at which awards were presented for outstanding contributions to advancing the cause of gay and lesbian human rights. Leading the list of those on the honorary dinner committee: Senator Alan Cranston of California, Senator Edward Kennedy of Massachusetts, Senator Daniel Moynihan of New York, Senator Paul Tsongas of Massachusetts, Senator Lowell Weicker of Connecticut. The keynote speaker at tonight's dinner was former Vice President of the United States, Walter Mondale.

"Times quite clearly have changed. The political clout of the gay community is now such that the advantages for a liberal Democrat at least of being associated in however limited a fashion with a gay political event—those advantages are apparently perceived as outweighing the possible fallout. Indeed... gay power is a political reality."

For the first two years of the Reagan administration, Steve Endean and his small band of field directors at GRNL spent much of their time attempting to bat down one piece of anti-gay legislation after another.

Senator Paul Tsongas of Massachusetts had introduced an anti-discrimination bill. Steve had been hopeful of enlisting co-sponsors to rapidly move that bill through the Senate while signing on representatives to the Abzug bill in the House. But the 1980 election saw the defeat of powerful and influential Democrats whom Steve had counted on, including George McGovern of South Dakota, Birch Bayh of Indiana, Frank Church of Idaho, and Warren Magnuson of Washington. The Republicans had won back control of the United States Senate for the first time in twenty-six years, thanks to right-wing organizations like the National Conservative Political Action Committee run by the gay, closeted Terry Dolan, and—of course—Jerry Falwell's Moral Majority. Steve knew GRNL and HRCF needed to elect more friendly candidates to both houses of Congress if ever he might fulfill his strategy to pass a gay civil rights bill.

He was determined to make 1982 a landmark year, and he could see his chance. A recession was dampening voter enthusiasm for President Reagan and setting up Democratic candidates for success.

Invigorated by the momentum of Congressman Jim Weaver's

win against a gay-baiting opponent in Oregon, Steve rolled up his sleeves, eager to position HRCF to bring considerable influence to the 1982 campaign season. The PAC's momentum accelerated with its first board meeting in October 1981, followed by a fundraiser in early 1982 hosted by wealthy benefactor Bob Alfandre at his elegant Kalorama Circle home in Washington.

A "who's who" of Washington's gay community gathered—perhaps for the first time—to explore how to harness the political process and bring the gay movement into the mainstream. The significance of that gathering rested as much on who showed up as the amount of money raised. Washington is the nation's capital—many of the attendees were recognized names still in the closet. *The Advocate* publisher David Goodstein and activist Jim Foster came from California to support Steve Endean's vision: to build a national organization that just might be able to deliver the political clout to confront the increasing anti-gay animosity of right-wing ideologues like North Carolina Senator Jesse Helms and Jerry Falwell's emerging religious right.

The challenge facing HRCF's first couple of years—before AIDS began raging through the community—was that so many people were deeply closeted. How could the PAC raise money from people who feared their identities would be revealed on Federal Election Commission reports?

The pressing question became apparent: how could the budding gay political movement encourage them to come out? This was a struggle HRCF would confront for the next decade.

The Municipal Elections Committee of Los Angeles, the first lesbian and gay PAC, was hosting large black-tie fundraising dinners to great success. But when the group attending the Alfandre event discussed the idea of holding a similar event, many wondered if members of the D.C. gay community in 1982 would show up at some fancy hotel in tuxedos with their boyfriends. So, a small committee led by Joe Cantor and art dealer Ted Cooper began asking people to quietly host private parties, inviting their network of friends. The goal was to organize fifty dinners that might raise a thousand dollars each, generating some fifty thousand dollars for HRCF. That was a magnificent sum of money then for a start-up organization that too many people would consider a pariah of the times.

Gay communities in other cities proved less shy than those in Washington. HRCF hired Jim Foster that year to head up major-donor fundraising and organize dinners around the country—including Dallas, Philadelphia, Boston, and, of course, New York.

Jim was a gay rights pioneer from San Francisco who had been discharged from the Army because of his sexual orientation and was now a Democratic political consultant. He had worked in the presidential campaigns of George McGovern and Jimmy Carter and the San Francisco mayoral campaigns of George Moscone, Dianne Feinstein, and Richard Hongisto. Ten years earlier, at five in the morning, he gave his historic speech on gay rights at the Democratic National Convention. Perhaps his most clever assessment of the gay community—and the reason for his great success as an activist—he shared with David Goodstein: "David, never forget one thing: What this movement is about is fucking."

Jim was charming and charismatic. He was a brilliant political strategist and one of the most successful fundraisers HRCF had at the time. Foster convinced Mike Farrell, known and beloved as B.J. Hunnicut on the television series *M*A*S*H*, to produce a video endorsing the Human Rights Campaign Fund for the first black-tie dinner in New York City in 1982.

But Jim was also overbearing and prickly, which tended too often to foster dissension among his ranks. That contentiousness came to a head shortly before the New York dinner, when the volunteer organizers threatened to leave if Jim stayed on. The timing couldn't have been worse—in the weeks leading up to any event, details are finalized, and the bulk of ticket sales are made. Steve couldn't afford to lose his team, so he and HRCF co-chair Jerry Berg arranged to have Jim leave the final weeks of work to the committee.

Steve wasn't about to jeopardize the success of the HRCF event in New York. It took a team to get former Vice President Walter Mondale to commit to being the keynote speaker. Several preliminary meetings with Mondale's "people" laid a foundation to one with the vice president and HRCF's "A" team: Steve Endean, Kerry Woodward, Jim Hormel, and former Legal Services president Dan Bradley, the highest-ranking government official in history (at the time) to declare his homosexuality publicly.

More than six hundred people attended the black-tie dinner.

New York media expert Ethan Geto convinced reporters that the number of attendees topped a thousand. Ethan had been an HRCF board member, but he stepped down to promote the dinner.

"Ethan could sell screen doors to submarine captains," Steve said of his PR guy.

The eyes of the nation turned to the emerging electoral influence of the lesbian and gay community, thanks to coverage by *The New York Times*, *The Washington Post*, and, of course, the *Nightline* program.

The greatest triumph the dinner brought our community was in the sheer joy folks experienced, starting with their arrival at the celebrated Waldorf Astoria hotel. Dinner in the Grand Ballroom of the Waldorf, world-renowned for its iconic Palm Court, lent a legitimacy that lesbians and gays hadn't experienced before.

Vivian Shapiro, a native New Yorker and eventual HRCF board co-chair, described her experience as transformative for someone who had been too often the brunt of derision and disrespect.

It was raining heavily as Vivian and her partner at the time approached the Waldorf. Their cab turned into the drive, and Vivian looked out the window to see a crowd of drenched protestors standing on the sidewalk holding placards. She turned to her partner and said, "Wow. Protestors. Something important must be going on at the Waldorf tonight."

She had no idea they were protesting her.

"It was the first time that I was inside," Vivian said, "and those schmucks were out there in the rain."

That black-tie dinner—and the others held around the country that year—gave the gay community ground-breaking legitimacy. Big New York unions had bought tables. Bill Lucy, the secretary-treasurer of the American Federation of State, County and Municipal Employees (AFSCME) International union, flew up from Washington for it. For the first time, straight politicians, corporate leaders, and heads of organizations saw hundreds of gay men and lesbians gathered in one of New York City's finest hotels, dressed elegantly and honored by those who had reached the pinnacle of respect in their fields. Essentially, they saw that night in the Waldorf Astoria's Grand Ballroom a group of people eminently likable and no less respectable than themselves.

Those straight community leaders gained newfound regard

for the lesbian and gay community, and we stood a little taller, too. The price of admission of a hundred-and-fifty bucks—a hefty investment for 1982—was worth it.

In addition to raising money through private donor requests and small events, HRCF attempted to develop a direct mail program to raise smaller donations from individuals around the country. The problem was, of course, identifying donors. Most potential givers were not out of the closet, so lists were hard to come by. No one had ever sent a letter nationwide to people who might be able to give to support gay rights.

David Goodstein refused to let go of the goldmine of a mailing list for *The Advocate*. Since so few prospects were out, Steve and his small fundraising team turned to porn lists, names gathered from the campaigns, and lists from straight progressive organizations to fight the repeal of the municipal civil rights ordinances and other anti-gay campaigns around the country. They combed voter lists for male-only households and households that had different surnames in certain neighborhoods. It was a tedious effort turned phenomenal when Alan Baron offered to help.

Alan Baron was a political savant—one of the most respected political minds in Washington, D.C., in the 1980s. While he never publicly came out, his close friends knew he was gay, and many of his colleagues knew it, too—and they didn't care. Alan was a Democrat, but he had friends on both sides of the aisle. They loved him for his astute understanding of politics, his encyclopedic memory of U.S. political campaigns, and his uncanny ability to predict future election results from that knowledge.

Alan Baron wrote "The Baron Report," a weekly political newsletter of polling information and anecdotal reports on the national campaigns. He also wrote an enormously successful direct mail appeal for HRCF that bears one of the more curious, circuitous, improbable stories in the annals of political fundraising.

Knowing Baron's extraordinarily successful track record in writing lucrative fundraising letters for Democrats, Steve asked Baron if he would craft one for the fledging gay political action committee. He had no money to offer Baron. Baron, intrigued by the possibility, agreed to write the letter anonymously—and he even agreed to raise the money to fund printing and postage.

Who knows why? Steve, of course, was nothing if not persuasive. And it was perhaps the first time anyone had invited Baron to become involved in gay rights.

"I'm writing to seek your help for PRIVACY RIGHTS '82, a new political action project designed to protect your rights from invasion by the self-righteous moralists," Baron wrote, mentioning "the threat to our personal rights posed by the Religious New Right and the moral majoritarians.

"Not since the blacklisting in the entertainment industry in the 1950s has there been as potent a threat to individual rights as exists in America today."

The five-page letter did not mention the word *homosexual* until the second page. It didn't reveal the beneficiary organization, Human Rights Campaign Fund, until the fourth.

"Our enemies—I don't think enemy is too strong a word for people who advocate the death penalty for homosexuals—have powers their predecessors could not imagine. Today's New Right leaders reach tens of millions of people via electronic broadcasting ... raise hundreds of millions of dollars through computerized fundraising techniques ... and recruit high-caliber, highly paid pollsters, and public relations experts to shape their messages and images."

The letter told the story of Congressman Jim Weaver's recent victory with the help of HRCF and the gay community in Oregon.

"If anybody should have gone down to defeat with Jimmy Carter in 1980, it was Weaver. But Weaver didn't lose."

The letter then noted that the reader could help HRCF support gay-friendly candidates around the country like it did Jim Weaver. It added the crucial message that HRCF and GRNL had been trying to convey since Joe Cantor wrote his report. Politicians could support gay rights if they knew that meaningful support existed for them, too.

"To build an effective political action committee," Baron wrote, "we need to raise $500,000 during the next twelve months.

"I hope you will join me—and such other Americans as Joel Wachs, the Republican President of the Los Angeles City Council; Donald Fraser, the Democratic Mayor of Minneapolis; Otis Charles, the Episcopal Bishop of Utah; Dr. John Spiegel, the former President of the American Psychiatric Association; Julian

Bond, the Georgia State Senator and black leader; and Gloria Steinem, the Publisher of *Ms.* and leading feminist—in our effort to stop the threat to our individual rights posed by the militant moralists," the letter concluded.

"The stakes are simply too high for all of us—indeed for any of us—to delay. Please take this courageous step and let me hear from you today.

"Sincerely yours,"

And at that point, the copy was blank.

Who could sign the letter? Who was well-known, perhaps even famous, to appeal to lesbian and gay contributors but non-threatening to liberal heterosexuals who might respond? What a statement of the times it was that Baron and Endean could not come up with a single name of someone who met those parameters and admitted to being gay.

One night, a group of his young protégés gathered at Baron's kitchen table to toss about possible names. Gregory King suggested Gore Vidal. Great choice, everyone agreed. He was well known, and everyone assumed he was gay. But no one knew Vidal to ask him. Sexual orientation was a delicate subject in 1981; a cold call was totally inappropriate.

Sean Strub was one of the clique of smart, young gay men who attended Baron's salons, a young political junkie whose first job on Capitol Hill was as an elevator operator in one of the Senate office buildings. Strub also frequented parties at Bob Alfandre's home, where HRCF had gathered its initial funding. A most fortuitous encounter had taken place the evening Sean met Tennessee Williams, described to him that night as "the greatest writer in the English language" and "world-famous and gay."

Just the signatory Baron was looking for.

And Strub knew Williams. He knew him well. Strub had Williams's address in Key West and had visited him there in the past.

Baron and Steve pressed Strub to persuade Williams to sign the letter. They offered to pay for his plane ticket to Key West. Williams invited Strub to meet him in New York instead, at the Elysée Hotel.

Strub arrived at two in the afternoon on an early summer day in 1981 with Baron's letter in his pocket. Williams met him at the door in his pajamas, holding a glass of wine. Inviting him in, the playwright reviewed the letter while Strub told Williams about Steve Endean and the Human Rights Campaign Fund. He told Williams how important his signature might be and that this seeming small errand to make the request was perhaps the most important thing Strub had ever done in his life.

Williams set aside the letter and proceeded to discuss his new project. Nothing more was said of the letter. Strub could not find another way to approach the ask. When a couple of hours passed, reluctantly, Strub headed to the door, prepared to take his leave—mission unaccomplished.

That's when Tennessee Williams called out to him.

"Don't you want your signature?"

Williams picked the paper up and scribbled his name at the bottom of the letter, mumbling that his lawyers would not be pleased.

They weren't, and they promptly called Baron to tell him that he was not authorized to use the signature. Being quick on his feet, Baron said the letter had already gone out, even though it had not. When it was mailed, the return was astronomical, and it continued to produce extraordinary results well beyond the typical lifespan of a direct mail prospecting letter.

Thanks to a persuasive major donor campaign, four enormously successful black-tie dinners, and that blockbuster direct mail appeal, the small band of activists led by the intrepid Steve Endean managed to raise enough money that year to make HRCF the seventeenth-largest independent political action committee in the United States after the 1982 election cycle.

Now it was time to spend it.

Alan Baron
By Gregory King, former communications director at HRCF

One spring in the early 1980s, John F. Kennedy, Jr., then a student at Brown University, asked his uncle for help in finding a summer internship in Washington, D.C. Senator Ted Kennedy sent him to Alan Baron. Alan was an unlikely Washington insider, a notable political commentator, and publisher of a widely read newsletter, "The Baron Report." Filled with details on the "what, when and why" of House, Senate, gubernatorial and presidential races, *The Washington Post* hailed it as "essential reading for conservatives and liberals." It made no difference to Senator Kennedy that Alan was perpetually disheveled and disorganized or that his diet consisted of Chinese takeout, pizza, hamburgers, and Dr. Pepper. What the Massachusetts senator cared about was Alan's encyclopedic knowledge of politics, his prodigious intellect, and the fact that he was fun to be around.

John Jr. was soon to learn what countless members of the Washington establishment already knew. The Baron, as he was known throughout town, was a human whirling dervish, spending his days giving speeches in corporate and union board rooms, offering political commentary on television, strategizing with liberal activists, and crafting enormously successful fundraising appeals for progressive causes. He appeared each Friday night on public broadcasting's *MacNeil-Lehrer News Hour*, providing the liberal perspective on the week's news. He created the rating system for the *National Journal* and was published regularly in *The Wall Street Journal*. He was a political savant, who in the pre-internet years of the 1980s, was able to retain in his brain a vast amount of information—polling data, electoral returns, fundraising totals—and draw insightful connections in the data. He was, according to his friend Sen. Dale Bumpers of Arkansas, "one of the best political thinkers in the country."

Alan's love of politics developed during his childhood in Sioux City, Iowa. He volunteered in Adlai Stephenson's 1956 campaign and had a personally autographed copy of *Profiles in Courage* as a keepsake from his work as a teenager in Kennedy's 1960 campaign. Alan came to Washington to study at The George Washington University. He worked on several successive presidential campaigns, including those of Iowa Senator Harold Hughes and Maine Senator Edmund S. Muskie. In 1972, George McGovern named Alan executive director of the Democratic National Committee—he was just twenty-eight years old. He joined McGovern's Senate staff after McGovern's landslide presidential loss to Nixon. Alan was fired in 1976 when McGovern learned Alan was running the "Anybody but Carter" movement from McGovern's Senate office. The firing made the national news, but McGovern and Alan remained friends for life.

Shortly after he left McGovern's staff, Alan began publishing "The Baron Report," which gave him a lucrative platform for engaging in his favorite activities: discussing politics and discerning unseen trends. He maintained contact with hundreds of sources around the country through scores of phone calls each week, checking in to find the latest poll results, the most recent staffing changes, and the emerging policy developments that made his newsletter such a useful source of information.

During an era when political opponents put aside their differences at the end of the working day, Alan hosted a weekly poker game at his home ten blocks from the Capitol. The regulars included Reagan White House Chief of Staff James A. Baker; Senator Daniel Patrick Moynihan's top aide Tim Russert, who later became the host of *Meet the Press* and head of NBC's Washington bureau; *The Washington Post* columnist David Broder; *The Wall Street Journal* columnist

Al Hunt; and NBC newsman Ken Bode. Harvard professor William Schneider, who served as a co-editor of "The Baron Report," and campaign veteran Mark Shields, who later replaced Alan on PBS, were regular guests.

Alan developed close friendships with political figures on both the left and the right. Ted Kennedy, Jerry Brown, and Barney Frank were good friends, but so were Reagan campaign manager John Spears, Reagan strategist Peter Hannaford, right-wing direct-mail pioneer Richard Viguerie, and Robert Novak, the influential conservative columnist and television commentator known, even by his friends, as the Prince of Darkness. Alan had close friends in Hollywood as well, including liberal activist Warren Beatty and television legend Norman Lear, who used the fortune generated by *All in the Family* and *Maude* to finance liberal groups, including, with Alan's guidance and advice, People for the American Way.

On other nights, Alan would turn his home into something of a salon for the expanding network of young gay staffers, almost all still in the closet, who worked behind the scenes in the executive branch, on Congressional staffs, with labor unions, trade associations, law firms, and lobbying shops. When Alan met Steve Endean, he became one of his most supportive allies in the effort to advance the cause of gay rights. He introduced Steve to his gay friends, who were instrumental in connecting Steve to others who could provide introductions on Capitol Hill and around the country who could be of help. When Steve created the Human Rights Campaign Fund, Alan offered to craft the direct mail appeal that would provide a regular source of income for the project.

Alan knew from experience how potent direct mail could be. A program he implemented for the Democratic National Committee raised $2.5 million from sixty thousand donors in 1980. Within four years, it was raising $13 million from half a million donors. Alan offered to pay for the initial HRCF mailing. Thanks to his former assistant, protégé, and friend Sean Strub—who later went on to a successful career as a publisher, entrepreneur, producer, and public official—the letter was signed by playwright Tennessee Williams. Sean knew Williams well enough to persuade him to lend his name to the first direct mail appeal for the LGBTQ community in history.

As no list of LBGTQ Americans existed at the time, Alan arranged to rent two mailing lists that he thought would have the names of many gays—a fashion catalog called "International Male" and the theater and entertainment magazine *After Dark*. In the five-page letter he crafted, Alan focused on privacy rights and the threat posed by the far right. "Not since the blacklisting in the entertainment industry in the 1950s has there been as potent a threat to individual rights as exists in America today," he wrote. "Our enemies —I don't think enemy is too strong a word for people who advocate the death penalty for homosexuals—have powers their predecessors could not have imagined." He explained the need for a powerful political action committee to "stop the threat to our individual rights posed by militant moralists." The letter, with Williams's signature, was an enormous success.

Alan continued to provide advice and support for HRCF and other gay causes. He drafted many of the Gay Men's Health Crisis's initial direct mail appeals during the earliest days of the epidemic. *The Baron Report* regularly informed insiders of the growing heft of the gay movement in politics. After former Vice President Walter Mondale spoke in 1982 at a Human Rights Campaign Fund dinner in New York, Alan wrote that the address "is unlikely to cause him problems," noting that the HRCF dinner "grossed $135,000 vs. $80,000 for the Pennsylvania Democratic Party's major annual fundraiser, also featuring Mondale, a week later."

After years of ill-health brought on by diabetes and several strokes, along with personal demons, Alan died in 1993 at the age of 50. In their history of the LGBTQ political movement in America, *Out for Good*, writers Dudley Clendinen and Adam Nagourney noted the importance of the letter crafted by Alan. "The gay rights movement and the religious right were joined now in a battle for understanding and public support that would continue through the 1980s and beyond." The battle that began with Alan's direct mail letter for the Human Rights Campaign Fund continues to this day.

HRCF was committed to being bipartisan, attempting to appeal to legislators on both sides of the aisle. The attempt was largely futile. Until 1980, both parties had liberal and conservative wings. We had hopes of winning the support of liberal Republicans, but few remained in Congress by 1980. Reagan's inauguration proved to be the beginning of the dramatic polarization we see in American government today. Most Republicans we found refused to support our community.

The PAC made its first contribution of the 1982 cycle to Republican Senator Lowell Weicker from Connecticut. His campaign staff was jittery about accepting money from a gay PAC during the primary, and they turned it down. This decision proved to be ironic—in five years, Weicker would be one of the community's most important champions and a lynchpin in persuading the government to fund AIDS medication.

The PAC jumped in to help another primary, this one in south Philadelphia, where two incumbents had been pitted against each other after Pennsylvania lost two House seats to redistricting. Congressman Tom Foglietta faced Congressman Joe Smith. Bets were against Foglietta in the newly drawn socially conservative district of Italians, blue-collar whites, blacks, and Puerto Ricans. But right in the middle, in Center City, lived a growing population of gays and singles.

"You could give Tom the pencil, and he couldn't draw a district where he could win," said one local Democratic legislator of the challenge facing Foglietta.

That was just the kind of challenge Steve wanted, and he convinced the HRCF board the race was perfect for them.

Foglietta won by a narrow margin of around fifteen hundred votes. Tony Silvestri ran the gay effort, and he acknowledged that gay money and gay support made the difference. HRCF was the largest single contributor to Foglietta's primary campaign. A picture of Steve Endean giving Tom Foglietta a check for five thousand dollars ran in gay newspapers across the country.

When interviewed by *Nightline* about accepting money and support from the gay community, Foglietta acknowledged he had understood the risk. "On the other hand," he said, "if we look at the record of politicians who have opposed gay rights, I think what we find is that those politicians tend to lose elections."

That campaign was the turning point for HRCF, according to the PAC's first board co-chair, Kerry Woodward.

"That was when other candidates started to take notice and say, 'Oh, that group has made a difference in that campaign,'" Kerry said. "And we were able to raise money and get people to door knock and volunteer. When a congressperson took a stand for gay rights and put their name on the bill as co-sponsor, and they were then attacked for it—we were able to come to their aid. They could see that it wasn't just an empty promise. That made a huge difference to our lobbying effort."

The top priority for the 1982 general election was the reelection of Barney Frank from Massachusetts. Frank was closeted when he joined the House of Representatives in 1981. He astounded Steve Endean when he came out to him when Steve was in Boston on GRNL business. Frank told Steve he wanted to live a life with other gay people and loosen the rules he had set for himself about how a gay politician should portray himself. Steve introduced him to the quiet gay social world of Washington, D.C., which brought together Democrats and Republicans, bureaucrats and military officers, heads of government agencies, and even directors of conservative political action committees, like the forever-closeted Terry Dolan.

So, Steve had a personal interest in funding Frank's 1982 reelection campaign. He also got personally involved with the local gay community in Frank's district and speaking with gay media. Frank, like Foglietta, had been redistricted into a race against another incumbent, but he won handily.

Steve's belief that Barney Frank's reelection was of paramount importance paid off in a huge way, so much so that I came to see him as perhaps our greatest champion. As his stature in Congress grew, he secured co-sponsors of the gay rights bill and his colleagues' votes in support of more money for AIDS and in opposition to hateful anti-gay amendments. Crucially important was the sound advice he freely gave and his willingness to speak at countless HRCF events. The latter was especially popular with our donors and prospective supporters because his remarks were so insightful and entertaining.

Barney Frank
By Joe Cantor, former campaign finance expert at the Congressional Research Service

The 1980 election represented a turning point for American politics, including the gay and lesbian civil rights movement. The election of Ronald Reagan and a Republican Senate shook the political world and ushered in a higher visibility for the role of the Christian right in American politics. Known by various names, including the "Moral Majority," social conservative groups not only took credit for the Republican electoral success but placed the burgeoning gay and lesbian civil rights movement clearly in their crosshairs. The founding of the Human Rights Campaign Fund that year could not have occurred at a more critical time.

One bright spot for progressive politics in 1980 was the election to Congress of Barney Frank, an outspoken liberal from Massachusetts. Frank came to Washington determined to fight for progressive causes, including lesbian and gay civil rights. Still in the closet, Frank had to negotiate some challenging hurdles to support gay civil rights without calling undue attention to his own personal life.

In meeting Steve Endean, HRCF's founder, Frank found a political ally he could both trust with his secret and with whom he could develop a pragmatic approach to the challenges facing gay civil rights. The two men found some kinship even in their personal styles, characterized by an absence of flashiness, little attention to social niceties, and a passionate but pragmatic commitment to the causes they sought to advance. Frank was the inside player, while Endean was the outsider seeking to bring gay civil rights into the political mainstream.

Frank got to work in Congress leading the opposition to anti-gay amendments to legislation, a common tool used by the right. He also worked on repealing anti-gay provisions already enshrined in law, such as the denial of immigration into the U.S. based on sexuality and, later, HIV status. As the AIDS epidemic emerged in the 1980s, Frank also led the drive for more government funding to combat this disease. He worked behind the scenes to accomplish many non-legislative objectives of the gay civil rights movement as well, such as ending the denial of security clearances based on sexuality. And along the way, Frank helped secure more and more co-sponsors to the gay civil rights bill, which at the time was perhaps the primary goal of the gay rights movement. A steadily growing number of cosponsors reflected increasing support among the American people.

In all these endeavors, Frank worked closely with HRCF and its staff in setting priorities and building alliances. He was HRCF's biggest supporter, making himself available to offer advice, speak at HRCF events, and raise money for the Campaign Fund. Frank felt a special connection with HRCF, its staff, and its members, some of whom formed the basis of his own personal support system as he faced life as a gay man in Washington and on Capitol Hill. He felt HRCF was not just lobbying him but lobbying *for* him as a gay man who had suffered too long in the closet.

Frank spent the first six of his thirty-two years in Congress in various degrees of hiding. When he came out in 1987, he became the first member of Congress to do so voluntarily, and the political world awaited the fallout. To the shock of many long-term political observers, Frank encountered few negative consequences. It may well be that by the time he unburdened himself of his secret, he had so impressed the political world and his colleagues with his gravitas and political skill that his sexuality was largely a non-issue. The inner councils of the Clinton and Obama administrations respected his insight, and even political opponents came to know that when he spoke, it was worth listening.

Frank was a media darling because he was so often quotable. Both witty and acerbic, he was willing to speak freely and in soundbites. Conservatives "believe that life begins at conception and ends at birth," he once remarked. As a member of the Judiciary Committee considering impeachment of President Bill Clinton in 1998, he sarcastically referred to the Nixon impeachment, saying that the committee's mission seemed to be, "What did the president touch and when did he touch it." He declared Antonin Scalia homophobic and a bigot who expressed his prejudice in his opinions.

Frank was unabashedly gruff, sending many, including reporters, away in tears. But he was fair about dishing out sharp comments to all, without regard to the political importance or social status of his audience. He was known for being short with his staff, lobbyists, even constituents.

"Patience, in my judgment, is a highly overrated virtue," he declared.

Annual surveys of Capitol Hill colleagues and staff invariably ranked Frank as both the smartest and the funniest member of Congress. The *New Yorker* declared him the wise guy and wise man of the Democratic Party. Political strategist Paul Begala once spoke at a fundraiser for a gay-rights group and said, "When I told my father, back in Texas, that I was speaking to an LGBT group, he said that sounded like a sandwich." When it was Frank's turn to speak, he told Begala that "only occasionally is it a sandwich."

How fortuitous that in HRCF's mission to propel the gay civil rights movement into the political mainstream, the organization formed an alliance with an inside player whose stature grew steadily in his sixteen terms in office. That this inside player would become the most prominent, openly gay elected official in the country added tremendously to his ability to help HRCF.

Barney Frank was far more than "a gay

congressman." He was a highly respected congressman who happened to be gay. He would come to epitomize what the gay civil rights battle was about: creating a climate wherein people could prosper in their careers, with their sexuality increasingly irrelevant. As Barney Frank's stature in Washington steadily grew, so did the stature of the Human Rights Campaign. It was a happy and fruitful partnership that produced immeasurable advances for the lesbian and gay community.

The 1982 election cycle was a watershed year for the new political action committee. On the *Nightline* program, Dan Bradley had predicted the extraordinary impact HRCF and GRNL would have on the upcoming elections, including a Democratic takeover of the Senate and a gain of twenty-six House seats.

Of the top twenty races HRCF entered, the average contribution to the candidate was more than four thousand-five hundred dollars. The PAC contributed over twelve thousand dollars to ten black candidates—more money than the Congressional Black Caucus PAC gave.

HRCF won 81 percent of the campaigns they supported, and GRNL signed up sixteen new co-sponsors of the gay civil rights bill.

Politics is an intoxicating but feckless paramour. Within months, Steve would face a crucifixion by those he considered his allies. David Goodstein, Larry Bush, *The Advocate, The Washington Blade,* and much of the gay media around the country all piled on. The onslaught was overwhelming and forced him to resign the leadership of GRNL and retain only his treasurer's position on the Human Rights Campaign Fund board. The next election cycle would bring the PAC down quickly, and establishment Democrats would abandon the gay community faster than fair-weather friends. The gay campaign fund had blindsided the religious right, and that so-called Moral Majority would recover from their losses quickly to take on the community with a ferocious vengeance.

Little did these political warriors fighting for the right to keep a job and rent an apartment realize that, along with the battle incited by a beauty queen hawking orange juice, a full-blown war on another front was already simmering. This conflict would be against an even greater, albeit invisible, nemesis—a deadly virus.

Chapter 6:
People Were Dying

On July 2, 1981, the *New York Times* ran their first story about a mysterious illness that would later be called AIDS.

> "Doctors in New York and California have diagnosed among homosexual men 41 cases of a rare and often rapidly fatal form of cancer. Eight of the victims died less than 24 months after the diagnosis was made. The cause of the outbreak is unknown.... [CDC spokesman Dr. James] Curran said there was no apparent danger to non-homosexuals from contagion. 'The best evidence against contagion,' he said, 'is that no cases have been reported to date outside the homosexual community or in women.'"

A year later, representatives of various gay, government, and health organizations decided on the term "acquired immune deficiency syndrome," or AIDS, at a Centers for Disease Control (CDC) meeting in Washington, D.C. In 1982, the mysterious syndrome killed 853 people in the U.S. and was rapidly reaching epidemic proportions among gay men.

At a White House press briefing in October 1982, reporter Lester Kinsolving asked Press Secretary Larry Speakes about a horrifying new disease ravaging the gay community.

"Larry, does the president have any reaction to the announcement by the Center for Disease Control in Atlanta that A-I-D-S, is now an epidemic in over six hundred cases?" Kinsolving asked, spelling out the acronym.

"A-I-D-S?" Speakes responded. "I haven't got anything on it."

"It's known as 'gay plague,'" Kinsolving explained.

The other reporters in the briefing room burst into laughter.

"No, it is," Kinsolving insisted. "It's a pretty serious thing. One in every three people that gets this has died, and I wonder if the president is aware of this?"

"I don't have it," Speakes replied. "Do you?"

More laughter from the press corps.

For the next two years, Kinsolving, a conservative member of the White House press corps, asked questions about the administration's response to AIDS. Speakes continued to respond with homophobic jokes and general indifference while the other reporters mocked him.

By the time President Reagan delivered his first speech on the epidemic in 1987, some thirty-six thousand Americans had been diagnosed with the disease, and more than twenty thousand had died.

Contrast the government response to AIDS with its earlier investigation into Legionnaires' Disease, a medical mystery that infected war veterans attending the American Legion convention in July 1976. Within weeks, just over two hundred veterans became ill, and thirty-four died. Mounting one of its most extensive investigations ever, the CDC identified the bacteria that caused the illness in five months. Not so with AIDS.

For a couple of years after the initial detection of a mystifying illness, first called gay-related immunodeficiency, or GRID, most of us were unaware of the impending "gay cancer" that would decimate our community. News delivery was practically stagnant in those pre-Internet days, moving at the glacial speed of daily newspaper production and delivery. Mainstream media posted next to nothing about it, in part because there was so little information to be gathered, as demonstrated by reporter Kinsolving's futile efforts to get some response from the White House. Rampant homophobia among reporters and media outlets was the primary reason for the media blackout. Medical journals attempted to unravel the puzzle of the disease, and infectious disease experts were busy fighting over what to call whatever was afflicting those "homosexuals" and who got credit for identifying it.

Even David Goodstein avoided the story until early 1982. He was confident the disease would run the same course as Legionnaires'—the cause would be identified quickly, and a cure would soon follow. "As I encountered each new revelation," the publisher of *The Advocate* wrote, "I kept expecting the clouds to open, organ music to boom a Bach requiem, and an outraged Jehovah to order me to stop fucking forthwith." (Goodstein evidently never forgot Jim Foster's admonishment that the movement was all about fucking.) But his editorial decision meant that AIDS was largely ignored in the nation's most widely read gay newspaper. He didn't want to alarm his readers—a judgment that no doubt cost lives. Every day gay men were unaware of the looming apocalypse was a day we delayed protecting ourselves. The death rate grew—slowly at first, but then exponentially and unabated.

It's impossible to imagine now, more than forty years later, how this lethal epidemic could have simmered for a couple of years, devastating our community virtually undetected. Consider March 2020, when the world was slammed with the alarming news that most businesses must close, and we were expected to shelter at home in an effort to thwart a novel coronavirus. This particular virus had been present in China for at least a month before Americans became aware of it. At first, Americans gave a casual nod to the looming epidemic by increasing their hygiene efforts. Then, suddenly, COVID-19 was all anyone could think about. It dominated the public mindset and decimated the lives of millions through illness, unemployment, and isolation.

AIDS similarly impacted the gay community. However, the difference was that it took years, not months—and thousands of deaths, not a handful—for the president to address the crisis.

Even the general public cast AIDS aside as something that was happening to "them." Except for the religious right. Jerry Falwell quickly zeroed in on the "plague of the century," as he called it. AIDS was "the judgment of God," Falwell said. "You can't fly into the laws of God and God's nature without paying the price." He called for the government to shut down gay bathhouses and to prohibit homosexuals from donating blood.

In the 1970s and early eighties, bathhouses were popular gathering places for gay men to meet partners, share saunas, and have sex discretely and often anonymously. Customers would pay only for the use of the facilities. Sex was between customers, and no money was exchanged. Bathhouses generally were considered to be much safer venues for men to meet for sex, especially when gay men were inordinate victims of assault and robbery.

Jack Campbell, a founding board member of GRNL and HRCF, co-owned the highly successful Club Baths, a national chain of bathhouses. Jack was passionate about politics, and he got involved in numerous gay issues, from leading the Dade County effort against Anita Bryant to running for office in Florida himself. He worked ceaselessly to advance the cause of lesbian and gay rights. His business made him wealthy, and Jack was a good giver. HRCF was just one of the many gay causes he supported. When we needed help, Jack always responded. Now and then, we had trouble making payroll at HRCF, and I would call Jack. His only question was how much I needed. It probably wasn't more than a few thousand dollars in those days, but I could always count on him dropping a check in the mail for a couple of grand. Nobody else would do that. And he never asked for anything in return. He never made any demands on HRCF; he did not expect invitations or compensation. Well, Jack did love having his picture taken with politicians, so I arranged that for him whenever possible, whether with Senator Ted Kennedy or another official he admired. Without Jack's incredible generosity, the Human Rights Campaign Fund likely would not have survived our many lean times.

Jack always provided a clean environment in his bathhouses. So, when the pressure came to shut down the baths around the country to curb the sexual behavior that might be spreading the disease, Jack insisted on providing condoms, much to the dismay of his business partners, who thought encouraging the use of condoms would discourage business.

Gay leaders throughout the country were alarmed by the conservative backlash against the baths. That reaction launched a fear that men with AIDS—and perhaps even all gay men—might soon be quarantined.

"It's happened before," warned a full-page ad placed in the *New York Native* by the Human Rights Campaign Fund in June 1983. "It happened in America, where for the 'common good,' Japanese

Americans were stigmatized and then quarantined ... We don't know the cause of AIDS ... We do know that fear of AIDS and its identification with the gay community may be the next epidemic. An epidemic of fear on the part of Americans threatens all of us in the gay community, regardless of our health or lifestyle."

Busy running both HRCF and GRNL, Steve Endean called AIDS "a weird new disease that seemed to be attacking the gay male community far more than any other population," brushing it aside to focus on the upcoming 1984 election cycle.

That would prove to be an ill-fated decision.

And, without hindsight, it wasn't necessarily a *bad* decision. He wasn't ignoring the crisis. Representing GRNL, he testified at a congressional subcommittee hearing sponsored by Representative Ted Weiss when the CDC reported two thousand cases and fewer than a thousand deaths. He noted, in particular, the discrimination that gay victims were experiencing.

"Hysteria is rampant," he told the committee on August 1, 1983. "People are combining their fear of the disease, their homophobia, and their racism... and punishing persons with AIDS by firing them from their jobs, by denying them housing, by denying them fundamental human rights."

Steve was recognized beyond Congress as well. The press acknowledged his impact on the 1982 campaigns and in the halls of Congress.

Washingtonian magazine listed him as one of "100 men and women in their twenties, thirties, and early forties who are likely to be among Washington's most powerful people of the future."

"His style is professional. When he talks tactics, it's as a seasoned lobbyist," wrote *The Washington Post* of Steve.

Larry Bush, a stringer for more than a dozen gay papers around the country, called him a key player in moving gays "out of the fringe and into the mainstream in political circles." And then, strangest of all, given what was to befall Steve in a few months, David Goodstein sang out his praise.

The Advocate named him one of "Ten People Who Made the Most Difference This Year" at the end of the 1982 congressional session. "On an absurdly low budget, Gay Rights National Lobby is producing miracles. Imagine what they could do if we really supported them," Goodstein wrote. "Increasingly, one hears from Congressional sources and others that GRNL is doing a job nothing short of miraculous."

By the end of the year, Steve estimated he had put in more than a hundred hours a week for months—common in the business of electoral politics that demands a feast of work in an election year and delivers famine in the off year.

And by the fall of the following year, Steve was out of a job—two, in fact.

A combination of events led to Steve's fall from grace. First, the extreme amount of time he invested in the 1982 election cycle drove him to exhaustion bordering on illness, and perhaps he subsequently made poor decisions. When he asked for an infusion of funds, some critics—including Goodstein and Voeller—accused Steve of giving away too much money, leaving HRCF in a precarious financial position. (Others would argue that a depleted bank account indicates that a political action committee has done its job of donating money to campaigns well.) He refused to renew Jim Foster's contract as a fundraiser, irking David Goodstein. Steve had suggested to Goodstein that they shift the HRCF fundraising operation to shore up GRNL's finances, which further enraged the publisher. Larry Bush accused Steve of paying too little attention to AIDS, which meant GRNL could not participate effectively in the complex appropriations process. Finally, Goodstein announced in *The Advocate* that he would withhold contributions from organizations that employed Steve, and he encouraged readers to do so also. The *Washington Blade* and gay papers around the country joined the incessant drumbeat for Steve to go.

And let's not overlook Steve's bristly and often demanding personality combined with tactics that could to some appear manipulative, making him an easy target for criticism at a time when no excuse was necessary.

Faced with this phalanx of opposition, Steve left the day-to-day management of HRCF in March 1983, but he stayed on as treasurer. He resigned from GRNL that fall, defending himself in his letter of resignation.

"I believe the attacks on me during the past nine months can largely be attributed to a political vendetta combined with a quest for power and control of our movement," Endean wrote in his letter of resignation from GRNL. Calling out no one by name, he continued, "They describe my unwillingness to take their marching orders as incompetence."

Being forced to the margins of the movement to which he had dedicated his life took its toll on him. When I came to head up HRCF in June 1983, not surprisingly, I found him under a great deal of stress.

Steve continued to serve as GRNL's executive director and on the HRCF board as the treasurer for the next several months. But our relationship was strained because I knew that he preferred someone else to lead HRCF.

Jack Campbell
By Steven Dwyer, former HRCF controller

In 1965, John "Jack" Campbell and friends purchased a bathhouse in Cleveland, Ohio, that they hoped would serve not just as a clean and safe place for men to have sex but also a social gathering space. From that first bathhouse, Jack developed the Club Baths, at its peak a chain of forty-two bathhouses spread across the country. Famously, when the Rev. Troy Perry remarked to him that Metropolitan Community Church had a hundred churches and thirty-thousand members, Jack replied, "Well, although we only have thirty churches, we have three hundred thousand members."

Jack had become involved in politics early, elected as president of the Young Democrats Club, first at the University of Michigan, then again at Kent State. In Cleveland, Jack organized a local chapter of the Mattachine Society. With his bathhouse empire stretching coast to coast, he became a national player both as a donor and serving on the boards of most of the national LGBTQ organizations, among them Gay Rights National Lobby, Human Rights Campaign Fund, National Gay Task Force, Fairness Fund, Lesbian and Gay Democrats of America, and National Gay Rights Advocates. Steve Endean wanted it recorded that the Human Rights Campaign Fund would not exist without Jack's very early generosity.

Jack moved to Miami in 1972 to open a new Club Bath location. Following a police raid on the club in 1974, he hired a lawyer and sued to have the charges against all parties dropped. He also filed suit against the Miami Police Department for harassment and won a court order opposing future harassment and a formal apology from the Miami Beach Police Department. In the fall of 1974, he made an unsuccessful run for a seat on the county commission.

In 1976, Jack was a co-founder of the Dade

County Coalition for the Humanistic Rights of Gays, a group focused on passing an ordinance outlawing discrimination against homosexuals in employment, housing, labor unions, and private education. When the ordinance passed in 1977, Anita Bryant fought back, establishing Save Our Children to collect 64,000 signatures to place a repeal measure before voters. Although Jack and the DCCHR waged a counter-campaign, voters overturned the ordinance after an ugly campaign.

Elected a delegate to the National Democratic Convention in 1980, Jack was active in the gay caucus and was suggested for a nomination to run for vice president. He declined and, in his place, the caucus put forth the nomination of Mel Boozer of the D.C. Gay Activists Alliance. Jack waged two more unsuccessful campaigns: for the Florida legislature in 1984 and mayor of Miami in 1989.

By the 1990s, Jack's bathhouse empire was crumbling. With the arrival of AIDS, some of the bathhouses were ordered closed as a matter of public health. Even in the cities where the baths remained open, the shifting gay public sentiment led to a decline in membership. Jack made an effort to rebrand the chain as health clubs under the name Club Body Center, and despite pushback from some of his partners, he was insistent on bringing safe sex education and free condoms into the clubs.

Jack Campbell died in 2014.

Chapter 7:
Vic Basile Takes the Helm

On a sweltering day in June 1983, I climbed a flight of stairs to a Washington, D.C., office in a small row house on D Street Southeast near the Eastern Market metro station—a neighborhood known for low rents and high crime. The second-floor office—just six hundred square feet—was the national headquarters of the Human Rights Campaign Fund. It was my first day as its executive director, and I was charged with nothing less than raising enough money for this small but aspiring political action committee to influence a majority of members of the United States Congress to approve legislation assuring lesbians and gay men equal rights under the law. It was a momentous assignment, and I was suitably intimidated. It didn't help that, on my desk that first day, I found a checkbook showing a balance of five thousand dollars and a stack of bills demanding at least that much.

Two full-time staff members greeted me on my first day. So did Steve Endean, still the executive director and lobbyist for the Gay Rights National Lobby, although his welcome wasn't all that warm. I was not Steve's choice for the job, but because he headed up GRNL and served HRCF as its treasurer, I had to find a way to work with him. While gay men are comfortable with being affectionate with each other, we are also accustomed to being shunned by the straight world, so I knew I could tolerate his aversion if I could not win him to my side.

I had worked as a community organizer, which taught me something about generating agreement among disparate communities and being confrontational when it was called for. I was married at that time, which, naturally, also taught me lessons in collaboration. Mary Ann is a wonderful woman who supported me in every conceivable way, even through our separation and eventual divorce. She continues to be supportive to this very day, a fact about which I am enormously grateful. I got the nerve to come out in 1979 when I was thirty-three years old. So, when I came out of the closet, I blew the door off! Even before our divorce was final, I got involved in Washington's gay community. I joined the Gertrude Stein Democratic Club and the Gay Activist Alliance (now Gay and Lesbian Activists Alliance), and I agreed to a major volunteer undertaking for GRNL.

My increasing visibility in the movement meant I needed to come out to my parents. They had been disappointed to learn of my divorce; they loved Mary Ann. This announcement might be an even bigger letdown. I suspected my mother would accept my sexual orientation in time, but I was concerned how my father would respond.

My dad, a first-generation American, dropped out of school after the sixth grade to support his family. A champion for the underdog, Dad was active all his life as a Democratic campaign volunteer. He saw a clear distinction between the parties. Democrats were the party of the working person, and the Republicans were the party of big business. It was all black and white: there was no in-between for him. Candidates loved having him go door-knocking with them. Given his gregarious personality, he could meet anybody on the street and have a conversation with them. He probably knew whoever answered the door, and if he didn't, he soon would. While I did not inherit his extroversion, I picked up his passion for politics.

When I came out to him, even though I was in my mid-thirties, he said nothing, bad or good. He remained quiet for months, struggling with my sexual orientation. I learned later that he even went to a psychiatrist for help in coming to terms with it—a bold move then for a man of his background.

But I always knew my dad loved me. I would call home and talk to him about my work, making a point to bring up a gay bashing or some other horror. I might share some of our challenges in Congress because I knew his personality led him to always back the underdog. At some point, it was like a switch was thrown, and he got it. From that moment on, he became very supportive. When I traveled home to visit my family, my then partner would sometimes go with me. Dad always referred to him as his son. I found that remarkable.

In the mid-eighties, the Northampton, Massachusetts, city council considered an anti-discrimination bill protecting lesbian and gay rights. Passage came down to the vote of one man on the council who was my father's age. Dad met with him about the bill—which was a big step for him—and the councilman changed his position to vote in favor of protecting our rights.

When the local Springfield paper featured Dad's decades-long political activism in a nearly full-page article, he discussed me—his gay son—and my work. I considered that a testament to how far he had come. His support for my activism in the movement was assured, and I couldn't be prouder of him—and more grateful.

When I met Steve, I worked for ACTION, then the federal umbrella agency for the Peace Corps and all the domestic volunteer programs. I was also president of the staff union, a local affiliate of the American Federation of State, County, and Municipal Employees (AFSCME), a progressive international union representing many of the lowest-paid public workers. It had come out early against the war in Vietnam. Dr. Martin Luther King, Jr., had gone to Memphis to help striking garbage workers represented by AFSCME when he was assassinated.

As the president of the staff union of ACTION, I had the opportunity to fight for the civil rights of a member of the LGBTQ community, as early as 1979. Kit, a popular temporary employee in ACTION's regional office in Chicago, decided to transition. Well-liked, colleagues were supportive of Kit's decision—until it came time for Kit to use the women's restroom. The women in the office were not pleased, and they complained loudly enough that Kit was fired.

Because she was a temporary employee, Kit had no right to union representation. But we represented her anyway, and we filed a grievance on her behalf. The grievance traveled up the chain of command of supervisors until it reached the director of domestic programs at ACTION. That person was John Lewis. Yes, *the* John

Lewis, the great civil rights leader who suffered grave personal injury marching for civil rights in Alabama and would go on to represent Georgia in Congress for more than thirty years.

I wrote Lewis a letter supporting Kit's grievance in which I drew parallels to the Black civil rights movement. I asked for a meeting, which he granted.

"Vic, I have read your letter," Lewis said as I walked into his office and before I could sit down. "You are absolutely right. We are rehiring Kit."

That man, I believe, was incapable of doing anything he thought was morally wrong, including discriminating against anyone for their sexual orientation or gender identity.

In 1982, Steve asked me to help GRNL organize a campaign to get a major union to take a positive stand on lesbian and gay equality. We chose AFSCME since it was so progressive and was, at the time, the largest AFL-CIO affiliate with 1.3 million members. An endorsement of legislation that prohibited discrimination against lesbians and gays surely would be noticed on Capitol Hill and in the larger political arena. We wanted to present a resolution at the 1982 international convention in Atlantic City.

In accepting Steve's request, I undertook my first formal challenge as a lobbyist and learned more than I ever anticipated about how power works inside large organizations. Unions are democratic organizations—the membership elects the leadership, and the leaders will respond to them in much the same way that elected government officials respond to their constituents. Unions are also hierarchical, so what the leadership wants it usually gets.

Our success required a two-prong effort—a strategy similar to lobbying Congress for a piece of legislation. We needed first to enlist a senior official in AFSCME to be our champion and then to create a groundswell of support among the membership.

I asked Bill Lucy for his help. As the secretary/treasurer, Bill was the union's second highest-ranking official and the country's highest-ranking African American union official. He is a genuinely nice guy and very approachable. I found it easy to get a meeting with him, even though I hardly knew him. It wasn't so easy to tell him what I wanted. I handed him a draft of my proposed resolution asking that "AFSCME endorse the passage of federal, state, and local legislation that extends basic civil rights in the areas of employment, housing and public accommodations to lesbian and gay citizens."

This was a big ask—in 1982, no other major union had taken a stand for civil rights for lesbians and gays. When I sat down with him and explained what I wanted and why it was important, he agreed to help. I was a little stunned with his ready assent—and thoroughly elated. I had enrolled my champion!

I did not understand at the time what "yes, I'll help" meant. I was naïve to this level of power, with no idea that Lucy knew the internal politics and the minds of his members far better than I did. I took very seriously my responsibility to demonstrate that the initiative had broad rank and file support. As I left the meeting, my mind was racing with thoughts about finding gay and lesbian AFSCME members around the country I could organize into that necessary vital groundswell. I immediately set to work.

I reached out to openly gay members in cities around the country and enlisted their help to win support in their locals. Soon, we were planning ways to expand our network. We worked to get as much support from the rank-and-file members as possible to effectively counter any potential opposition at the convention.

Our little crew of passionate activists arrived in Atlantic City full of anticipation and ready to do battle to ensure the passage of our resolution. I had had little communication with Bill Lucy since my initial meeting, so I was relieved to see the resolution on the agenda. It was scheduled to come up on the second day, which gave us some time for last-minute planning and organizing.

The moment arrived for Bill to approach the podium and address the delegates. He said a few words about the resolution and why it was important. Then, in the blink of an eye, it passed on a voice vote with not one objection from the floor. Really, not one of the two thousand delegates said a negative word. There might well have been some negative thoughts, but they went unspoken.

My fellow activists and I were, of course, jubilant. AFSCME had once again lived up to its progressive reputation and was now the first major union to formally support gay and lesbian equality.

Strangely, our victory felt a little anti-climactic. All of the organizing, all of the preparation, all of the anticipation—and it was over in a flash. We had achieved our win when I garnered Bill Lucy's endorsement. I learned once again how power influences politics and brings about real change. It was a lesson I would not soon forget.

I do not know specifically what Lucy did to "grease the skids" so that the resolution passed without dissent. I suspect it was a combination of his leadership, the universal respect he enjoyed from the rank-and-file members, the progressive culture of the organization, and maybe even the support our efforts provided. Whatever the circumstances, he deserves the credit for making that historic event happen, and as a result, he will always be one of my heroes.

I brought that monumental victory back to Steve, and he was, of course, elated.

I had a lifelong love of politics, something I inherited from my father. I worked for civil rights and anti-poverty efforts as a VISTA Volunteer and later at ACTION, but the fight for LGBT equality was personal, and I was passionate about it.

I longed to be part of the national lesbian and gay movement, and in the early 1980s, formal organizations were just emerging. In those days, I could move from my government job to a position heading up a political organization in the movement more easily because there were so few of us who had experience in government and politics, who were willing to be out, and were brave enough to venture into the uncharted territory of lesbian and gay rights.

It paid to be young, then, too. Washington was a town fueled by the energy of young idealists, willing to put in long hours for little money. In my late thirties, I was on the older side, believe it or not.

Now the movement has grown so much that any paid position is highly competitive, demanding specific skills and deep experience.

Those early years were an exciting time to be involved in the beginning of a historic shift, and I'm not the only one who caught the vision. I'm told nearly a hundred people applied for the position of executive director of the Human Rights Campaign Fund, and it came down to me and Steve's pick, Jerry Weller, who was a founding HRCF board member. For whatever reason, the board chose me. I was somewhat surprised since the most critical function of a political action committee is to raise money, and I had little experience at that. You also must know how to get that money into the right hands to harvest the most influence. That meant knowing politics on the Hill, something I knew, but not terribly well. I expect my experience as an organizer and my activism in D.C. gay politics, combined with my passion and calm but persistent demeanor, qualified me for the job. Delivering the AFSCME endorsement no doubt demonstrated my ability to deliver results. Not to be discounted was support from some significant influencers, including Tony Silvestri, a Philadelphia lesbian and gay activist; Joe Tom Easley, a law professor at Antioch Law School; and Dan Bradley, who, as I have mentioned, was the highest-ranking government official in history to declare his homosexuality publicly.

On my first day, Steve greeted me cordially and congratulated me on getting the job. He promised to bury the hatchet, so to speak, because he wanted us to work well together. I had my doubts, but I took him at his word. My great admiration for Steve Endean came much later.

Chapter 8:
Sadness and Some Silver Linings

The HRCF board had a seemingly insignificant practice that turned out to be instrumental in transforming the organization's emphasis. We participated in an activity that came to be known as "sharing," where each member spoke about what was happening in their lives. To Steve, and also to me, it seemed a bit "California touchy-feely."

In fact, hearing a little about each other's ups and downs, including some personal struggles, brought all of us closer to each other. Members generally opened up, revealing very personal things because they trusted each other. They knew that what they shared in the room stayed in the room. We learned more about each other as individuals and formed bonds that we would come to need in tough times. The camaraderie was invaluable.

I valued that support. I once discovered a spot on my nose that I feared could be a Kaposi's sarcoma lesion. I was deeply concerned that I had seroconverted. This was especially confounding because I was in a monogamous, committed relationship. When I discovered it, I was at a board meeting, far from my personal doctor. Fortunately, one of our board members was a medical doctor, who quickly put my mind at rest. It was not AIDS-related.

That practice of sharing, particularly about our too-common experience of AIDS, brought the epidemic directly into our board room in a visceral, undeniable, heartbreaking way.

The day Steve Shellabarger told us his partner was sick was beyond devastating.

Once a year, the HCRF board met in Washington, D.C. The board members enjoyed coming to Capitol Hill, where the political fervor is palpable and invigorating. For the other quarterly meetings, we would travel to promising cities—San Francisco, Palm Springs, Seattle, Ft. Lauderdale, Dallas, even Fire Island—using the visits to network and help build an active HRCF presence. I particularly enjoyed going to Columbus and Dallas, which have large and vibrant lesbian and gay communities, thanks in no small part to the efforts of Steve Shellabarger of Columbus and John Thomas of Dallas. I found both men delightful and engaging. They were so popular that folks—straight and gay—eagerly participated with them in growing their communities. Everyone enjoyed hanging out with Steve and John.

Steve Shellabarger came to HRCF almost under duress. A popular schoolteacher, Steve was very much in the closet—or so he thought, until the day in 1983 when a letter landed in his mailbox from the Human Rights Campaign Fund. As he tells the story, he opened the envelope to find a letter asking him to help organize in Columbus.

"What in the hell is this?!" he bellowed, waving it at his partner, who also was named Steve. "Have I gotten on a mailing list for some gay group?"

He was truly appalled—and a little frightened.

He knew he could not teach school and be out in Columbus, Ohio. Ohio had a sodomy law dating back to the Victorian era. Being outed could cost people their jobs.

"I was still teaching school," he said, "and I just could not believe that someone gave my name to a gay group."

"How on earth did he get on that list?" he wondered. He called the only friend he knew who might have shared his name. Indeed, his friend, Michael Gelpi, had passed his name on to me. Michael knew Steve would be sympathetic with our mission and perhaps even embrace it. Steve believed conservative towns like his would never provide a welcoming environment for openly lesbian and gay people. He understood that headway for the gay community had to be made the way any significant group made progress at the national level: by working within the system through lobbying and the financial support of such organizations as HRCF. So, Steve agreed to help.

By 1987, the sounds of timers and beepers and buzzers marked HRCF board meetings. A quarter of our members were taking AZT medications requiring timely dosing. Every hour, someone's timer would go off, prompting the owner to reach for his prescription bottle and glass of water in what was in most cases a futile gesture to beat the virus. You could almost sense a collective sigh of sadness triggered by those soft alarms. Each of us was grateful to have that dear friend with us, and each wondered if this might be the last time we all would be together.

Board meetings started on Friday nights, which became dedicated to supporting each other through the crisis, so we could clear our minds and get to work Saturday morning to win our battles in Congress. Too many friends were diagnosed as positive, and it seemed as though we were going to funerals every week. We all became very close, and to hear the trials each was going through was heart-wrenching. It was cathartic to get all that emotion out of the way, supported by the few and only people who could truly understand.

The worst night I can remember was when Steve Shellabarger shared two pieces of news—one good and the other devastating. Steve was not out to his family in Columbus—and he had just learned that his partner was HIV-positive. He simply could not deal with having to come out to his family and bury his partner at the same time. So, he went to his family members and told them he was gay. Then he came to the board meeting to tell us his Steve was dying.

Both men taught for the Columbus city school district, which had no healthcare policy for employees who contracted HIV. One evening, Steve Shellabarger invited the district's union leaders to his home. He told them his partner was dying, and they needed help.

Steve is a delightful, generous, charming, even charismatic man who can generate support for just about any cause. But this was the most challenging ask of his life so far. He put his job on the line to get help for his partner, and as it turned out, for lesbian and gay education employees across the state. Right there in his living room, Columbus education union leaders developed a supportive policy that the Ohio Education Association would follow for years.

That was the twisted blessing of AIDS. It brought people out of the closet, and it forced family and friends to confront reality. Thankfully, most rose to the occasion. But some family members struggled, even to the very end.

Todd Cosper was on the HRCF staff when he got sick. He went to live with Philip Dufour, our field and events organizer, and Philip's partner because he had no one else to care for him. His mother finally took him in just before he died—an all-too-familiar scenario.

Sometimes, men themselves struggled to admit they were HIV-positive. Steve Smith was a lobbyist for HRCF who graduated from Harvard Law when he was just twenty-two years old. He was a good-looking guy with a wonderful partner. And then he got sick. He was very private about being positive. He never told me, but in a conversation one day, he let me know he was sick without directly saying so. He kept working, even as he grew more emaciated, until he could work no longer. He died shortly after he left HRCF.

Perhaps one of the greatest impacts of AIDS was that it pushed gay men imbued with privilege to stop hiding behind their money and get involved. The government had turned its back on us, and we were forced to take care of our own. Even mainstream social service organizations whose missions demanded they care for the sick ignored the plight of people with AIDS and refused outright to care for them.

If it can be said that the virus had any benefit, it was that we learned to build organizations to provide much-needed social services, including food, healthcare, and companions who would spend time with people with AIDS. The Gay Men's Health Crisis in New York, the Whitman Walker Clinic in Washington, the San Francisco AIDS Foundation, and many more sprang up around the country almost overnight. As a community, we also stepped up to support them with our money. The AIDS crisis demanded we open our wallets to give, and we did, in donations ranging from ten dollars to contributions in the thousands.

Another bittersweet gift was one that our community still enjoys. AIDS brought lesbians and gay men together. As the gay community struggled to process incredible trauma, grief, and homophobia, as families left sick members to die alone, groups of lesbians banded together to support and tend to the men dying from AIDS. They even organized blood drives to make sure there would be enough to meet the demand for those with HIV and AIDS.

AIDS brought several significant lesbians to our board. When I asked Ellen Malcolm, founder of EMILY's List, to serve on the board, she was just learning about AIDS, and she was amazed to discover the lack of government attention to the disease. I think her desire to do something about AIDS and dissolve any perceived barriers between lesbians and gay men inspired her to join us. And that work started at her first board meeting in Dallas, where she, Hilary Rosen, and Vivian Shapiro together became a force to be reckoned with.

Billy Bernardo was a beloved board member and a quintessential gay man who had quite a knack for humor. When Ellen walked into the board meeting on Sunday morning, Billy was telling a story about a gay man he had met the night before whom he called "a major lesbian." Ellen didn't get why many in the room were in stitches as Billy stood at the front of the room performing a schtick on "this major lesbian."

"Billy, excuse me," Ellen interrupted. "What is a major lesbian?"

The room grew quiet. The expression on Billy's face clearly showed he knew he was busted.

After that, the men realized they needed to be a little bit more considerate of the lesbians in the room. Our board meetings took on a more inclusive and respectful tone after that.

Billy succumbed to AIDS in an unspeakably tragic way. He had lost his partner to AIDS after terrible suffering. Billy was HIV-positive, and when the Kaposi sarcoma lesions erupted, Vivian Shapiro flew from New York to Los Angeles with her partner, Mary Nealon, for the weekend to cheer him up. He was expecting them, but when they arrived, no one answered the door. They called his phone, but no one answered. Vivian was confused and concerned, so she found someone who could let them into Billy's apartment. They found him hanging from a bedpost. Billy knew Vivian, someone who loved him, would find him.

These were desperate times, and AIDS was an almost certain death sentence then. Suicide was all too common—and totally understandable.

AIDS also transformed HRCF's fundraising program when we established the AIDS Campaign Trust. People were dying. By the mid-eighties, gay men who were unwilling to support civil rights legislation were eager and willing to underwrite our lobbying for federal funding for AIDS research, education—and a cure. Even straight people were more willing to give to this dedicated fund.

Fundraising was one of HRCF's primary activities because a political action committee is only as good as the money it can raise. As executive director of HRCF, I made raising money my mission so we could contribute as much as the law allowed to candidates for Congress. Electing gay-friendly members could secure the millions in funding we needed from the federal government for treatment, research, and education about AIDS. We needed money *for* members of Congress to get money *from* members of Congress.

While we wouldn't earn legal employment protection until 2020, now people were dying. Somehow the overriding commitment of the Human Rights Campaign Fund quietly shifted protections from discrimination to fighting the epidemic.

We had been in a fight for our jobs. Now we were in a fight for our lives.

Chapter 9:
Yellow Kitchen Gloves at 1600 Pennsylvania Avenue

It was late winter in Washington, cold and gray. The day had started routinely enough when the receptionist yelled to me that Dan Bradley was on the phone. Calls from Dan weren't unusual, although they were less frequent since he had stepped down as board co-chair of the Human Rights Campaign Fund. In that role, he called a couple of times a week about everything from routine updates to advising me on dealing with various issues and crises—and to simply lend moral support. Whenever and for whatever I needed him, he was always available. Dan was calming when I felt overwhelmed, ready with well-reasoned advice when I was unsure how to handle a particular situation, and always quick to deliver either with a bit of humor. I can't recall ever seeing him angry or stymied by a vexing problem.

However, since his positive HIV diagnosis about a year earlier, the calls were less common, and each time we spoke, it was clear that he was getting sicker, his weakening voice a giveaway. But today was different. I sensed energy and enthusiasm that I hadn't heard in him for a long time.

"I'm coming to Washington," he declared, "to pound on the White House gates to tell Ronald Reagan that he needs to do something about AIDS. I don't care whether he meets with me or not, but he's going to know that I was there. I don't care if anyone goes with me or not, but I am going to do this."

If he actually followed through on his threat, he would most certainly be arrested, but that was the point. He was planning to commit an act of civil disobedience at the White House.

Dan was angry and upset with the Reagan administration's complete inaction on AIDS. It was 1987—six years and twenty-thousand deaths into the epidemic. The president had uttered the word *AIDS* in public only once (in response to a reporter's question), and he hadn't proposed spending any money to fight the disease. We needed funding for AIDS research, treatment, and education programs, and we needed it yesterday.

The media gave the issue little more than passing attention as illustrated by homophobic jokes that occurred at a routine White House press briefing in 1982.

That interaction between the president's press secretary and the elite press corps, as much as anything else, explained the media's near-silence and our government's inaction on AIDS. At that point, more than six hundred people were reported to have died, and nearly all of them were gay men. Some were Haitians. A few were IV drug users. All were from groups disparaged by the larger society, who assumed they got AIDS through their own immoral, irresponsible, and/or illegal behavior.

Dan knew he was dying, just as so many of his friends had already done, but he was determined not to go quietly. Although it was good to hear him with so much emotion in his voice because it meant that he must have been feeling better, anger was not a quality I associated with him. Dan's personality was always even-tempered and warm; friendly but not effusive; serious but also light-hearted, supportive but still a little distant. Our conversations usually left me feeling good, smarter, and wanting more. This one left me feeling desperate to help.

To my question about how we could help, all he would say was that he didn't care if he did this alone—he was going to do it. I took this as a green light that he welcomed participation by others. I began thinking of how to organize around his protest.

My first calls were to board co-chairs Vivian Shapiro in New York and Duke Comegys in Los Angeles to let them know what Dan was planning and to get their buy-in to provide support. Not only were they supportive, but they also wanted to help organize and participate in whatever we planned. Duke announced his plans to attend to the eighth annual National Lesbian and Gay Health Conference in Los Angeles, at which he was the keynote speaker.

"We have tried rational discourse for six long years, and it simply hasn't worked," Duke told the conference attendees. "If reason alone can't do the job, then radical action—such as sit-ins and demonstrations with hundreds, even thousands of us going to jail—is our only recourse. It is time that we challenge this president directly. I know that I am personally ready to go to jail to save my life and the lives of my family and friends. I just cannot take any more death."

My next few calls to other board members, fellow activists, and colleagues in other organizations revealed just how deep and wide the anger was and that protesting the administration's gross nonfeasance was the least people could do. It was as if a boil was festering and needed to be lanced.

The word spread quickly, and support swelled. Activists and established movement leaders from across the country wanted to join Dan outside the White House. Within days, the Human Rights Campaign Fund transformed its very establishment-oriented political work into assuming central command for the first significant act of civil disobedience over the AIDS crisis. Indeed, interest grew so rapidly that we became concerned about keeping the protest peaceful. We repeatedly reminded interested protesters that this effort was to bring attention to the government's indifference and the thousands of needless deaths resulting from the Reagan administration's inaction.

Because the International AIDS Conference was being held in Washington, we chose its opening day, June 1, for our demonstration. We considered this serendipitous because many members of the gay community and reporters from media outlets all over the world would be in the city for the conference. Dennis Lonergan, who managed communications for HRCF, was asked to coordinate media to ensure maximum coverage.

As the day approached, details of the action solidified. We applied for and received a permit to rally in Lafayette Square, across the street from the White House. We advised everyone willing to hop the barricades into the street and be arrested to bring fifty dollars in cash for the disorderly conduct fine—their "get out of jail" fee.

It was a sunny, hot, and humid day—typical June weather for Washington. Several hundred of us showed up, dressed professionally in suits and skirts, as Steve Endean expected of any lesbians or gays who wanted a voice in the civil rights debate. In that sense, we were channeling the example set by Frank Kameny, and by Dr. Martin Luther King, Jr., in the fight for civil rights before him. We assembled that morning in the New York Avenue Presbyterian Church. As the church where President Abraham Lincoln worshiped and Dr. King preached against the Vietnam War, it was a fitting venue from which we started our march to the White House.

After some discussion about what was about to unfold and brief civil disobedience training, we followed Dan to the door. We headed up New York Avenue to Lafayette Square, across Pennsylvania Avenue, and directly in front of the White House. Dan hung onto my shoulder for support to walk the two blocks.

I marched alongside Jean O'Leary, who headed up National Gay Rights Advocates, a nonprofit law firm protecting lesbian and gay rights. Jean was a former nun who, in 1977, organized the first meeting of gays in the White House with Carter aide Midge Costanza. Together, we carried a large wreath denoting the twenty-thousand Americans who had died of AIDS at the time.

Also joining us were Troy Perry, Larry Kramer, Virginia Apuzzo, Sean Strub, Leonard Matlovich, David Mixner, and Urvashi Vaid.

Tourists and onlookers made our crowd look even larger, doubling the number to roughly five hundred. Reporters from *The Washington Post*, *USA Today*, and other media outlets covered our protest. Because of the International AIDS Conference, it was easy to draw media, including international media. The Washington D.C. police looked on, too, as Dan made his remarks.

Dan spoke from a raised platform HRCF field director Philip Dufour had brought to the site, along with a P.A. system.

"I've lost a lot of friends, and I'm sure the president has lost a lot of friends," Dan told the crowd, gathering every bit of energy his sick body would allow. "It's not just gay Americans who will die of AIDS.

"Our surgeon general and our doctors have issued incredible recommendations and plans of action," he said in a voice that occasionally quavered. "At least he [Reagan] ought to read the surgeon general's report."

Following his remarks, sixty-four of us scaled a concrete barrier in front of the White House, stepped into the middle of Pennsylvania Avenue, and sat down on the street. Philip had cleverly thought to bring squares of carpet to protect us from the hot pavement.

"Testing is not a cure for AIDS" and "Reagan, Reagan, too little, too late," we chanted, waiting for the police to arrest us.

Good fortune struck as the police donned bright yellow rubber kitchen gloves, apparently so that they wouldn't catch AIDS from us. For different reasons, of course, the media and the gay men found the gloves irresistible.

"What we did was reasonable," the assistant police chief later told a reporter who questioned the gloves. He claimed it was standard procedure for police officers to wear gloves when handling prisoners since some of those arrested had AIDS. But the city's public health commissioner said he told police officials that gloves were unnecessary during most routine arrests because officers would not be exposed to any blood or body fluids that might carry the AIDS virus.

Loving the photo opportunity the yellow kitchen gloves lent to the scene, photographers recorded video and snapped photos. The gay men, delighted with the chance to note the fashion *faux pas*, chanted, "Your shoes don't match your gloves, your shoes don't match your gloves …"

Eventually, the chanting died down, and the police commander warned us that we would be arrested if we didn't move out of the street. Everything grew quiet—even among the hundreds of observers. None of us moved, and we were warned again. Still, no one moved.

I kept checking on how Dan was doing because he was not well, and the June day was sweltering. Quite a few members of our little group of "civil disobedients" were either HIV-positive or had full-blown AIDS, but adrenalin levels were high, and that most likely helped to keep everyone stable.

D.C. police are very experienced with demonstrations. They were professional—neither hostile nor friendly. Well, except for the yellow rubber gloves. Soon they moved in, those white plastic handcuffs in their hands, and began arresting us for disorderly conduct. With our hands secured behind us, we were loaded inside waiting police transport vehicles—some into small vans and others into a school bus painted white with police markings—presumably to be transported to jail.

We ended up at what appeared to be a police processing facility. We were separated by gender and placed into two large cells. Rather than somber or frightening, the experience turned out to be hilarious—imagine about forty gay men in one large jail cell! Gay wit was at its finest, and the noise from the women's cell suggested that our lesbian compatriots were having a fun time too. Even the police seemed to be enjoying the humor.

After a couple of hours, they began to process us for release. We handed over our fifty dollars in cash to pay the fine and went on our way. It all went without incident, and soon we were free again.

Amid the frivolity, though, there was some seriousness as well. Dan was on his feet and doing his best to participate. While the experience pleased Dan immensely, I am sure it also took a toll on his fragile body. To no one's surprise, he succumbed to AIDS the following January. He made a dying wish that his gravestone be inscribed with the words, "Here lies a gay civil rights lawyer." Sadly, his surviving siblings refused to grant his wish.

Two miles away at the Washington Hilton, Vice President George H.W. Bush spoke that day to more than six thousand scientists and health professionals at the third international conference on AIDS. Unwilling to promise much more than lip service to "an all-out war against the disease" of AIDS but "not against the victims of AIDS," he was booed for his proposals of routine testing of federal prisoners and immigrants, aliens seeking permanent residence, and anyone seeking a marriage license.

At the conclusion of his speech, Mr. Bush, obviously annoyed at the booing, leaned over to the assistant secretary for health next to him and asked over a live microphone, "Who was that? Some gay group out there?"

Clearly, the Human Rights Campaign Fund had a lot more work to battle the insensitivity of the Vice President and convince the Reagan administration that we needed more help—a lot more help. Randy Klose stepped up.

Dan Bradley
By Vic Basile

Among the reasons I so desperately wanted the executive director's job at HRCF, none was more important than the opportunity to work for LGBT equality with Dan Bradley. In 1982, he simultaneously came out and resigned as president of the Legal Services Corporation. President Jimmy Carter had appointed Dan to the position in 1979. At the time, he was the highest-ranking government official in history to declare his homosexuality publicly. The announcement was covered widely by the national media and prompted *Harper's* magazine to feature him in a cover story by civil rights historian Taylor Branch titled "Closets of Power."

Dan's life story could easily have been written by Horatio Alger. Despite being raised in a Georgia Baptist orphanage where life was highly regimented and discipline enforced according to the Old Testament, he developed an outgoing and friendly personality that made him popular at school. His classmates also saw his natural leadership qualities and elected him class president every year of high school. Upon entering Mercer University, his personality and natural propensity for politics got him elected freshman class president. As he described those who elected him, "I knew their names, faces, majors, where they came from, and their activities at school. I made it my business to know."

Subsequently, he enrolled in Mercer Law School and soon found himself drawn to advocacy on behalf of the poor. As a newly minted lawyer, he represented migrant farmworkers before joining the federal Legal Services program as a staff attorney, where he quickly moved up in the ranks. Florida governor Reubin Askew recruited him to be the state's racing commissioner, President Carter then tapped him to serve as president of the Legal Services Corporation, ensuring low-income individuals and families have access to quality legal aid.

Legal Services had been a thorn in the sides of Republicans for many years, and they repeatedly, but unsuccessfully, tried to kill the program. With Reagan's election, they thought the program could finally be eliminated, but Dan proved to be as adept a lobbyist as he was an administrator and advocate. His actions were widely credited for saving the program, and it continues to function to this day.

When Dan decided to come out, he knew that his action would likely give Republicans the leverage they needed to kill the program, so he chose to resign. He moved to Miami, where he practiced law, traveled the country speaking on behalf of LGBT equality, and joined the boards of the Gay Rights National Lobby and HRCF. Soon after, he was elected co-chair of the HRCF board, a position he held when I came to head the organization.

During an appearance on *Donahue*, Jerry Falwell told him that gays were condemned to hell unless they gave up their ways. Dan responded: "When I die and get to the Pearly Gates and St. Peter takes out his checklist on who is admitted to heaven, he is not going to ask my sexual orientation. He is going to ask, 'Did you do your good deeds? Did you help your neighbor? Did you help the poor?'"

Chapter 10:
I Want to Live

Randy Klose and I were sitting together on one of the upper bunks of the jail cell that housed us and our compatriots after our civil disobedience arrest, when the police donned yellow kitchen gloves to handcuff us and load us up in vans. Despite the jokes and laughter that permeated the cell, I noticed that Randy had gotten quiet. That was unusual because no one who knew him would ever accuse him of lacking gay humor. He could be as campy as anyone. Finally, he started talking about what might come next.

He correctly saw that our march on the White House to protest the Reagan administration's six years of ignoring the AIDS crisis, successful as it was, would be for naught if we failed to capitalize on and build the momentum. A few great media stories helped create public awareness and put a little pressure on the Reagan White House, but the public's attention span is short. In Randy's view, there needed to be a more robust plan to build on what we had accomplished that day if we were ever going to see any leadership from the administration on funding for AIDS research, treatment, and education programs.

Of course, he was right, but all HRCF's available resources were focused on lobbying Congress, where we had leverage. We had none at 1600 Pennsylvania Avenue, and at that point, I could see no way to break through that wall.

"I want you to find a lobbying firm that can get us into the White House," Randy said.

I looked at him, a little perplexed. HRCF was a small PAC

with a couple of lobbyists on staff since the Gay Rights National Lobby had merged with HRCF in 1985. (More on that later.) So now Randy wanted me to hire what would surely be an expensive outside firm to supplement our work?

"This isn't about gay rights," he said. "It's about AIDS. I want to live."

Ahh. All I could say was "okay" before he admonished me.

"And don't go shopping at Kmart! Don't worry about the cost. I'll cover it."

This was a substantial financial commitment – lobbying firms with that kind of reach do not come cheap, but if there was a chance to cut through the resistance, the rewards could be huge. With administration backing, the full weight of the government could be brought to bear in the battle. That could translate into significant funding increases and an end to the homophobic amendments that were crippling prevention programs. The possibilities were far too tantalizing and promising not to pursue.

Finding the right firm was challenging, but after consulting with Hilary Rosen, defense industry lobbyist and HRCF volunteer Tim Furlong, and others, we approached Wexler Reynolds, one of the most sought after and powerful firms in Washington, and one with what was at the time a novel approach to lobbying. Nearly all firms were associated with either one party or the other, but not both. Wexler Reynolds changed the paradigm and gambled that, together, their different party affiliations would give them access to all of the levers of power regardless of which party held the White House and Congress. Anne Wexler had been a highly respected Democratic operative for many years and an assistant to President Carter. Nancy Clark Reynolds had worked for Ronald Reagan when he was governor of California and had become a close family friend and confidante.

After some back and forth, we came to an agreement and left with our costly lobbying firm on board. How on board they were remains debatable. They did open a few important doors on Capitol Hill and provided some beneficial strategic advice, but they were less successful than we had hoped with our primary White House prize. And they were pricey—some months costing as much as $30,000. It is hard to say whether Reynolds was unwilling to spend the necessary political capital or that she was simply unable to make inroads. In fairness, Gary Bauer, the president's influential domestic policy advisor, was notoriously homophobic and conceivably could have blocked Reynolds from reaching the admittedly elusive goal we sought. He later led James Dobson's Family Research Council, an organization notorious for its opposition to gay equality.

The political game is a long one. It costs money to play—and a lot of it. A political action committee exists for the primary purpose of making campaign contributions to influence the outcomes of elections. To do so, money needs to be raised—the more raised, the more influence the PAC can have.

When the Human Rights Campaign Fund was established in 1980, campaign finance rules limited contributions from donors to $5,000 per year, and that money could come only from individuals and other PACs. Although Steve Endean had been able to get early seed money from Jim Hormel, Dallas Coors, Jack Campbell, and a few others, many more would have to be found if the Campaign Fund were to become a serious political player.

For help, Steve turned to his longtime friend Terry Bean, who got GRNL's major donor program off the ground. Terry is a natural-born salesman who I believe could sell just about anything to just about anyone. He is also passionate about LGBTQ equality; he has been out and in the battle for five decades. Those two qualities made him the ideal person to ask people for large contributions. That ability was not lost on Steve, and he secured a commitment from Terry to raise money for the Campaign Fund. Terry took on the role with gusto, traveling to any city where he could find potential donors who were willing to meet with him.

Steve knew the importance of getting the PAC onto a firm financial footing as soon as possible. For the 1982 elections, he was able to count nearly $610,000 in receipts from all sources, an eye-popping equivalent to $1,690,310 forty years later and more than double what the fundraising plan had projected. One hundred nineteen candidates shared $145,000 in direct contributions from HRCF.

Its early courting of wealthy benefactors earned it the nickname "Human Rights Champagne Fund," a moniker folks bandy about even today. As a PAC, by definition, HRCF was designed to be a money machine. If it was to be taken seriously, it needed to raise significant amounts of money.

HRCF took some heat from Larry Kramer and others for its commitment to fundraising and mainstream politics over street activism and more confrontational protests. But other organizations in the movement were leading terrific activist protests in response to the AIDS crisis. In 1987, Larry Kramer founded ACT UP, the AIDS Coalition to Unleash Power, to organize and mobilize the LGBTQ community to demand an effective AIDS government policy.

I saw my job as one of raising as much money as possible so HRCF could persuade Congress to pass a lesbian and gay civil rights law. While we never relinquished that commitment, within months of my coming on board, it was eclipsed by the need to generate funding for AIDS and save lives. Randy Klose handed over his wallet to open the door to the White House for us. Plenty of others ponied up to get us access to Congress.

I sought out people who could and would raise money to recommend for board consideration. A multitalented, politically savvy board would be a luxury. I didn't seek out board candidates for their expertise in politics or activism—though most of them were politically savvy. A lot of nonprofits do—they find wonderful, supportive people. But you can't run a successful PAC without money. We survived on our ability to donate to campaigns. Today, four decades after its founding, each of HRC's board members promises to give or raise fifty-thousand dollars in contributions annually. We certainly didn't have that expectation while I was the executive director. But each board member gave what they could afford. And much of the board meeting discussions were dedicated to fundraising.

Ironically, AIDS was a catalyst for opening the wallets of major donors, emboldening many to come forward who might otherwise have remained closeted. As Randy Klose exemplified, their money had protected them from discrimination, but it didn't protect them from the virus.

Randy Klose came from Texas, where his family owned all the Dairy Queens in Texas and Oklahoma. After reading an essay in which Larry Kramer of ACT UP said he wanted to know why wealthy homosexuals were not responding to the crisis, Randy said, "I read the article and said to myself, 'Here I am.'"

I first met Randy in Los Angeles through HCRF board co-chair Duke Comegys, a wealthy art collector and fundraiser who had led the board of the Los Angeles Gay and Lesbian Community Services Center, for which he had raised substantial sums. Duke hosted a luncheon at his home in Bel Air for several of his friends who could write big checks. He spoke about HRCF and our efforts to secure more funding for AIDS research and treatment at the event.

Randy arrived at the lunch in his Rolls Royce. I don't think he was more than twenty-eight years old. He didn't say much, and he didn't stay long, but he wrote us a check for $10,000. Duke pulled me aside.

"Cultivate him," he whispered to me. "He can give a lot more."

So I did. I invited Randy to Capitol Hill and introduced him to Senator Lowell Weicker, the chair of the appropriations subcommittee responsible for AIDS funding. I then introduced him to House Majority Whip Tony Coelho, who, as he was shaking his hand, smiled and said, "Dairy Queen, huh?" The next stop was in New York to meet the renowned AIDS researcher Dr. Mathilde Krim, who encouraged him to become more involved with HRCF. Dr. Krim founded the American Foundation for AIDS Research with Elizabeth Taylor. These meetings convinced Randy that HRCF was a credible organization that, given adequate resources, could influence government policy and funding.

After that, Randy started to write bigger checks. I think his second check may have been for $50,000. By the time he died in 1992, I'm sure he had given us a million dollars and raised millions more. We became his home away from home, and he soon bought a house in Dupont Circle so he could play a more active role in HRCF and our work. Randy was committed to the lesbian and gay community and the battle against AIDS, and he could demonstrate that through HRCF in a way he could not in Los Angeles in the eighties.

Randy wasn't interested in sitting in his beautiful Beverly Hills home and writing checks. He organized. He lobbied members of Congress, and he was instrumental in the passage of the Federal AIDS Research and Information Act (S1220) in 1988. The Act added millions of dollars to the NIH's AIDS research budget, added 750 positions the newly created Office on AIDS within the Department of Health and Human Services (HHS), and authorized money for prevention programs. He went to practically every major town in this country and encouraged people to organize Federal Clubs. He was a worker, and his passion for HRCF made him a better fundraiser.

At every single board meeting, Randy stood up and reminded us of why we were there.

"Look," he said, "we're not raising money for some hospital here. This isn't the opera, you know. This is our lives. These are our friends. This is our family."

No wonder there were so many tears at board meetings. Randy went from being a fancy rich kid to a fierce warrior—a transformation that inspired all of us. He essentially set the bar for what I came to consider "extremely significant." He, in turn, considered HRCF extremely significant.

As Randy told me defiantly that day in the Washington jail, he wanted to live. And live he did—fully and much longer than most in those days. I believe his involvement with HRCF and unshakable commitment to the struggle literally added years to his life.

Wealthy donors like Randy formed one of the pillars of our success. Another important group of professional men gathered in two houses at Pajaro Dunes on the Monterey Peninsula in California. Jerry Berg brought them together after California voters had rejected the "No on 6" campaign, an initiative to ban gays from teaching in public schools. Most of them were fairly closeted at the time. They decided at that meeting to do some polling to learn more about the gay community in California. They organized a dinner at one member's home and sold twenty tickets for $1,000 a plate to pay for the research. These men were affluent, influential, and very committed to building the gay community.

They continued to meet over the years, using their skills, money, and connections to contribute to the fight for gay equality. Among them were Jim Hormel, Chuck Forester, David Goodstein, Jim Foster, Larry Bye, Jerry Berg, and Bob Sass, all of whom were instrumental in developing HRCF. These men knew how to use the political system and gain access to influential politicians. For example, as then-Mayor Dianne Feinstein's liaison to the gay community, Chuck Forester brought issues important to the San

Francisco gay community directly to her. Chuck would go on to join the HRCF board and eventually serve as co-chair.

These men bought tickets to the events. They helped put on the dinners. They played a huge role in the establishment and growth of the Human Rights Campaign Fund.

As committed as I was to raising money for our movement, it never got easy to ask for it directly. Steve Shellabarger loves to remind me of the story of a fundraising dinner he hosted in Columbus early in my tenure at HRCF, which I attended. Columbus philanthropist Sue Greer, who had a gay son and a lesbian daughter, became deeply supportive of our efforts after her son was diagnosed with HIV.

I had my eye on Sue that night in Columbus. At what I thought was the right time, I turned to Steve and quietly mentioned I was going to make a request of Sue.

"Do you want to come with me?" I asked Steve. As important as these direct appeals were, and as often as I made them, it was never easy for me to ask someone for thousands of dollars. I was appropriately uneasy, and I appreciated having Steve at my side for moral support.

Together we approached Sue, and after some pleasant chitchat, I looked at her directly.

"Sue," I asked. "Would you consider making a contribution to the Campaign Fund for $10,000?"

I could feel Steve squirming a bit next to me. No one else would pick up on it, but I knew Steve well, and knew when he was nervous. Or maybe I was sensing my own anxiety, which I hoped wasn't evident. After what seemed like an eternity but probably lasted only the few seconds it took her to comprehend my request, Sue replied.

"Sure," she said.

And she pulled out her checkbook and wrote a check for $10,000.

Steve and I thanked her, of course. I pocketed the check and turned away.

"Damn," I said to Steve under my breath. "That was too easy. I should have asked for more."

Early in 1985, word got around that someone from Omaha had shown up in D.C. with $10,000 that he wanted to give to a national organization fighting AIDS. In 1985, a contribution of that size was virtually unheard of, so word about it spread quickly. The donor had chosen the Gay Rights National Lobby as the beneficiary of the gift.

Don Randolph, a self-described "illusionist," delivered the check, claiming he raised the money doing drag shows at a bar back home. However, with his scruffy beard and very masculine appearance, it was difficult to imagine Don in drag, let alone raising all that money while performing.

The check was drawn on the account of The Imperial Court of Nebraska, an affiliate of the International Imperial Court System (IICS), a network of independent "empires" located throughout North America. The larger empires produce very elaborate and grand annual balls to raise funds benefitting the LGBTQ community and coronate a new empress and emperor. This, of course, only added to the cryptic nature of the donor and the gift.

Six months later, Don returned to Washington with $10,000 more for GRNL, and not surprisingly, was invited to join GRNL's board. A short time later, GRNL merged with HRCF, and Don was immediately invited to join our board.

Arriving at his first meeting with another $10,000, he confided to me that, although he technically raised the money at a drag show, it was almost entirely from a single anonymous donor.

A few months later, Don called me to say that the anonymous donor wanted to come to Washington to see exactly where his money was going. Of course, I knew this was a very big deal and that a successful meeting might produce not only another $10,000 but possibly a steady stream of gifts. To ensure that we made a positive impression, I asked Hilary Rosen, our lobbyist, and political director Eric Rosenthal to prepare presentations on the status of AIDS treatment and care issues in Congress and relevant campaigns that we were following and in which we were likely to become involved.

When Don and the mysterious donor arrived, I finally learned that his name was Terry Watanabe. A mere twenty-eight years old, he owned Oriental Trading Company, a catalog business that sold inexpensive toys, novelties, and party supplies. He had taken over the business from his father by the time he turned twenty-one and transformed it from a small carnival supply company to one much broader, marketing directly to the general public. Over a few years, it had grown to become one of Omaha's largest companies.

I could see that he was very nervous, even more than I was, so I made some small talk, hoping it would help relax both of us. Then I asked him if he would like to hear more about our work from Hilary and Eric, but instead, he asked if there was somewhere just the two of us could talk. So we went to my office. After an hour of conversation, he reached into his jeans pocket to retrieve a crumpled piece of paper that turned out to be a personal check, wrote it out, and handed it to me. I nearly passed out when I saw that it was for $50,000. I was expecting another $10,000, or if we were incredibly lucky, maybe $25,000, but not an astonishing $50,000.

Then came the wrinkle: the money had to go to a tax-deductible 501(c)3 organization. HRCF was a political action committee that had only recently begun to lobby with the acquisition of GRNL. Contributions to neither organization were in any way eligible for tax deductions. HRCF did not have a foundation in which to deposit the check, and Terry was quite resolute in his desire for the tax deduction. I offered to take a third less (the approximate value of the tax-deduction) if he would make the contribution in "hard money," which may be spent without restriction, but does not qualify the donor for a tax deduction because it is being used directly for the election or defeat of specific candidates. He insisted on the deduction.

It isn't all that difficult to establish a 501(c)3 entity. It simply takes a little time to get documents prepared, and then there is the long wait for IRS approval. More to the point, though, was the need to create a purpose for the new entity that complemented the mission of HRCF. The money, however tempting, would be little more than a distraction if we failed to accomplish that goal.

Fortunately, we had a research and polling project we were eager to start. So many members of Congress would privately say that they were with us, but they couldn't afford to be public about it for fear that it would be used against them in the next election. This was despite the fact that no House or Senate candidate had ever lost a re-election bid because of their support for gay issues. If we could document this through compelling research and polling, it would theoretically make it easier for elected officials to be more supportive. A 501(c)3 arm would be the perfect vehicle to do this kind of work because it could use tax-deductible money, which is much easier to raise, to pay for it, and $50,000 would be more than enough to fund it.

The possibility that we could miss this great opportunity if there were no place to put the funds made me desperate to find a solution. Then it occurred to me that perhaps another nonprofit organization could hold the money for us until we got our own established. It seemed like a great idea until I tried to think of an organization that would do us this considerable favor—and one that was sure to give the money back when we could legally accept it. Finally, I remembered that my friend Ellen Malcolm, founder of EMILY's List, which funds campaigns for pro-choice Democratic women, had a private foundation, and she gladly agreed to help. With the money secured, we were able to begin mapping out the research and polling project. Terry's gift was more than monetary. It prompted us to establish a tax-exempt foundation so that HRCF could offer tax deductions to those donors who wanted them.

Meanwhile, I had not completely given up on helping Terry understand the importance of hard money (non-tax-deductible and thus harder to raise) to the battle against HIV/AIDS. The only source of enough money to effectively conduct research and to care for those who were sick was the federal government, and until his 1986 budget, Ronald Reagan proposed no money for these purposes. What little federal money that had been appropriated came from Congressional initiatives. The fact that spending for research and treatment was increasing was due to effective lobbying by HRCF, the National Gay and Lesbian Task Force, AIDS Action Council, and others. In addition, it reflected successes in electing our friends to Congress and getting our enemies out. All of these hard-won gains were only possible through the use of hard money.

After I had found a temporary home for Terry's gift, he, Don, and I went to dinner. With the alcohol flowing, I again attempted to explain why hard money mattered so much. He asked questions that revealed that I wasn't making much progress. He seemed doubtful that it made any real difference.

"Give us $5,000 of hard money, and I'll show you what we can do with it!" I blurted in frustration.

As soon as the words left my mouth, I desperately longed to stuff them back in. The man had just made our largest gift by far, and here I was, demanding more.

That was it, I thought. *He is going to ask for the $50k back.*

Instead, he reached into his pocket, pulled out another crumpled check, wrote it out for $5,000, and handed it to me. Swallowing hard, I managed to say thank you as I put the check neatly into my pocket.

Early the following day, Terry and Don were on a plane headed back to Omaha. Although I tried to reach Terry several times over the next few months, he was completely unresponsive. It was like he simply disappeared. Finally, maybe a year later, I got a phone call from his assistant telling me that Terry was in Washington and asking if I could have dinner with him. Naturally, I agreed.

At dinner, I opted not to ask him for another gift, thinking it was better to get to know him more and build a trusting relationship. I learned that he was a Republican, which wasn't surprising given that he was a successful businessman from Nebraska, and that his political views were driven exclusively by economics. He was refreshingly not very political, and he just wanted to help in the battle against AIDS.

After dinner, we decided to do a little barhopping. As the evening wore on, Terry asked if I was going to ask him for anything, to which I responded that I would not.

He reached into his pocket for a check and handed it to me. It was for another $50,000, and this time it was hard money, meaning that it was completely unrestricted so, among other things, it could be spent on political activities.

Randy Klose
By Steven Dwyer

For some, activism is a calling. For Randall "Randy" Klose, it was a matter of survival. As he explained, he had never really faced discrimination until he had AIDS, and then his world abruptly changed. As an heir to the Texas Dairy Queen franchise, growing up, he pursued a career in theater and had settled into a comfortable life in New York. Post diagnosis, living with a president who didn't care about helping gays with HIV/AIDS, he discovered that he was no different from other gays, except that he had access to better health care. The line "I am sick of gay men who won't support gay charities" in Larry Kramer's essay "1,112 and Counting" hit a nerve, and Randy rose to the challenge, checkbook in hand.

While perhaps best remembered for his role as co-chair of the Board of Directors for the Human Rights Campaign Fund, Randy accomplished much more through his actions and philanthropy.

When Richard Berkowitz, Michael Callen, and Dr. Joseph Sonnabend wrote the groundbreaking pamphlet "How to Have Sex in an Epidemic," their funding requests to amfAR and the Gay Men's Health Crisis were turned down. However, a donation from Randy made the publication of this safer sex manual possible, and no doubt saved lives and changed the conversation about AIDS in the gay community.

In 1987, Randy became a member of HRCF's board of directors. He became so involved in the life of HRCF—from conducting fundraising seminars to performing carpentry around the office—he moved to Washington, D.C. When the organization participated in the protest at the White House, he was among those to be arrested. As a board member, Randy was very opinionated on what should be undertaken, but unlike many, he backed up his opinions with his checkbook and his active participation. When he suggested that HRCF hire a lobbyist, he stepped up with funding to pay for one.

Few know that Randy filed as a plaintiff along with Donald Knutson and the National Gay Rights Advocates in a class-action civil lawsuit against the National Institutes of Health, the Food and Drug Administration, and the Department of Health in Human Services for alleged "improper conduct" in the area of testing and approval of experimental AIDS drugs. The lawsuit charged that NIH improperly favored NIH-supported drugs and set stricter standards of approval for non-NIH-sponsored drugs.

His efforts contributed to the passage of the first federal AIDS law, the 1988 Federal AIDS Research and Information Act. The two chief Senate co-sponsors of S.1220, Edward M. Kennedy and Lowell P. Weicker Jr., praised him for his actions.

Randy supported the International Lesbian and Gay Human Rights Commission and traveled with them in 1991 to Moscow. The group participated in the first Russian Gay Pride and brought along computers and equipment to help establish a Russian gay press.

Knowing that in politics, money brings access, he was an early supporter of Bill Clinton's presidential campaign. He not only provided personal donations, but he sought to engage HRCF and other LGBTQ organizations in the campaign. Using his fundraising prowess, he helped bundle individual contributions to the campaign to show the power of gay support. Sadly, he passed from AIDS shortly before the 1992 election. He was only thirty-seven years old.

Chapter 11:
Dinners and Drinks

HRCF's now iconic black-tie dinners were first held in 1982. The prototype for the dinners came from a now-defunct California political action committee, the Municipal Elections Committee of Los Angeles, or MECLA, which, according to the *Los Angeles Times*, quickly established the lesbian and gay community as "one of the most powerful new minority groups in California politics."

Coupling a black-tie dinner and political pragmatism quickly provided MECLA with phenomenal success. It also demonstrated that well-known politicians and even a few celebrities would attend a very public gay and lesbian event, thus providing invaluable visibility, stature, and legitimacy. Plus, the high-ticket price not only meant more money for candidates but also revealed the community's financial clout.

That's just what we wanted to do for the Human Rights Campaign Fund.

To the delight of everyone associated with the first HRCF dinners in 1982, we soon realized how much fun it would be to get out of the gay bars and throw a party. Inviting LGBTQ people to dress in evening gowns and tuxedos at a fancy hotel for dinner, drinks, and dancing—while doing good for the community—was revolutionary for us at the time.

The New York dinner featured Vice President Walter Mondale, the frontrunner for the 1984 Democratic presidential nomination, as the keynote speaker. At the time, it was risky for anyone seeking national office to attend such an event, but Mr.

Mondale came, and more than six hundred people paid $150 a plate to hear him. The evening attracted national media attention from *The New York Times, The Washington Post, USA Today,* and *Time* magazine. ABC News's *Nightline* devoted an entire show to emerging gay political clout and featured interviews with Steve Endean and Dan Bradley.

"Nothing like that had ever happened before," said Vivian Shapiro, who worked in advertising in New York, was on the dinner committee, and would soon co-chair the HRCF board. "In that one night, everything seemed to change," she said. After joining the board, Vivian crisscrossed the country, speaking at events and raising a considerable amount of money for the organization.

Boston and Philadelphia held similar events in 1982, featuring keynote addresses by noted politicians; many local elected officials also attended.

Jim Foster went to Dallas to ask his friend John Thomas, who had recently moved from Miami to Dallas, to hold a dinner in Dallas. John Thomas (for some reason, folks tended to call him by his first and last names) worked for the (now-defunct) *Dallas Times Herald*. He was the head of human resources for the paper, which made sense because he was just such a likable guy and cared about everyone he met. He had a deep passion for politics, particularly gay politics. When he was in Florida, he was active in the Dade County effort to retain the gay rights ordinance that Anita Bryant's Save Our Children campaign defeated.

John was the perfect point person to organize the first dinner in Dallas. He asked Mike Anglin and Ray Kuchling to join them, and Jim presented the concept of the dinner. The men knew they were taking on a risky project. At $150 each, the tickets were pricey for 1982 (they are $400 now), and the money raised would benefit some organization in Washington nobody had ever heard of. These guys were very busy in several other gay community efforts, including launching the AIDS Resource Center. But the men recognized the need for a strong presence in Washington, D.C. And the three of them would have to guarantee the cost of the expensive hotel banquet room.

"I guess the more the three of us talked about it, the more we goaded each other into the *possibility* of saying yes," Mike Anglin has said about that first dinner. "It did seem like it could be, at least, a fun project to try, even if it didn't raise any money. And it was clear that nothing of this sort had ever happened before in the Dallas gay community.

"John said we should only do it if all three of us were willing to take it on as an active priority. We each had to commit to it all the way through to the end. Ray jumped in first and said yes ...but only if John and I both said yes."

Then John said, "What the heck. They can't shoot us for trying."

The three agreed to participate—with a caveat. They would donate half the proceeds to local lesbian and gay nonprofits and send half to HRCF.

After the first meeting with Jim, they started to organize a good-sized steering committee. Fellow activist Dick Weaver had an extensive network of friends in the community, and the next night he hosted a gathering at his apartment to enroll a team to get the ball rolling.

Such pre-event parties became instrumental in the success of the black-tie dinners around the country. Hosts entertained potential table captains, and the table captains committed to paying for a table or filling a table with ten paying guests. The evenings were always festive, offering an opportunity for lesbians and gays to gather socially someplace other than a bar. Folks would announce their intention to buy a table to the group, encouraging others to do the same. Perhaps an element of friendly competition prodded them, or maybe it was the free-flowing alcohol. Whatever it was, these pre-dinner parties always contributed to the enormous success of the dinners in Dallas and around the country.

Perhaps no one held a more successful table captain party than Bob Alfandre, who hosted a gathering to prepare for the second Washington, D.C., dinner at his Kalorama Circle home. Bob was an eclectic guy born in Brooklyn. After college, he worked for the CIA but quit when he realized a gay man had no future as a spy. Instead, he made his fortune building houses in suburban Washington. It was a tender evening for Bob, as he had just lost his partner, Carroll Sledz, to AIDS. His emotions were high and his commitment to a successful evening was strong. He knew if he could get one person to commit to buying a table, it was a lot easier to fill all the tables. So Bob did what he did best—he asked.

Bob had a theatrical streak in him, and he could make you laugh one minute and cry the next. First, he shared a little about why the Campaign Fund and our work to get federal funds to fight AIDS were important to him. Next, he shared a bit about Carroll's fight against the virus. Then Bob captivated us with a poignant Shakespeare quote, evoking his memory of and love for Carroll.

"When he shall die, take him and cut him out into little stars, and he will make the face of heaven so fine that all the world will be in love with night, and pay no worship to the garish sun."

He had the room in tears. And he waited just the right amount of time to let the poignancy of the moment sink in before he spoke again.

"So," Bob asked, "who will buy a table?"

Everyone did.

That single table captain party tripled attendance at the Washington dinner from the year before.

Bob Alfandre
From the Rainbow History Project,
RainbowHistory.org

Bob Alfandre's legacy lies in his generosity of time, money, and spirit. He grew up in Washington, D.C., served in World War II, and did a brief stint with the CIA. He left the spy agency during the early days of the McCarthyite witch hunts, convinced that his life as a gay man would make career advancement impossible. Instead, he focused on the modest construction company he inherited from his father, Joe Alfandre. With his brother, he became a major participant in D.C.'s postwar economic boom. The Aldre Construction Company built large housing developments in suburban Washington. Bob used his wealth to become a prominent philanthropist for the LGBT community.

Through the 1970s, eighties, and nineties, he opened his home for many benefits and causes, giving early support to local and national gay and lesbian organizations, such as the Whitman-Walker Clinic, the AIDS Quilt, and the Human Rights Campaign. Beyond his work on behalf of these organizations, Bob was a major supporter of gay and gay-friendly local politicians, helping many in their first elections to city-wide positions.

During the height of the AIDS crisis, Bob bought a small home in Washington and converted it into a hospice for those who had nowhere else to go. Almost entirely at his own expense, Bob financed the day-to-day operations of the hospice. He named it the Carroll Sledz House, in memory of the partner he lost to the epidemic. The house had eight beds. Bob recalls that during the height of the crisis, not one sat vacant: "There was always someone to take an empty place."

Through subtle persuasion of his circle of Washington's gay social elite and his largesse, Bob raised millions of dollars for the Whitman-Walker

Clinic and is largely responsible for the Elizabeth Taylor Medical Center, opening in 1993. The in-house pharmacy there is named in his honor.

Like many gay men of his generation, when Bob was young, he had married a woman and had a family. When he met Carroll Sledz and fell deeply in love, Bob divorced his wife and moved out of his Georgetown house and into Sledz's Capitol Hill apartment. But Bob and his wife remained friends. In recent years, he remarried his wife. He has two daughters; one runs the family business while the other founded a ballet company in Newport, Rhode Island.

On June 12, 2014, Bob Alfandre passed away at his home in Washington, D.C., after a long struggle with cancer.

Dallas hosted their first dinner that year at the Fairmont Hotel and has held a dinner every year since. The first dinner drew one hundred forty people paying a $150 a ticket and netted $6,000.

Dallas is one of only two cities in the country—with Boston—that has hosted a dinner every year since 1982. (They held dinners each year except 2020, when COVID-19 prohibited all large gatherings.) It is now the largest local fundraising dinner for the LGBTQ community, distributing over $1 million. More than three thousand people attend the event, which sells out months in advance.

The number of black-tie dinners grew every year after Philip Dufour joined the staff and helped to organize them in Seattle, Atlanta, and Chicago. In 1997, under the leadership of Elizabeth Birch, the Washington dinner became a national dinner and welcomed President Bill Clinton as the keynote speaker. He became the first sitting president to address an LGBTQ audience. In 1998, Vice President Al Gore became the first sitting vice president to keynote a dinner. Later, Philip invited Tipper Gore to attend dinners in Raleigh, Nashville, New Orleans, and Salt Lake City.

The dinners also gave attendees a chance to enjoy an elegant event with a friend, lover, or partner in a public way they otherwise would never have done. And they could dance!

Meeting planner Joan Eisenstodt negotiated all our hotel contracts. She and Philip Dufour traveled to Boston before one of the early dinners on a site visit. They discussed the requirements needed for the dinner, including what would be necessary for music and dancing.

"Dancing?" the hotel event manager asked her. "You mean like men dancing with men?"

Joan assured him that was precisely what she meant.

"Oh, we don't do that here," the manager insisted.

"Oh, yes, you will," Joan insisted. "Let me remind you that you have signed a contract with us. Whoever wants to dance will dance with whomever he chooses."

And they did.

The black-tie dinners in the 1980s encouraged lesbians and gays to get involved in the movement by reinforcing a sense of mainstream legitimacy.

"It was just a couple of hundred people, but it was amazing," said Ellen Malcolm, founder of EMILY's List, of her first dinner in Washington. "This was *my* dinner! To get all dressed up and go to a hotel with our friends—it felt like we were living a 'normal' life, fully visible to the world. As the dinners grew, so did the pride and the excitement of being there. The people who came to speak were extraordinary. It was just wonderful."

"I came out as a lesbian thirteen years ago," said one woman attending a dinner. "But in many ways, I view my political coming out as having happened at my first HRC dinner. Writing my first check was my way of saying, 'I matter. I can make a difference.'"

The Human Rights Campaign Fund dinners began to legitimatize the gay community in the eyes of politicians, who were accustomed to generalizing the movement as long dominated by street activists. Apparently, seeing lesbians and gay men dressed in evening attire made us more "acceptable" in the eyes of straight power brokers. Indeed, those dinners set a standard for gay fundraising and gay visibility, and they enjoy phenomenal success across the country to this day.

Today, keynoting a black-tie dinner is a prized opportunity, but that wasn't always the case. Dallas can command pretty much anyone they want for a dinner now—they have enjoyed hearing D.C. Congresswoman Eleanor Holmes Norton; actress and Dallas native Morgan Fairchild; Gerry Studds, the first openly gay member of Congress, and even former governor Ann Richards. But one year, a noted author did not show up. So, board member Vivian Shapiro, who came from New York simply to attend the dinner, took the dais and ad-libbed her way through the evening to a standing ovation.

New York City, from the first dinner with Mondale, drew notables deeply committed to civil rights. At the dinner in 1983, the speaker was the Reverend Jesse Jackson. I went in a limousine to pick Jackson up at his hotel. We were about twenty minutes early, so the driver—a big, burly guy with a strong Brooklyn accent—pulled over to wait. I was already a little nervous because it was my first dinner as HRCF's executive director, and New York is a tough town. The driver wanted to talk, and he wanted to know what event we were attending. Wishing to avoid any distracting unpleasantness, I wasn't too eager to come out to this guy, so I told him Jackson was in town for a political dinner.

"Oh, what kind of political dinner?" the driver asked.

"Well," I said, trying to decide how much to tell him. "It's a human rights dinner."

"What kind of human rights?" he asked.

I evaded for as long as I could until, finally, I just thought: *Oh, what the hell?*

"It's a gay and lesbian dinner," I admitted.

All was quiet for a minute while we both contemplated my confession.

"Oh," this big guy with the strong New York accent said. Then the tone of his voice brightened. "That's pretty good. I'm kind of AC/DC myself. Okay!"

I learned that night never to trust stereotypes.

Perhaps my most memorable dinner—other than the night President Clinton spoke in Washington—was in New York in September 1986. That night, Coretta Scott King stepped to the podium to deliver the keynote address.

"My dear friend Winston Johnson asked me to be here this evening, and I am here to express my solidarity with the gay and lesbian movement."

And as incredible as it was to hear Mrs. King announce her support for our movement, I was even more proud that she acknowledged Winston Johnson.

Winston first met Mrs. King on April 5, 1968, when Eastern Airlines, for whom he worked, flew her husband's body to Atlanta the day after his assassination in Memphis. Winston worked with VIPs and celebrities who visited the first-class lounge between flights, and over time he became good friends with Mrs. King, who traveled frequently to build the King Center. Winston never came out to her—or anyone at work—until 1986, when the U.S. Supreme Court upheld Georgia's sodomy law. Now it had become personal.

"There's something we should have talked about years ago," Winston told her. "Leon [his partner] and I are a couple. We've been together since 1964."

And then he asked her the question that made me so proud of him that evening.

He asked her to speak to the HRCF dinner in New York City that September.

"Well, tell me where and I'll be there," Mrs. King replied.

The afternoon before the dinner, Winston and I picked her up at LaGuardia Airport, and she shared a conversation she had with her husband about gay rights. King was close to Bayard Rustin, the Black civil rights activist who was also gay, advisor to King, and the chief organizer of the 1963 March on Washington at which King delivered his "I Have a Dream" speech. She told me that her husband said the lesbian and gay movement was the next major civil rights struggle.

Winston later invited President Jimmy Carter to speak at a dinner. He declined, likely dissuaded by his political minions. Carter always was personally supportive of our movement, but publicly he was too quiet, unfortunately, until later in life he came out in support of marriage equality.

Winston Johnson
By Terry Bird, friend of Winston Johnson

Winston Johnson grew up in Greenville, Florida, where his father, Bethel Johnson, owned a successful hardware store. Winston and his next older brother Hjalma Johnson told me about the times in 1955, 1956, and 1957 when hometown celebrity singer Ray Charles would return to Greenville each year in a new Cadillac Eldorado convertible.

Fighting depression and fear of the Johns Committee, Winston dropped out of the University of Florida. (The Johns Committee, formally known as the Florida Legislative Investigation Committee, investigated lesbian and gay students and faculty in Florida public schools.) In 1963, he joined the U.S. Navy Reserves on active duty at Millington Naval Base in Millington, Tennessee. He took a job with Seaboard Coast Lines railroad in Jacksonville and met Leon Allen, who also lived in Jacksonville. They started their loving relationship in April 1964 and decided to move to Atlanta in 1967 for a better life, taking an apartment as "roommates." Winston and Leon met when homosexuality was not discussed openly, and gay men stayed in the closet if they wanted a career. Their move to Atlanta was to distance themselves from family (Leon's close-knit Syrian Catholic family and Winston's large Southern family) and for the opportunities a big city offered.

Winston was soon hired by Eastern Airlines ["EAL"] to work in customer service during what he called "the halcyon days of air travel." His first assignment was driving the EAL Lincoln sedan to pick up VIP passengers and deliver them to their flight right on the tarmac. He met Hollywood celebrities and politicians as well as successful businesspeople.

Winston told me the story of his friend Rodney, who held a managerial job at Winn-Dixie: one day in the 1980s, the top executives called Rodney in and told him they had hired a staff detective to follow him. "You are often seen going to the opera with other men," they said and asked him if he was a homosexual. When Rodney admitted that was so, they told him they did not hire homosexuals and fired him.

Stories like that from Winston and Leon and other true accounts of discrimination raised my consciousness, so when the first Human Rights Campaign Fund fundraising dinner was proposed for Atlanta in 1988, Winston immediately signed up as a table captain and made sure that his other friends, including me, did too. That dinner was a success, and Winston was an ardent supporter of HRCF for the rest of his life.

In his twenty-four-year career at EAL and later in sales at Carey Limousine of Atlanta, Winston came in contact with many well-placed people, politicians, and show business celebrities. He met Coretta Scott King the day after her husband was assassinated; they became friends after that.

One seminal event in Winston's advocacy came after Jimmy and Rosalyn Carter invited Winston and two coworkers at EAL to a White House State dinner around 1978. Still in the closet at that time, Winston attended by himself. Other people took their spouses. After President Carter left office, Winston came out to President and Mrs. Carter. He told President Carter how much his partner Leon would have enjoyed the White House dinner and how he wished he could have said, "I have a life partner, Leon Allen. May I bring him?" Jimmy Carter was saddened to hear this and sympathetic, telling Winston he would have supported him in that request.

And as the years went on, Winston became more open about his sexual orientation, talking with Coretta Scott King and other civil rights leaders, including John Lewis, Julian Bond, and Xernona Clayton.

When Oprah Winfrey and Stedman Graham were delayed for hours in Atlanta, unable to fly Chicago, they spent the afternoon with Winston, and he told them about his life as a gay man.

After Eastern Airlines ceased business in 1990, Winston became sales manager at Carey Limousine of Atlanta, a job he did well with his Rolodex full of connections to well-placed people. However, after five years, Leon's Parkinson's disease worsened, and Winston resigned from Carey to become Leon's primary caregiver for the next twelve years until Leon died.

In addition to his political activism with HRC, at the end of his life, Winston fought for the full spectrum of end-of-life options. Suffering terminal cancer, he decried the fact that Georgia had no "right-to-die" laws. "I am not afraid of dying," Winston said, "I just want to avoid the pain. A few years ago, in an emergency room, I was in excruciating pain for twelve hours, and the doctor refused to treat my pain appropriately. I, a man in my seventies, cried and writhed in pain. When one is terminally ill, if that person is of sound mind, it should be up to that person to decide when they can take no more."

Winston always was offended by injustice, whether it came from discrimination because of race or sexual orientation. He used his connections as opportunities to try to convince people with power that we should make our society fair for all people.

Nobel Peace Prize-winner, and Holocaust historian and survivor Elie Wiesel addressed HRC's New York dinner in 1989.

"Those who are bigots do not stop at classes and races or at gays or lesbians," he said. "Those who hate you hate me. So why should I not be here to speak to you about self-respect and civil rights?"

Some cities weren't ready to host large public dinners at hotel ballrooms. Instead, they held cocktail parties in private homes. These more intimate affairs tended to have a lower cost of fundraising. Often the hosts covered the expenses so HRCF could receive all of the proceeds.

San Francisco's first event was in 1985 in a loft. In Los Angeles, Duke Comegys, Randy Klose, Billy Bernardo, and Sheldon Andelson, a prominent banker who was a Democratic Party activist and donor, threw private cocktail parties. Some cities, like Washington, D.C., and Columbus, at first hosted smaller parties and receptions. Washington's first dinner took place in 1984, and Columbus didn't hold a formal dinner until the late 1980s.

In 1984, I went to Columbus for their first fundraiser, a cocktail party. Steve Shellabarger invited attendees to bring an appetizer and fifty dollars. His friends donated the alcohol and flowers, which they auctioned off at the end of the evening. I went home with $6,000. It was a good night.

The following year, Columbus held another fabulous cocktail party which Dagmar Celeste, the wife of the Ohio governor, attended, doubling attendance, and cementing the community's legitimacy in the eyes of the top officeholder in the state.

"I always knew if we were going to make political progress," Steve Shellabarger told me, "We had to be successful in the same way that every minority group in history in the United States of America has ever made it. And that's through the political process and doing things like everybody else does, like the Jewish community has done, like the black community has done, like labor. We had to do it not simply through demonstrations, not through wild, crazy stuff. If gay people were going to become accepted, we had to make friends in the right places. We had to raise money. We had to campaign; we had to make friends and lobby. We needed to follow the political process and make it work for us, as it had worked for others."

Vic Basile and Steve Endean, circa 1988

Photo by Doug Hinckle, courtesy of the Washington Blade.

From left: Vic Basile, Kate Clinton, Leslie Tolf, Hilary Rosen and Vivian Shapiro. Washington HRCF dinner, 1986.

Photo by © JEB (Joan E. Biren)

Billy Bernado, Randy Klose and Vic Basile, 1987 March on Washington.

Photo courtesy of Vic Basile

Winston Johnson and Coretta Scott King, New York HRCF dinner, 1986.

Photo by Pamela Camhe

Chuck Forester, Vic Basile and Duke Comegys,
HRCF board meeting, Key West, 1988.

Photo courtesy of Vic Basile

Steve Smith, Karen Friedman, Eric Rosenthal, Steve Endean, 1991.

Photo courtesy of Gregory Gibbs

Dan Bradley, photo taken several months before his death in 1988.

Photo the *Miami Herald,* 1987, McClatchy.
All rights reserved.
Used under license.

"White House AIDS demonstration", June 1, 1987.
From left: Jean O'Leary, Vic Basile, Dan Bradley,
Leonard Matlovitch and Rev. Troy Perry.

Photo by Patsy Lynch

"White House AIDS demonstration", June 1, 1987.

Photo by Patsy Lynch

Tim McFeeley, 1991

Photo by Patsy Lynch

President Bill Clinton and HRC Executive Director Elizabeth Birch, HRC National Dinner, 1987.

Photo by Chris Klepbonis (Courtesy of the Human Rights Campaign)

Chapter 12:
Marvin Collins and the Federal Club

Not too many months into my tenure as HRCF's executive director, I met Marvin Collins, a Republican political operative from Texas. Marvin had managed George H. W. Bush's campaign for the United States Senate in 1970 and then became the executive director of the Texas Republican Party. That was followed by a stint at the American Council of Life Insurers as their chief counsel, a job he left out of sheer boredom. Marvin was a highly skilled campaign operative, and lawyering for the life insurance industry wasn't enough to get his adrenaline flowing.

Marvin was also gay and drawn to the fledgling lesbian and gay movement, even though he was mostly closeted (and, sadly, remained so until he died in 2005). After some discussions, he suggested that he join the HRCF staff as a full-time volunteer. I very enthusiastically agreed.

Once on board, his incredible organizing skills quickly emerged when he suggested that I go on the road to recruit local lesbian and gay leaders to organize support in their respective communities. He then set about what I viewed as the nearly impossible task of finding people who would both host me and arrange a small meeting where I could talk about HRCF and, hopefully, enlist their active participation. Within a couple of weeks, he had found willing hosts in twenty-four cities across the country and arranged a calendar for my travel.

In short order, I was off on my neatly organized six-week journey. Columbus, Ohio, was one city that was unbelievably successful, of course, as this was when I met Steve Shellabarger and his partner Steve Marquis, known to their many admiring friends as Steve and Little Steve. To this day, Columbus remains one of HRC's most important cities, and it was Steve Shellabarger who made the magic happen there.

At the end of my tour, HRCF had many new volunteers committed to spreading the word and, most importantly, raising the money needed to give to candidates, build the organization, and lobby for federal AIDS funding. For his part in creating the tour, Marvin more than proved his worth. If he did nothing else for us, this one initiative gave us so much momentum. But fortunately, that was not his only contribution.

While I was on the road, he thought about how we could turn small donors into big donors. His idea was to create an exclusive "club" that people could join for a gift of $1,200 per year or one hundred dollars per month. The concept certainly wasn't unique. Even GRNL had a major donor club, but not our still-nascent PAC.

Marvin's idea to recruit members was to send a highly personalized letter to current donors who regularly contributed and to one-time donors of at least $250. These people numbered less than one hundred. Most on our seven-thousand-five-hundred-person donor list gave far less, so expectations were low. Indeed, my fundraising naivete made me think no one would respond to what seemed to me to be such a bold and crazy request of a hundred dollars a month. In return for their gift, the letter promised access to the latest inside political reports plus two tickets to the black-tie dinner of their choice—nothing more. To add an air of exclusivity, we called the club the Insiders' Group. (Later, we would rename it the Federal Club.)

We received about a half dozen replies, to my amazement and delight, giving it a very respectable response rate of about 6 percent. Marvin's crazy letter had worked, my skepticism was unfounded, and my respect for him grew even more.

Mike Grossman, a Dallas real estate broker, was the first to reply, and that made him the first member of the Insiders' Group, a title he richly deserves. Mike later joined the board and provided outstanding leadership and support to HRCF, as well as to me. Mike has always been one of the brightest stars in the Lone Star State's gay community. He has been instrumental in countless significant projects supporting the gay community in Dallas. His activism is virtually boundless.

We knew that there were some especially generous people among our donors, and we began to analyze what had happened in our first solicitation so that we could grow the program. Of course, a face-to-face direct ask is always a far more effective fundraising tool than even the most personalized letter. We faced the sobering challenge of finding significant numbers of potential large donors to solicit. How and where would we find them?

Seeing the success we had with Marvin's letter, board members quickly engaged in planning how to launch the program in their respective cities. Michael Gelpi from Columbus was one of the first to capitalize on it. He and Steve Shellabarger invited a small group of friends to a brunch at which they recruited a dozen new members, including themselves. Suddenly, there were eighteen members of our fledgling Insiders' Group.

Shortly after that, I got a phone call from Dallas attorney Don McCleary, who posed an intriguing question: Would I consider hiring a congressional staffer, the brother of one of his close friends, if he raised the money for his salary? I had no idea who Don McCleary was, let alone the staffer, but we desperately needed more staff and had no money to hire anyone. Sensing my hesitancy, he provided a little more background and assurances that this was a serious offer. After some back and forth, we agreed that the young man would call me to arrange an interview, and I would get back to Don after the meeting.

Not long after, I received a call from Philip Dufour, who was serving as the communications director in the office of Democratic Louisiana Congresswoman Cathy Long, and we arranged a time to get together. When we met, I discovered early in the conversation that he spoke with an air of self-confidence, had excellent people skills, and was politically savvy. I left the meeting impressed and feeling confident that Philip could make a significant contribution to the organization. After doing a little due diligence, we brought him on board as a field organizer, which included helping to grow the Insiders membership.

True to his word, Don immediately went to work to raise the funds to cover Philip's salary. Once he knew about the Insiders, he decided that it provided the best vehicle for him to fulfill his commitment. He pitched the idea to Randolph Terrell and Larry Pease, who volunteered to help recruit other members in Dallas. They created a list of key businessmen and set a date for an Insiders brunch at the posh Crescent Club. Now the ball was rolling. Before the brunch, Don and his team invited each to lunch or brunch to explain what the event was about, so everyone who came knew that they would be asked for a $1,200 non-tax-deductible contribution. (Remember the importance of "hard money," which we could give directly to specific candidates, lobbying, and other political activities.)

In February 1987, I flew to Dallas for the event, and I took Bob Alfandre, who, as I've described, was a man with more than a bit of theater running through his veins, to exploit his legendary ability to secure commitments. I was amazed to see more than seventy guests walk through the door. Bob made such a compelling pitch that it motivated forty-nine attendees to sign up.

Don had more than met his commitment, but he did not stop. He saw his Crescent Club success as only the beginning of what Dallas could accomplish—and he was right. He created the sense that joining the Insiders' Group was the "thing to do" by making it social as well as political. The Dallas Insiders, as the group named themselves, held regular lunches and other social events where members could meet each other and even do a little business. Members were encouraged to invite guests who might be interested in joining, and many did exactly that.

Atlanta soon followed with an event at the Ritz Carlton hosted by Joe Blount. While not as big as the Dallas event, it nevertheless produced many new members, and a couple contributed significantly more than the $1,200 membership fee. One of those was Edie Cofrin, who wrote a check for $10,000. She said she was simply responding to board co-chair Vivian Shapiro's closing request from her pitch, asking attendees to give as much as they could afford. Edie suspected that she was most likely capable of doing more than most of the other attendees, so she very generously checked the highest box on the donor card.

Through the grapevine, I had heard a little about Edie and her philanthropy. Among several other initiatives, she had anonymously bought and donated a home to house people with AIDS. Her involvement with and commitment to HRCF continued to grow. She went on to join the board of governors and then the foundation board on which she continues to serve. Much later, when plans for a building developed, she again stepped forward and made the lead gift.

Much to our collective amazement, the Insiders Group, now the Federal Club, was on a roll and furnishing HRCF with a substantial flow of new money. With it, we were able to retain Hilary Rosen as our first lobbyist. She, as a seasoned lobbyist who had close relationships with many members of the House and Senate, was able to open doors that had previously been closed to us. A year later, after Hilary moved on to a senior position at the Recording Industry Association of America, but stayed close to the organization and helped to train Steve Smith and Carlton Lee who we had hired to replace her.

As the Federal Club grew and expanded across the country, its structure evolved to accommodate multiple giving levels, encouraging larger gifts, and providing additional recognition for major contributions. As of this writing, there are nearly 5,700 Federal Club members in all but three states, plus the District of Columbia, Puerto Rico, and the U.S. Virgin Islands. There are just under eleven hundred Federal Club Council members contributing $5,000 or more. Combined, their gifts to HRC total $16 million annually. To add some perspective, at the launch of the program in 1985, the organization's total income from all sources was about $400,000. Indeed, the organization's entire donor list was not much bigger than today's combined Federal Club/Council membership.

We finally had a solid plan to solicit ongoing major gifts. For this, the Human Rights Campaign has Marvin Collins to thank. I want to note how very challenging this must have been for Marvin to take such an active role in the PAC. He came of age in an era when coming out would have been tantamount to suicide—at home and work. Many older gay men spent their lives in the closet and lived with an ongoing fear that those they were close to would learn the truth. As a result, they were not comfortable with the gay movement, even though they knew how important it was. Marvin was very intense, and he maintained strict secrecy around his personal life. But he loved making gay friends, and he wanted to contribute to the movement. HRCF provided him that opportunity.

It also allowed him to come out in his own way to the former president of the United States, George H.W. Bush. Marvin was close friends with the Bushes. One day he asked for a meeting with his former boss, and they visited for nearly an hour.

"What are you doing with yourself these days?" Mr. Bush asked Marvin.

"Well, sir," he replied after a moment. "I'm working for gay rights."

Apparently, the former president was not fazed. It's funny how people just seem to know these things about us.

"Well, that's good," was the reply. And that was the end of that.

I take great pride in thinking our little organization gave him the confidence to share himself authentically with his former boss. And no doubt, if Marvin were alive today, he would rightfully take great pride in knowing what had become of his idea that launched the largest fundraising vehicle the lesbian and gay political movement has seen.

(Let me address parenthetically the impression many hold today that HRC is an organization of and for the wealthy in our community. While today the Federal Club and Council have some six thousand people committing at least a hundred dollars a month, these generous donors are a small subset of the entire HRC donor list of 500,000 people who give at least thirty-five dollars a year. Folks can become a "partner" for a monthly gift of five dollars—the amount of a minimum donation to public television. Large donations may buy buildings, but small donations enable the PAC to fulfill its commitment to working for equality in Congress, business, and around the country.)

The generosity of many wealthy lesbians and gay men helped HRCF win significant electoral victories that year and establish the financial groundwork for the escalating AIDS fight.

Now that we had some decent money coming in and a solid foundation to keep it coming, I was ready to start spending it.

Don McCleary
By Elizabeth Birch, former HRC executive director

In every way, Don McCleary was a privileged son of Texas. He was handsome and had the drive, intellect, and swagger to rise to the top of Dallas's elite social and legal class. But Don was different in one critical way: he was born gay. For men of his generation who came of age during what would become a "coming out" revolution, such consciousness about one's sexuality would create a dramatic fork in the road of life. Should one stay quiet and enjoy all the fruits of privilege or speak the truth and put one's career at risk? This was especially true in Texas. With great resolve, Don chose his path and became an inspiring champion of gay rights. And, even as he disrupted Dallas society, he helped set in motion a culture of giving in the broader LGBTQ community.

In 1987, Don McCleary was instrumental in the explosive growth of the Human Rights Campaign Fund Federal Club. Modeled on the giving programs at organizations such as the American Defamation League and the American Red Cross, this major donor program created a vital new revenue stream to fund significant portions of HRCF's lobbying, organizing, campaign, and public education work.

In 1991, Don joined the HRCF Board of Directors. Don was the co-chair when I was hired to lead the organization in 1995. That was my good fortune. I had been laser-focused on developing a new logo as part of a fresh repositioning of the organization. Of all the logos we tested, I favored the simple equal sign. In focus groups and surveys, a slightly more complicated version of the logo edged out the simple one. When Don reported the results to the board, he picked up that I was not happy.

"What's the matter?" he asked.

"It's the wrong logo," I said. "The correct logo should be as simple and iconic as possible. It should be the kind of logo that you can put on a building or a backpack, and it will pop and inspire."

He said simply in his Texas drawl, "Your judgment is why we hired you, darlin'."

He invited the board to support my choice, and they did.

Don brought the same passion for equality to his law firm, Gardere Wynne Sewell LLP, as managing partner from 1991 through 1995. His leadership propelled Gardere into local, state, and national public affairs and an expanded focus on humanitarian initiatives and pro bono work. To broaden the talent base at the firm, Don instituted a progressive cultural diversity program, including an aggressive push to hire minorities and women.

Don was a favorite of Texas Governor Ann Richards. He championed the campaign of his law partner, Ron Kirk, who went on to become the first African American mayor of Dallas. In 1995, the Dallas chapter of HRC recognized his work in fighting discrimination, presenting him with their Kuchling Humanitarian Award, named in honor of the late Raymond Kuchling, a leading activist in Dallas' LGBTQ community in the 1980s. That same year, Governor Richards and Mayor Kirk presented Don with the Anti-Defamation League's Jurisprudence Award for his support of cultural diversity. In his acceptance speech, he said, "We always struggle between diversity and dogmatism, between tolerance and tyranny, between understanding and narrow ideology. Each of us must contribute to the creation of a society in which the individual's dignity is preserved."

Don McCleary was forty-seven when he died in 1996 of complications associated with AIDS in Dallas. I was with him a great deal in his last days.

"America has lost a champion of basic fairness and common decency," I said in delivering his eulogy. "Don worked tirelessly so that one day, all Americans will enjoy full equal rights, freedom from discrimination and the unconditional love of their families ... We owe it to his memory to continue his work."

HRC's McCleary Law Fellows Program is named for Don McCleary.

Chapter 13:
Gays Speak Out

The Human Rights Campaign Fund's phenomenal success in the 1982 election fueled my commitment, determination—and even fervor—to grow support for lesbian and gay rights when I came on as the executive director in June 1983.

The 1984 election cycle promised our community even greater success. The Democratic Convention would be held in San Francisco, considered the most gay-friendly city in the country. The party and its candidates reached out to our voters as never before, actively and openly seeking our money and votes. The party was on record as opposing discrimination against homosexuals in employment, immigration, and the military. Half the candidates seeking the presidential nomination promised at the very least to sign onto our civil rights bill. The Democratic National Committee established a Gay and Lesbian Caucus. Even the Republican National Committee held meetings with representatives of gay organizations.

"No American citizen ought to be denied equal protection," said Gil Gerald, a co-founder of the National Coalition of Black Gays and a founding HRCF board member.

"Human rights, and that includes gay rights, is no longer a debatable issue within the Democratic Party," said Ann Lewis, political director of the Democratic National Committee. "Gays now have a track record in which they have worked in our campaigns and demonstrated what they have to offer to our party and the political process."

"All of us are God's children," said Rev. Jesse Jackson, who had spoken at our 1983 black-tie dinner in New York City. "There can be no basis for denying civil rights or civil liberties. Public policy must protect personal preference."

"Nineteen-eighty-four will be a threshold year for gays in politics," Dan Bradley predicted. "There will be no turning back."

The first part of Dan's prediction turned out to be dead wrong. Democrats suffered setbacks at all levels of electoral politics in 1984. Walter Mondale's devastating defeat (he lost by 18 percentage points, winning only the District of Columbia and his home state of Minnesota) was dissected ad infinitum. The generally accepted assessment was that the campaign paid too much attention to courting special interests, including lesbian and gay voters.

So, the Democratic Party abandoned the lesbian and gay community—for a while, at least.

"We were very cognizant this year of the negative impact of the special interest label on Walter Mondale," said Ken Mulley, political director for the National Education Association. "He was portrayed, in fact, as more or less kowtowing to the unions who endorsed him."

"The perception is that we are the party that can't say no, that caters to special interests, and that does not have the interests of the middle class at heart," said Dick Lodge, Tennessee's Democratic Party chair.

"Blacks own the Democratic Party," Harry McPherson, a former aide to Lyndon Johnson, complained. "White Protestant male Democrats are an endangered species."

"We have to realize that we're getting out of touch with normal, regular people," a Democratic consultant said. "We're forgetting that the white middle-class is rejecting us. We're being wagged by the tail of Jesse Jackson, of feminists or gay activists. The average voter is asking, 'What about me?'"

My favorite asinine perspective derived from a loser's hindsight came from another Democratic party leader.

"We ought to be just as concerned with the farmer on the tractor as that guy with an earring in his left ear."

The lowest blow came in April 1985 from Paul Kirk, the chairman of the Democratic National Committee, after he met with Alabama Governor George C. Wallace, an ardent segregationist. Kirk promised Wallace that the party would moderate its views to regain lost ground by concentrating on the economy and defense.

"Fringe issues and lifestyle issues such as gay rights cannot be the priority in the dialogue of a major party," Kirk said after meeting privately with Wallace. "It must focus on central issues such as the economy, a strong defense, jobs, and education for our children if it hopes to reclaim its rightful heritage."

The party went on to purge its special-interest caucuses, including the Gay and Lesbian Caucus.

The 1984 election results devastated me professionally and personally. Although there were a couple of negative articles in gay press, I was never subjected to the kind of media assault that befell Steve Endean. And while the board and staff were fully supportive, I, nevertheless, deeply questioned my ability to lead HRCF. What lifted me out of the doldrums was remembering Steve's assured commitment to the long haul, that ours was a fight that would take years, even decades. He was simply the most tenacious but pragmatic warrior in this fight for civil rights, and he knew it was a long game. I took inspiration from what he called his Rules of the Road, in which he said that "we will win by capturing the middle and taking the 'political center' from our moralistic opponents." He admonished us to be persistent: "We must never, ever give up. We must understand that we will win the war even if we lose battle after battle."

And I was bolstered by Dan Bradley's promise that there would be no turning back.

Most people did not fully appreciate that lesbian and gay civil rights legislation would protect more—lots more—than the rights of sexually active gay men. Our community faced innumerable violations of personal rights, including lesbian mothers fighting for custody of their children in divorces, boys who were victims of anti-gay violence, and all of us who feared we could lose our jobs or our homes on the whims of a bigoted boss or landlord.

The so-called pundits overlooked a critical factor in their election analysis of the Democratic losses. Mondale had captured the allegiance of national organizations' leaders, but not necessarily of the people—the grassroots memberships of their organizations. By mobilizing constituent support of lesbian and gay voters, I could see a path to reestablish our relationship with the Democratic Party and achieve our goals of generating funding for AIDS and getting civil rights legislation passed. Of course, we always sought an opportunity to support Republican candidates, but few showed interest in our outreach.

As Dan Bradley foretold, there would be no turning back. The next challenge for HRCF was to build grassroots involvement to generate constituent pressure on Washington.

The lesbian and gay community struggled to express its views to lawmakers—for obvious reasons, with so many in the closet. But our silence hurt us. The religious right and conservatives never seemed to have trouble making their voices heard in an avalanche of mail, and they got results. They still do. But those of us on the left are too often less willing to take the time to express our demands to our elected representatives, leaving us overlooked, ignored, or rejected. And why not? If we don't care enough to write a letter about important issues like our lives or our jobs, why would an elected official support us and endure the virulent objections of the religious right?

Somehow HRCF needed to find a way to be heard.

Three critical pillars—money, lobbying, and constituent mobilization—increase the success exponentially of any political organization. HRCF had established a solid foundation for bringing in money.

Then, in 1985, I saw a chance to acquire an established, dedicated lobbying organization: the Gay Rights National Lobby.

When Steve Endean left GRNL following incessant attacks on his competence and judgment by the *Advocate*, the *Washington Blade*, syndicated journalist Larry Bush, and David Goodstein, he left a leadership vacuum. The Lobby hired a succession of replacements to head up the organization, but none was successful. Just a year after Steve's departure, it became clear GRNL was on the verge of closing. The board asked if the National Gay and Lesbian Task Force would consider a merger, but NGLTF declined. Then GRNL board member Paul Kawata approached me to learn if HCRF would consider bringing them on. GRNL had a donor list of some seven thousand names, which I deemed of great value. It was hard to get names and addresses of lesbians and gays who would welcome mail from us. I was reluctant to see that asset disappear if GRNL folded.

GRNL also had Terry Watanabe's friend Don Randolph on the board. Don had already brought GRNL $20,000. I was eager to recruit him to join the HRCF board.

But GRNL also came with a sizable debt—some $30,000, which was a lot of money in 1985. I didn't want that debt, but I wanted that list. I was willing to take the risk and find a way to eliminate, or at least reduce, the debt.

And we did. The owner of the largest gay disco in Washington, a straight man named Marty Chernoff, learned about the debt, and offered to help us. He called the GRNL creditors and told them the organization was going out of business. He negotiated reductions as payments in full. We were able to reduce the debt to a third, and that was a price we could manage.

So for $10,000, we got a donor list of around seven thousand names and an office of used furniture. But most importantly, we acquired an entity that would become our lobbying department.

We also got Don Randolph as a new board member, as I had hoped. When he arrived at his first board meeting with another check from Terry for $10,000, he essentially paid for the GRNL acquisition.

Meanwhile, Steve Endean went to work for the AFL-CIO for about a year after leaving HRCF and GRNL. When he couldn't bear being out of the movement any longer, he returned to GRNL as their consulting lobbyist. In that role, he stumbled on a program the National Organization for Women used successfully to generate constituent involvement. By calling a particular toll-free number, members would authorize Western Union to send letters to legislators in response to a specific matter or legislation. These letters were called "mailgrams," and they were modeled after telegrams but delivered the next day rather than immediately. In the days when long-distance phone calls cost money, only businesses could afford fax machines, and email was nonexistent, mailgrams could flood a congressional office with constituent fervor overnight.

Steve immediately saw how Western Union's "Action Hotline" service could provide the third pillar of HRCF's political operation. Members of Congress from Los Angeles, San Francisco, and New

York certainly knew they had gay constituents in their districts. But all too often, representatives from Nashville or Houston or Tulsa would say, "Well, I don't have any of those gay people in my district." Steve had found a way to get "those gay people" to send overnight letters proclaiming, "I live in your district. I care about these issues, and I'm lobbying you on this particular issue." For many [members of Congress], it was the first communication they had from a constituent about a gay issue. If they heard from one or two hundred, they noticed.

When he could not convince the GRNL board to take an interest in the program, he launched it himself in 1986.

"I decided my only option was to leave the Lobby and try to build the grassroots pressure and network we needed somewhere else," Steve said.

He called his new program the Fairness Fund, and he made generating constituent mail to Congress its sole purpose.

Individuals participating in the Fairness Fund mailgram campaigns called a toll-free hotline and chose whether they wanted to send a message related to AIDS or civil rights. The Western Union operator read to the caller three fifty-word mailgrams, and the caller would choose one to send to their representatives on Capitol Hill. The first mailgram cost $4.50, and additional ones cost $4. The fee was charged to the caller's telephone phone bill. The Fairness Fund prepared appropriate messages to respond to critical events, and they changed to coordinate with legislative priorities and strategy.

The Fairness Fund soon proved the impact mailgrams could have on Congress. The first real test of the mailgram hotline occurred during the fight over the nomination of Robert Bork to the Supreme Court when it generated some 3,500 mailgrams to Capitol Hill in opposition to the judge, who in a 1984 ruling wrote that "private, consensual homosexual conduct is not constitutionally protected."

Steve and his team traveled to Pride parades, AIDS Memorial Quilt displays, the March on Washington, and other events to sign people up for the program, promising to notify supporters of an important issue so they could call Western Union to send a mailgram. Carrying a clipboard to record names and addresses, he approached people wearing a T-shirt with "Speak Out" printed on the front. On the back were the words "Cheap and Easy." So very Steve. The program grew, but at a high cost to Steve, literally. He bankrolled the Fairness Fund on his credit cards until he had to declare bankruptcy.

David Goodstein had died of cancer in 1985, but animosity and insufficient financial support continued to haunt Steve. I don't know why. Perhaps his intense, irrepressible bulldog nature put people off. I know it did me, at times. But I never thought of him as anything but a hero to our movement. He did get some financial support, and a matching grant from former HRCF board member Jim Hormel enabled him to hire Steve Dwyer and Lee Bush to build the program.

After a while, we were able to provide the Fairness Fund with space in the HRCF office. In 1987, Randy Klose convinced me to negotiate a merger, enabling Steve to concentrate on grassroots mobilization and building our field operations instead of constantly worrying about raising money. Steve came back into the HRCF fold as our field division director, bringing Lee Bush and Steve Dwyer with him, expanding our efforts to achieve a national civil rights anti-discrimination bill and taking on the ever-growing fight for federal support of AIDS research and treatment.

Soon the program evolved, and we brought it in-house, renaming the national mailgram campaign "Speak Out." Instead of receiving a charge on their phone bills, participants paid us directly and in advance to send three critical overnight letters when key issues arose. The new format gave us several advantages. We kept most of the money donated to run the program, pay associated expenses, and pay canvassers. Later we made enrolled Speak Out participants members of the Human Rights Campaign Fund.

The program reached many who did not consider themselves "political" or "activists" and just wanted a discreet way to participate. Steve told of a man in Cleveland who had thrown a "Speak Out" party in his home and signed up twenty of his friends to authorize mailgrams. "But I'm not an activist, you understand," the man insisted.

"If you don't reach beyond the activists," Steve said, "you won't mobilize and harness the support of the fair-minded majority.

You have to get the vast number of people who don't want to be political and convince them they don't have to be 'activists' to make a difference."

Speak Out enrolled an astounding twenty-five thousand people in 1989, primarily through direct canvassing at events by Steve and his team. A year later, that number doubled, and it doubled again in 1991. In 1993, Speak Out delivered its millionth mailgram.

Thanks to Steve Endean, the constituent mobilization program joined our political action committee and lobbying endeavor to successfully establish the third pillar of the Human Rights Campaign Fund's mission. With a PAC, a lobby, and constituent mobilization, we were poised to become a political powerhouse.

Often, when Speak Out volunteers experienced pushback in signing up participants from event organizers who accused them of promoting a political cause.

"This event isn't political," might be the objection the event organizers claimed.

The canvasser's reply?

"I'm not a gay activist. I'm an AIDS activist. AIDS is not political."

And therein lies the silver lining of the AIDS tragedy. Too often, we heard that most people would never have been willing to come out and put their names on constituent mail to their congressional representatives but for AIDS. AIDS blew open the closet for thousands of gay men and brought them to action. Their money might have protected them from discrimination, but it could not protect them from the virus. The mailgram campaign and Speak Out gave them a voice. Their friends and loved ones were dying, and they wanted to take a stand and influence public policy.

They discovered, as I had realized years earlier, that they weren't in a fight for their jobs. They were in a fight for their lives.

Chapter 14:
To Know Us Is to Love Us

AIDS accelerated the trajectory of the lesbian and gay rights movement during the 1980s, taking us from abhorred and ignored to embraced and even loved. Sure, this may be an exaggeration, or at the very least true only for some of us. But nothing moved lesbians and gays into the public consciousness and the beginnings of public acceptance more than when family, friends, and neighbors who loved them learned they had contracted a mysterious virus for which there was no treatment, much less a cure, and for which death was all but certain.

The devastating virus brought with it fear, sadness, loneliness, and death. To be sure, too many were abandoned when family members learned they had AIDS. On the other hand, our nation's growing awareness ushered in a rapidly transforming consciousness. As the media began reporting more on the epidemic, straight people quickly learned people with AIDS were in their families. They were their friends and coworkers—people just like them. It was the best of times, and it was the worst of times.

Perhaps the most agonizing yet transforming eye-opener was Hollywood heartthrob Rock Hudson's announcement in July 1985 that he had AIDS. Until this news, AIDS was considered a disease that "fairies on Santa Monica Boulevard got." Almost overnight, the U.S. realized that AIDS was a grave danger to the national health, and something had to be done about it.

As soon as I heard the news, I foresaw the bittersweet impact this would have for the gay community. I wanted to express my gratitude to Hudson for his willingness to publicly acknowledge that he had AIDS at this most vulnerable time. I contacted Marty Richards, a Broadway and Hollywood producer. He and his wife, Mary Lea Johnson, a Johnson & Johnson heiress, had hosted a fundraiser for HRCF at their mansion in Southampton on Long Island.

"He's pretty sick," Marty said when I called to ask if he could give me Hudson's address.

"Well," I replied, "I just want to thank him for being public about having AIDS."

Marty gave me the address, and I sent my acknowledgment, assuring Hudson that his courageous personal action would make a difference beyond what anyone could anticipate.

And it did. Suddenly, the world learned this beloved and famous Hollywood celebrity had AIDS. To have a star, especially one who was such a heartthrob, contract the virus—not that anyone would have wished this—became very helpful. It put a face on AIDS for millions of people. The more people could identify with those who had the disease, the more we could deflect the stigma, and the easier it became to recruit straight people to help fight against it.

Once again, the Reagans refused to get involved in the AIDS crisis, even for their close friend. Hudson had traveled to France seeking experimental treatment, but he was denied admittance to the military hospital because he was not French. Hudson's publicist sent a telegram to the White House requesting help. "Only one hospital in the world can offer necessary medical treatment to save the life of Rock Hudson or at least alleviate his illness," the telegram said. "Commanding general of Percy Hospital has turned down Rock Hudson as a patient because he is not French. Doctor Dormant in Paris believes a request from the White House or a high American official would change his mind. Can you help by having someone call the commanding general's office at the Percy Hospital at the above number?"

But a young Reagan staffer declined assistance in a reply to the telegram. "I spoke with Mrs. Reagan about the attached telegram. She did not feel this was something the White House should get into." Mrs. Reagan reportedly said that they "had to be fair" in terms of treating Hudson the same as anyone else.

Hudson's death two months later broke the hearts of stars and fans alike. On the day Hudson died, October 2, 1985, Congress set aside $190 million to research AIDS. Private contributions added millions more to support research and to care for those who were sick.

Hudson left $250,000 to establish the American Foundation for AIDS Research (amfAR), founded by Mathilde Krim and Michael S. Gottlieb. Hudson's longtime friend, actress Elizabeth Taylor, served as the founding national chairperson.

Some health professionals feared treating the sick men. In response, many lesbians took care of their dying gay brothers. They cared for them in hospitals and at home. They donated much-needed blood. Most importantly, they offered them love and care. Nothing drew these two, often-discordant, sides of our community together like the AIDS crisis.

Thus, AIDS was an adversary with a silver lining. Straight people began to see gay men with compassion. Still, it was killing far too many gay men, and it demanded every tool we could bring to the fight, and specifically money. Nothing was going to beat this virus without a whole lot of money—in amounts that only the federal government could provide.

Despite their extraordinary commitment and their dogged efforts to raise private funds for education and care, private organizations like New York City's Gay Men's Health Crisis, the first community-based AIDS service provider in the U.S., would never be able to bring enough resources to fight the disease. We needed money for research, education, and the development of effective medications to beat AIDS. Private donations would never be able to provide the amount of money necessary to address the virus. Only the checkbook of the United States government could fund the fight against the epidemic.

Enter the Human Rights Campaign Fund. AIDS was a political imperative demanding a congressional initiative, and we, along with other groups, were poised to take it on. As a political action committee, we could contribute money to candidates who would support the AIDS fight in Congress. Acquiring GRNL's lobbying activities empowered us to meet with members of Congress directly. Through the Fairness Fund's constituent mobilization efforts, tens of thousands of lesbians and gay men became politically active, telling their national representatives they cared about AIDS and demanding their action.

HRCF was a fledgling organization when I joined as the executive director. Organizations have lifecycles, and I came to this one in 1983 while it was small but nimble.

I was ideally suited to building it, to identifying the right people and convincing them to join us in this monumental challenge—and I was eager to do so. I was in my late-thirties—old enough to identify those with talent and inspire younger, idealistic comrades to join our effort. This was the way of Washington, D.C., in the eighties, and perhaps it still is. People in their twenties come to town with a dream of joining up with a scrappy organization to change the world. They are willing to invest the hours and the enthusiasm for a cause and a small paycheck, never knowing the outcome but relishing the challenge.

Even amidst the devastation of diagnoses and disease and death, of suicides and sorrows and sometimes-daily funerals, these were also exhilarating days for those of us in the gay rights movement. This was especially true for our mighty little PAC in the battle for access to the nation's purse strings. I don't brag or exaggerate about our role—it was no small undertaking to get the federal government to allocate the money needed to beat this scourge, and it was HRCF's mission to do exactly that. Other groups, like ACT UP, were more vocal, more visible, and their activities were essential. But our monumental charge at the Human Rights Campaign Fund was to get money for AIDS research, education, and treatment. Like any effective political organization, we did it quietly, trudging the halls of Congress and monitoring committee hearings, contributing to the campaigns of influential legislators and friendly candidates, and building a base to amplify the voices of lesbians and gays.

An overriding purpose was driving us as if we were called to accomplish a task no less than changing the world. Indeed, the next decade would demonstrate exactly that. We would see the world change for lesbians and gays.

Our lobbyists were an essential part bringing about that change. Armed with a deep knowledge of the issues and the ability to generate campaign contributions, they were able to access key members of Congress and their senior staff. But perhaps more important than having knowledge and money are the trusting relationships lobbyists have with members and staff – the longer and more trusting, the better. And for us, there were no better people with those relationships than Hilary Rosen and Tim Furlong.

We were making progress, and that was exciting. It's hard to admit we were having so much excitement amidst such tragedy. But we were on a mission.

There was a sense of timelessness to the fight for gay rights and the subsequent battle against AIDS, Larry Bye suggested when we reflected on those days and the six-page plan he had sketched for HRCF at a GRNL board meeting in 1980. There was an almost ethereal sense that the goal might be in the unforeseeable future, but the goal was inescapable—a destiny.

"I don't think we ever thought about time," Larry said when I asked him about his memories of the early days of HRCF. "It was an odd, time-free zone. There was a timeless sense—in that it didn't matter whether it took fifty years or a thousand years. We were going to do this, but it wasn't about ever getting anywhere. It wasn't that we didn't have a goal. But this fight was about who we were. And we were going to do this for our own sake."

HRCF's first political director, Eric Rosenthal, similarly echoed his impression of the timelessness of those early days of HRCF.

"I remember it being a building time," Eric told me. "Our expectations were modest. We were happy with any victories that we achieved. You know, you don't win it all in a year or two. We saw it as the beginning of a building process within the political sphere."

"We never thought it was ever going to happen," Larry said. "That wasn't what was important. If somebody had said to us, 'You guys realize this is going to take forever, right?' that wouldn't have fazed us. 'Yeah, okay, so what?' we would have said. 'What do we need to do tomorrow?' It wouldn't have mattered."

But now, with AIDS inflicting a guaranteed death sentence on so many of us, it did matter.

I note here a few points of federal action (or lack of action) to explain what we were up against during the most frightening days of this disease.

In 1982, Congressmen Henry Waxman and Phillip Burton introduced legislation to allocate $5 million to the Centers for Disease Control and Prevention for surveillance and another $10 million to the National Institutes of Health for AIDS research. A year later, Congressman Ted Weiss held hearings on the federal response, at which Steve Endean testified on behalf of GRNL.

In September 1985, President Ronald Reagan mentioned "AIDS" for the first time in response to a reporter's question, saying he supported research into AIDS. He said the effort was a "top priority" for the administration and defended the paltry $126 million for AIDS research in his 1986 budget.

In 1986, the National Academy of Sciences issued a report calling for a $2 billion investment for what they called the "national health crisis." The U.S. Surgeon General, C. Everett Koop bucked the administration's wishes by issuing a groundbreaking report calling for education and condom use. President Reagan reluctantly approved it, but he did not like its content or its conclusions, which were too graphic for the religious types and demanded too much pressure to do something. There was great resistance to distributing the report to the general public. In May 1988, Koop mailed a CDC brochure entitled "Understanding AIDS" to every household in America. The president was not crazy about that move either.

"One of the things that's been wrong with too much of our education is that no kind of values of right and wrong are being taught," Reagan said, affirming the position of Senator Jesse Helms and Representative Bill Dannemeyer, who devoted their legislative efforts to ban the use of federal funds for AIDS education materials that "promote or encourage, directly or indirectly, homosexual activities." As a result, we found ourselves in a years-long battle with what we would call "No Promo Homo" amendments on virtually every AIDS funding bill submitted to Congress.

It took until 1987, nearly five years after the virus was identified, for Reagan to deliver his first major speech on AIDS. By this time, 36,058 Americans had been diagnosed with HIV, and more than twenty thousand had died.

"Even with thirty-thousand AIDS cases last year," said Congressman Waxman, who led what seemed like a perpetual battle with the White House for more money, "the administration was asking the Congress to cut back on the funding for research to deal with AIDS."

Indeed, in 1987, the administration requested $213 million. Congress nearly doubled that number to $416 million. (Compare that to the almost $35 *billion* the federal government allocated in 2019 to fight AIDS.)

In 1990, Reagan would apologize for his neglect of the epidemic while he was president. I considered it poor consolation. Little could make up for his notoriously awful leadership on the disease, as his administration opposed every positive step in the battle, from funding to policy.

In 1985, I hired Eric Rosenthal as our assistant for programs and development and soon promoted him to political director. Much of Eric's work involved whatever needed to be done. He became the fourth staff member to cram into our small second-floor office above the real estate office near the Eastern Market Metro station, joining Marilyn Braithwaite, who managed the money; Killian Swift, our administrative assistant, and me. His first responsibility was to analyze political campaigns and assess them for HRCF support. He also helped with fundraising and organizing the Washington black-tie dinners.

Eric and I were driving somewhere early in 1985—neither of us remembers the particulars, but it was probably a trip to a nearby congressional district to support a friendly candidate. With plenty of time to talk—and no cell phones to distract or email demanding responses—we turned to wondering how HRCF could best convince Congress to appropriate the many millions of dollars needed to tackle AIDS. We wanted to give AIDS an immediate, prominent role in the organization without ignoring our commitment to gay civil rights issues. That's when we came up with the idea of a dedicated fund to support AIDS-related legislation and funding. We called it the AIDS Campaign Trust, or "ACT on AIDS."

People from around the country donated to the fund—perhaps some because the name omitted the word "gay." Many straight people felt they could support the AIDS fight without supporting gay people. (I cringe a bit as I write this because it sounds so disrespectful of our community. But that's how it was then. Even deeply caring people in the mid-eighties bore strong judgment against us. Or perhaps they simply were afraid of being identified as supporters of gay people.) We hoped we could attract support even from members of the gay community who might be afraid to support gay issues—so many were at least partially closeted at that time. Also, we wanted to make it easier for straight people and members of Congress to provide support since a health issue was easier to support than gay civil rights at that time.

The AIDS Campaign Trust became a vehicle around which we researched the issues and formulated guidelines—essentially a litmus test—allowing us to evaluate the positions of candidates and members of Congress for HRCF support. Looking back, I can see that establishing the AIDS Campaign Trust was the point at which HRCF committed to this new mission, shifting the bulk of our time and resources to lobbying and electing members of Congress who would fight this dreadful disease. No formal decision was made to make the shift. There was no official board vote. We never stopped working to pass a civil rights bill. We just altered our focus in a seamless transition guided by a sense of urgency and inevitability. It was a change to which our community responded. The sense of urgency generated significant donations to the AIDS Campaign Trust in response to requests we made in direct mail and gay media around the country.

A final bittersweet story from the AIDS epidemic is Eric's. Eric worked on AIDS policy throughout the eighties and with his partner, Jeffrey, volunteered to care for babies with HIV at the National Children's Hospital. There they met a five-month-old baby named Joshua, whose mother was dying of AIDS. They took him home and cared for the little boy until, when he was three years old, Joshua died of AIDS. This experience so moved Eric that, at thirty-seven years old, he enrolled in medical school. He now works as an emergency-room pediatrician.

Ironically, shifting our focus and resources to AIDS irked Steve Endean till the day he died of AIDS. That man never gave up on his dream of having equal rights codified for lesbians and gays. Calling HRCF "preoccupied" with AIDS, he grudgingly conceded the need to "set aside our civil rights agenda to address the AIDS crisis."

He eventually credited the AIDS crisis as the reason for the phenomenal success of the Fairness Fund.

"People told me that most people they knew would not be willing to be out enough to have their names put on constituent mail to their congressional representatives," Steve noted. "In hindsight, I am convinced that gay men particularly wouldn't have signed up in large enough numbers had the AIDS crisis not dragged them by the thousands from their closets. The onslaught of AIDS showed how much was at stake in life-and-death terms, in influencing public policy."

Even as our donor base grew, HRCF didn't have a lot of money—our budget was maybe half a million dollars. It was my job to keep the staff focused on where we invested that money and how to best use our resources of time and talent.

To expand our impact, we sought to create coalitions with like-minded progressive organizations to build awareness of our work among political influencers. GRNL was invited to join the Leadership Conference on Civil Rights (now called the Leadership Conference on Civil and Human Rights), as long as it agreed not to ask them to take on lesbian and gay issues. The U.S. Catholic Conference and the AFL-CIO had objected to our membership. They were two of the largest and most powerful member organizations and critical to LCCR's funding. Steve Endean worked hard to pry open the door to that invitation when he headed up GRNL. After much discussion, he convinced the Catholic Conference leadership that he wasn't looking for an endorsement of the "gay lifestyle," and the group withdrew their objections to our membership in LCCR. The AFL-CIO would accept our membership if we agreed not to push for a Leadership Conference endorsement of the national gay civil rights bill within two to three years.

We also established relationships with other progressive organizations, including the National Committee for an Effective Congress and Independent Action, both of which are independent progressive political action committees, the United Food and Commercial Workers Union, and the Service Employees International Union.

Perhaps one of the most impactful of our alliances was with amfAR. I collaborated with co-founder Dr. Mathilde Krim on our respective efforts to secure more AIDS funding from Congress. In 1986, she introduced me to Richmond Crinkley. Richmond was the former director of the Vivian Beaumont Theater at Lincoln Center in New York City and producer of the Tony award-winning *Elephant Man* on Broadway. He was also on the board of trustees at the Kennedy Center in Washington.

Richmond had lost several friends to AIDS and was eager to join the fight. His particular interest was research, and he had devoured every article he could find in an array of medical journals. By the time we met, he already knew far more on the subject than most of us in the activist world and was enthusiastic about sharing the knowledge with anyone interested.

Richmond could see the value of getting the latest information on AIDS into the hands of people who could make a difference, particularly opinion leaders, reporters, supportive elected officials, and researchers. I agreed we would support him with subscriptions to medical journals, a computer, and office support. He would compile all the relevant articles he could find and send them to HRCF. These press packets provided up-to-the-minute, authoritative, and comprehensive coverage of medical aspects of the AIDS crisis. We would reproduce and distribute them monthly in a service we called MedPac to opinion leaders, reporters, supportive elected officials, and researchers who need such information but might not have had ready access to it.

In HRCF, Richmond saw a willing partner and a means to an end. I saw a brilliant man who could contribute mightily to the effort. His work would contribute to HRCF's first significant legislative victory—a special Congressional appropriation of $47 million in funding to distribute experimental drugs, particularly AZT.

In 1986 we started sending people to work in key campaigns, offering to organize local lesbian and gay communities to volunteer for the candidates and offer staff support. As a result, we could influence elections, in addition to giving scarce dollars directly. Every campaign relies on volunteers, so our support was welcome.

We also met with candidates who came to Washington requesting money. We would talk to them about our issues and decide if they were supportive and whether we thought they had a chance to win. Then, we would make contribution decisions based on that.

The 1986 election cycle was much more successful than in 1984.

We raised $886,000 for HRCF from events, regular contributions from members of the Federal Club, and direct mail from 17,000 individuals. This made us the largest national gay and lesbian political organization in the United States and one of the nation's twenty largest independent political action committees, and well within the top sixty of all five thousand PACs in 1986.

The AIDS Campaign Trust disbursed more than seventy-five thousand dollars. Total congressional funding for AIDS increased by more than 70 percent in 1986. I like to think the Campaign Trust contributed to that.

HRCF gave more than a quarter of a million dollars to qualified candidates in the 1986 election—more than we had contributed in the previous five years combined. Every incumbent co-sponsor of the lesbian and gay civil rights bill on the ballot won re-election. Of the ninety-nine candidates receiving support from HRCF, 74 percent won. Unfortunately, only seven Republican candidates supported our issues and received contributions.

HRCF ended the year with eight full-time professionals on staff. We began "loaning" members of our staff to campaigns to help organize. That year, we had staff members working in eight campaigns, including that of the late John Lewis of Georgia.

We counted a number of notables on our advisory board, among them Washington, D.C. mayor Marion Barry, San Francisco mayor Dianne Feinstein, Atlanta mayor Andrew Young, Bill Lucy of AFSCME, actor Mike Farrell, Gloria Steinem, Episcopal presiding bishop Edmond Browning, and Joseph Rauh of the Leadership Conference on Civil Rights.

At last, in 1986, I was able to contract with Hilary Rosen to lobby for us, to drive our initial focused effort in directly impacting legislation. I hired Steve Smith and Carton Lee as full-time lobbyists when Hilary left. (She stayed on as a board member, and a very valuable one.)

Lobbying on Capitol Hill in those days required working "inside the system," meeting directly with members of Congress and their staff. A successful lobbyist has close relationships with a number of members of Congress. They also are skilled at proposing language for legislation that helps—or at least does not threaten—the member's reelection. It was a slow process of relationship-building compared to just delivering a large check with a handshake. Congressional offices often relied on outside groups to do their work for them, presenting them with facts so they could better understand the issues. They were willing to listen and learn.

Hilary called this "evolutionary politics" because the process was slow, the hallowed halls of the Capitol day in and day out; meeting people in their offices, in committee hearings, and in the cafeterias, crafting relationships over time. It often took years to bring elected officials along. We learned the art of compromising to find common ground on AIDS funding, even if a member of Congress didn't like gays.

Gay and lesbian staffers frequently provided brave backup that made the difference, often risking their jobs and coming out to their bosses in advance of a vote. They exercised small acts of courage when they begged them to vote for the funding allocations. They were as gutsy as Larry Kramer's ACT-UP followers marching down the streets of Fifth Avenue to protest for more government action on AIDS.

In just five years, HRCF had the foundation it needed to make our community heard. We rolled up our sleeves and went to work to enlist champions to our cause.

Mathilde Krim
By Vic Basile

I can't recall exactly how or when I met Dr. Mathilde Krim, although it was most likely in 1985 at an AIDS event of some kind, perhaps an HCRF fundraiser that she often attended. I do vividly recall her warmth, charm, sincerity, determination, and intelligence. Above all, I felt her genuine kindness and caring. And just beneath the surface, it was clear she was a woman on a mission without a moment to spare.

Later I learned she was a wealthy research scientist of considerable stature, power, and influence. She was married to Arthur Krim, chairman of Orion Pictures and a former Democratic Party finance chair. They were a power couple, to be sure. Their Upper East Side brownstone in New York City was a command stop for Democratic presidents and those who sought to be president. A political blessing from Arthur Krim meant many thousands of dollars in campaign contributions and an opening of other important doors.

Dr. Krim was deeply involved in AIDS research, having co-founded the AIDS Medical Foundation, the first private organization concerned with fostering and supporting AIDS research. By the time we met, she had turned her attention to the political struggle: the fight to get the government to provide more money for research and treatment and to stop anti-gay amendments that made the battle even more difficult. At the time, both were extremely heavy lifts. Homosexuality was still viewed as a perversion by most people, and AIDS was seen as a gay disease. Right-wing political activist Pat Buchannan summed up the prejudice when he described AIDS as "God's retribution on the gay community."

Dr. Krim felt otherwise. With passion and fervor, driven by teenage memories of World War II Nazi atrocities, which she said had sensitized her against injustice, she joined the fight against discrimination toward people with AIDS and gay people generally. She was among the first to recognize that this new disease raised serious scientific and medical questions and that it had the potential to develop into a deadly epidemic. In an interview with the *Los Angeles Times* in 2000, she said, "In those early days, they were literally dying in the streets. Gay men who had AIDS lost their jobs and their apartments—their families turned away from them. It turned my stomach, it really impacted me, and I decided this was something not to be tolerated." And she didn't, bringing her remarkable intelligence and enormous political influence to the fight.

She dedicated herself to increasing the public's awareness of AIDS and became personally active in AIDS research.

In 1985, Dr. Krim joined forces with Elizabeth Taylor and created the American Foundation for AIDS Research (amfAR), serving as its founding chairman. Together, they were a powerful force, raising hundreds of millions of dollars for research, even securing a recalcitrant President Reagan to headline an amfAR event in Washington in 1987.

In recognition of her decades-long work in the battle against AIDS, President Clinton honored Dr. Krim with the Presidential Medal of Freedom in 2000. In another great honor for her tireless efforts, the National Portrait Gallery accepted into its permanent collection two photographic portraits by noted photographers Annie Leibovitz and Joyce Tenneson.

Mathilde Krim died on January 16, 2018. Her endless compassion and kindness, pure grace, and extraordinary ability to move mountains had few parallels in the struggle. Perhaps the best description of her caring, even humble, nature can be found in a quote she gave to *The New York Times in 1988*: "Everybody thinks of at least one person whom he has lost or is afraid for. And I am no different. I have my little list."

Chapter 15:
Enlisting Champions

FEDERAL RESPONSE TO AIDS

Intergovernmental Relations and Human Resources Subcommittee of the Committee on Government Operations

The AIDS epidemic continues its cruel, relentless pace. The most recent data from the Centers for Disease Control reveals almost 2,000 reported cases and 730 fatalities in this country alone. The number of cases is still doubling every 6 months. The young age of the victims and the debilitating nature of the disorder deepens the human tragedy of AIDS. And there is little sign that researchers are close to unraveling the mystery of the epidemic.

For far too long, our collective response, societal as well as governmental, to the crisis was haphazard and inexcusably slow. But within the last few months, the consensus for urgent and exhaustive action has solidified. The Federal Government, in fulfilling its duty to protect the *Nation's* health and safety, must mobilize its enormous resources to meet this challenge as quickly as possible. Moreover, Congress, the administration, and the Public Health Service must act aggressively to provide care and compassion to the victims with respect to their right to confidentiality.

This forum will enable representatives from many groups involved with AIDS to share their concerns and insights about the epidemic with Federal officials. At the same time, it will afford the administration an opportunity to describe its activities and respond to concerns that may be raised. I believe that such an exchange will increase Government responsiveness to those affected by its decisions. In this situation, the quality of these decisions may determine whether people live or die.

> Opening Statement of Chairman Ted Weiss,
> New York House of Representatives
> August 1, 1983

With the Reagan administration refusing to acknowledge the epidemic and even laughing about it from the press secretary's podium, I knew our only hope to generate the amount of money we needed to tackle AIDS was to lobby the United States Congress. Fortunately, a handful of legislators saw the impending health crisis in its early days and launched an effort to confront it. HRCF embraced them immediately.

In August 1983, Congressman Ted Weiss of New York held a congressional hearing on AIDS. I had just come on board as HRCF's executive director, and Steve Endean represented the Gay Rights National Lobby at the hearing, along with the National Gay Task Force, Lambda Legal, and Gay Men's Health Crisis.

The previous spring, Congressman Henry Waxman of Los Angeles held a day-long hearing at the Los Angeles Gay and Lesbian Community Services Center, a great source of board talent and financial support for HRCF.

"I want to be especially blunt about the political aspects of Kaposi sarcoma," Waxman said that April day. "This horrible disease afflicts members of one of the nation's most stigmatized and discriminated-against minorities. The victims are not typical Main Street Americans. They are gays, mainly from New York, Los Angeles, and San Francisco.

"There is no doubt in my mind that if the same disease had appeared among Americans of Norwegian descent or among tennis players, rather than among gay males, the response of both the government and the medical community would have been different."

Indeed.

I was determined to back up these two pioneering advocates, Weiss and Waxman, and find more allies on Capitol Hill who would bring the full force—and funding—of the federal government to the fight.

As I was learning more about how things get accomplished on Capitol Hill, Tim Furlong told me that if we were ever going to move the needle on AIDS legislation and especially on funding, we needed to develop champions in Congress—lawmakers who would ensure that the government engaged fully in the battle against the virus. Tim was a successful defense industry lobbyist who came to Washington from Texas to work for Senator Lloyd Bentsen. He also had AIDS and wanted to apply his ample lobbying talents to the battle against the disease. He began volunteering for HRCF in 1985, and because he was so talented, we later hired him on a retainer.

Tim was the one who introduced me to Hilary Rosen, who had just left a Washington lobbying firm, uncertain of her future. I knew her talent and her experience. A lobbyist's currency is in who she knows and her "access" to decision-makers. One of Hilary's was the influential conservative Utah senator, Orrin Hatch. With Tim's encouragement, I approached her before she decided what she would do next, advocating for her decision to start her own lobbying firm. Hilary became HRCF's first lobbyist, and we were her first client. We both consider the relationship a fortunate one, which continues to this day.

At the time, finding members of Congress who would be willing not simply to vote with us but actually to lead on either gay or AIDS issues was no small order. More often than not, the mere possibility that otherwise liberal legislators might be perceived as "pro-gay" could precipitate a stampeding herd of terrified politicians. Our friends in Congress needed to know that we would have their backs when they voted to beat back crippling anti-gay amendments. We needed support from members of Congress who were seen as leaders by their colleagues or who held important committee assignments.

To me, the whole idea seemed like a bridge too far. But to a savvy and skilled lobbyist like Tim Furlong, success was possible if we could convince our prospective champions that we would not put them in harm's way unnecessarily and that we would be solidly in their corner at election time. The former problem was addressed with relative ease because Tim was a known and trusted quantity on the Hill. The latter was more challenging because we would need to raise at least an additional $50,000 (roughly $121,000 in 2021) beyond what we had already budgeted for campaign contributions. The best place I knew to find that much money and to find it quickly was Los Angeles. At the time, the lesbian and gay community in Los Angeles had perhaps the most sophisticated and successful fundraising culture in the country.

From day one, it has always been foundational to HRCF's strategy to provide financial support to friendly members of Congress for their campaigns, but our entry into lobbying imposed a new set of rules. We were ratcheting up our political game. Winning was going to require substantially more resources: people, as well as money.

To meet the immediate challenge, I depended entirely on HRCF board co-chair Duke Comegys, the wealthy art collector and fundraiser who had led the board of the L.A. Gay and Lesbian Community Services Center. Duke hosted a fundraising lunch for HRCF—the one at which I met Randy Klose, and I spoke specifically about our new strategy, the legislative outlook, and some of the threats from aggressively homophobic members like Senator Jesse Helms of North Carolina and California Representative William Dannemeyer, who represented Orange County, just south of Los Angeles.

After the guests left, Duke handed me checks that totaled $50,000, and I quickly headed back to Washington. Who knew fundraising could be this easy? Actually, it resulted from Duke's very savvy prep work; he had carefully picked his guests and primed them to give.

Tim was naturally delighted with my success, and together we planned the next steps. We wrote $5,000 checks—the maximum campaign contribution allowed per election—to each of half a dozen or so members of Congress we wanted to be our champions. Among the first were Connecticut Senator Lowell Weicker, who chaired the Labor, Health, and Human Services Appropriations subcommittee, and California Congressman Tony Coelho, the majority whip. As the majority whip, Coelho was well-positioned to round up votes to defeat anti-gay amendments and to pass larger appropriations for AIDS research, education, and treatment, a job he did skillfully.

"We just want to show our appreciation for all of your support," I would say as I handed over the envelope. "We know you don't necessarily need this money, but we're very grateful for your help and want to show our appreciation."

Then I delivered the kicker.

"Who else would like to get money from us?" I would ask. "We will write a check to their campaign, and I'll give it to you to pass on to them."

It was a superb way to enlist the congressperson's support for our cause and make new friends for HRCF. They relished handing out the thousand-dollar checks we would write to their colleagues. Since members of Congress like being the source of campaign contributions to their colleagues because it gives them greater influence, this was a particularly popular move.

Lobbyists today are often looked upon (unofficially, of course) as an adjunct of the legislator's campaign fundraising team. The profession has developed into a system of legalized bribery that exchanges campaign cash for legislation and rules that favor the lobbyists' clients.

Back in the 1980s, though, lobbying was a bit more nuanced. Contributing to congressional campaigns was a primary function. But political action committees like ours were pioneering how we could maximize our limited funds, as HRCF did when we offered to contribute lesser amounts to our champions' colleagues.

HRCF lobbyists—first Tim Furlong and Hilary Rosen, and then the firm Wexler Reynolds and staffers Steve Smith and Carlton Lee—more significantly supported congressional staff with information, and we helped them draft legislation. Nobody knew the issues facing the lesbian and gay community as we did, and few Hill staffers would or could take the time to learn. So we met with them—and sometimes with members of Congress directly. We made phone calls, and we provided in-depth educational materials to which they could refer. This information became especially valuable as the AIDS crisis heated up and Congress considered increasing appropriations year after year.

We also served as a whip organization. In Congress, each party in each house has a leadership position formally known as assistant party leader but called the "whip." The whip counts votes, keeps track of the number of votes for and against a piece of legislation, and "whips up" support for or against it. As lobbyists, Hilary, Steve, and Carlton stayed in close contact with Hill staffers to assess the status of bills and share that information with everyone who needed to know it.

Steve Smith made a particularly significant contribution when, in 1987, Reagan nominated Judge Robert Bork to serve on the U.S. Supreme Court.

Bork served as a circuit judge for the United States Court of Appeals for the D.C. Circuit from 1982 to 1988. In *Dronenburg v. Zech* in 1984, Judge Bork wrote an opinion upholding the Navy's discharge of a sailor for being gay. Noting that James L. Dronenburg had "an unblemished service record and earned many citations praising his job performance" in nine years as a Korean linguist and cryptographer with a top-secret security clearance, Bork stated that "legislation may implement morality" in sexual matters and that the courts had no business creating new constitutional rights to engage in sexual activity. Governmental penalties against homosexual conduct could logically be struck down, he said, only if "any and all private sexual behavior" was constitutionally protected, "a conclusion we are unwilling to draw." Bork went on to attack the Supreme Court's entire line of authority, beginning with *Griswold v. Connecticut,* which articulated a constitutional right to privacy in matters relating to sex and procreation.

Senator Edward M. Kennedy rallied Democrats to defeat Bork—with the help of a tape-recording Steve Smith found of a lecture Bork gave in 1985 at Canisius College in which Bork stated, "In the field of constitutional law, precedent isn't all that important."

But Bork had previously assured the Judiciary Committee that he respected the need to uphold "long settled" Supreme Court precedents on civil rights.

Senator Kennedy played the recording on the last day of the Bork hearings.

"He asks us to judge him on his record as a judge," Kennedy declared of Bork, "but in his own speeches as a judge, he has shown little respect for the past decisions of the Supreme Court. Again and again, on the public record, he has suggested that he is prepared to roll back the clock ... Who is the real Robert Bork?"

The Judiciary Committee voted 9-5 against the Bork nomination, which ultimately went down to defeat in the full Senate with a bipartisan vote of 58-42.

As an aside, Anthony M. Kennedy was appointed to fulfill the Supreme Court vacancy. In Kennedy's tenure on the court, the justices handed down three major decisions upholding the rights of lesbian and gay Americans. In 1996, in *Romer v. Evans*, the court invalidated a Colorado law that preemptively barred any attempt to protect lesbian and gay rights; in 2003, in *Lawrence v. Texas*, they ruled that gay people could not be criminally prosecuted for having consensual sex; and in *United States v. Windsor*, they declared unconstitutional the Defense of Marriage Act. Justice Kennedy wrote all three opinions.

Keeping Bork off the Supreme Court had a greater impact on LGBTQ rights than any of us could have foreseen. HRCF's contribution, thanks to Steve Smith unearthing that fateful recording, was critical to that victory.

Some might see lobbying as the darker side of politics, the part not discussed publicly, but like it or not, pounding the marble halls of Congress is how things generally get done on Capitol Hill. Campaign contributions bought our lobbyists access and some assurance that we would be heard. Therefore, our lobbying also led to the substantial increases in the funds appropriated by Congress for AIDS research and drug treatment we saw in the current and subsequent years. It would be difficult to overstate the importance of Tim's strategy transforming us into a player of significance. We got the attention of politicians when the Reagan administration was proposing to spend *zero* dollars on a disease that was ravaging our community and before LGBTQ issues were seen as legitimately part of the greater civil and human rights struggle.

Lobbying is effective. It doesn't get the headlines like street activism does—or fire up the adrenaline of those activists. Yet, working within the system generates positive results in ways that angry activism rarely can, as the defeat of Robert Bork and the confirmation of Justice Kennedy demonstrated. Perhaps that single serendipitous event—one that may never have had happened without HRCF lobbying—is the reason we have marriage equality today.

HRCF crafted an excellent and mutually supportive relationship with Tim Westmoreland. As a lawyer and a staffer for Henry Waxman, Tim organized the hearing at the Los Angeles Gay and Lesbian Community Services Center. He soon after became the congressman's chief counsel and point person on the AIDS issue.

Tim predicted early the avalanche AIDS would inflict on the lesbian and gay community, eclipsing the fight for gay civil rights. His expertise is in public health, and he is gay, giving him an almost prescient understanding at the time of what was to come.

"You're going to be swept away if you don't pay attention to this," Tim advised Steve Endean, who was eschewing the immediacy of the epidemic as he continued to beat a persistent march for equality. "This is going to overcome civil rights."

"Tim Westmoreland, Representative Waxman's key point person for AIDS, may have done more in combating this dread disease than any human being alive, with hardly any credit for his tremendous work," Steve Endean said, eventually agreeing with Tim's early warning and acknowledging his largely unrecognized impact on AIDS funding.

Steve was right. Serving on the staff of the Subcommittee on Health and the Environment of the U.S. House of Representatives, under the chairmanship of Congressman Waxman, Tim Westmoreland called the attention of Waxman and, thus, the United States Congress to the urgent crisis that was looming in the gay community.

The director of the Centers for Disease Control and Prevention in 1982 introduced Tim to Dr. James Curran, who was investigating an unusual outbreak of Kaposi sarcoma and pneumocystis pneumonia among gay men. Curiously, the initial cases happened to be from Waxman's district in West Hollywood. Through his position on Waxman's committee staff, Tim suggested that Waxman hold a hearing in hopes of generating funding to research the outbreak. That first hearing occurred a few months later at the Los Angeles Gay and Lesbian Community Services Center when just three hundred cases had been identified and a hundred deaths reported. Dr. Curran, by then the head of the CDC's Task Force on Kaposi Sarcoma and Opportunistic Infections, estimated at the hearing that tens of thousands of people might be affected by the disease.

As word of Dr. Curran's projection became more widely known, fear spread among the gay men's community. At the time, no one knew what caused the disease or how it was transmitted. Equally disturbing was the reaction of anti-gay politicians and religious leaders. Some called for quarantining gay men, firing them from their jobs and evicting them from their homes. Even many gay-friendly elected officials lacked the courage to be publicly supportive.

On May 18, 1983, Congress finally passed a bill that included $12 million specifically targeted for AIDS research and treatment. I cite this to demonstrate the importance of HRCF's efforts to move Congress. The money we might raise in the community from fancy dinners and cocktail parties could never touch the level of financial support the federal government brought to fight the epidemic. And this initial allocation was just the beginning of a lengthy effort to generate more. It would take another five years of lobbying and enlisting champions in the House of Representatives and the Senate to pass S. 1220, the Acquired Immunodeficiency Syndrome Research and Information Act, which for fiscal year 1988 authorized some $700 million in research and education funds.

Enlisting and supporting those champions became the focus of our lobbying work at HRCF. Early champion Henry Waxman defended his commitment to the AIDS fight to a reporter who questioned his motivation "just because he had a lot of gay men in his district." His response, Tim Westmoreland told me, went something like this:

"I'm doing this because I chair the Committee on Public Health, and this is the major public health issue in America.

"Secondly, if I were doing it for my constituents, why would you think that's a bad thing? You're not surprised when the congressman from Pittsburgh works for the steel industry. They are my constituents. I'm supposed to advocate for them.

"And the third thing is, I'm a Jew. I know what it means when society doesn't care what happens to you."

I don't think we could have expected a more outstanding champion than Congressman Henry Waxman. Nevertheless, we found plenty more willing to stand up for the gay community in our fight for AIDS funding, including Representatives Philip Burton, Tony Coelho, Barney Frank, Bill Green, John Lewis, Nancy Pelosi, Gerry Studds, Ted Weiss, and Senators Lowell Weicker and Edward M. Kennedy.

Our nemeses were many, but few were as odious as North Carolina Senator Jesse Helms and California Congressman William Dannemeyer.

Called an anti-gay crusader, Bill Dannemeyer made national headlines for his attacks on "militant homosexuality" and his demands that AIDS patients be quarantined and that people with AIDS be barred from jobs in health care in the early years of the epidemic. As the ranking Republican on the House Energy and Commerce Committee's subcommittee on health, he promoted his homophobic agenda, opposing the inclusion of AIDS patients and gay people as protected classes in anti-bias laws and supporting new anti-sodomy laws.

"God's plan for man in this world is Adam and Eve, not Adam and Steve," said the congressman from then-arch-conservative Orange County, California. "We must either defeat militant homosexuality, or it will defeat us."

Dannemeyer placed his notorious statement called "What Homosexuals Do" into the Congressional Record in June 1989:

"Activities peculiar to homosexuality include: Rimming, or one man using his tongue to lick the rectum of another man; golden showers, having one man or men urinate on another man or men; fisting or handballing, which has one man insert his hand and/or part of his arm into another man's rectum; and using what are euphemistically termed 'toys' such as one man inserting dildoes, certain vegetables, or lightbulbs up another man's rectum."

One Hill staffer reported that the item was so popular you couldn't find a copy of the Record anywhere without those pages ripped out. The *Washington Post* said it "gave details about the lovemaking techniques of some homosexuals."

Representative Barney Frank was nearly as blunt in a

comment he made about Dannemeyer's statement. "Your Orange County Congressman Bill Dannemeyer gave a description in the Congressional Record of how a penis is inserted in an anus. I think a more interesting question is how the people of Orange County inserted an anus into the House of Representatives."

"He was a mean and hateful person," Congressman Waxman said of his colleague from California.

Seated next to him at a hearing, Waxman once asked, "Bill, what are your thoughts on masturbation?"

Dannemeyer replied, in all seriousness, "I don't think there's anything we can do about it."

Dannemeyer submitted amendment after amendment, attempting to attach unacceptable restrictions to AIDS bills in the House, such as mandatory AIDS testing and criminalization of HIV transmission.

Senator Helms was equally reprehensible.

One day in October 1987, Helms marched into the Oval Office and handed President Reagan a small brochure. The graphically explicit pamphlet was part of the Gay Men Health Crisis's "Safer Sex Comix" series, targeted at adult gay and lesbian readers, portraying safer sex in as positive, upbeat, and erotic a light as possible.

"Mr. President," declared Helms, "I don't want to ruin your day, but I feel obliged to let you look at what is being distributed under the pretense of AIDS education material." According to numerous newspaper reports, the president opened the booklet, looked at a couple of pages, closed it, shook his head, and hit his desk with his fist. This single brochure was just what the nation's conservatives had been looking for: proof that the fight against AIDS was just another way for lesbians and gays to advance the "homosexual agenda." Never mind that the Gay Men's Health Crisis used public money only to advance activities acceptable to government agencies. Private contributions paid for more controversial projects like this pamphlet.

"I may throw up," Helms said. "Some senators believe the AIDS epidemic is so bad that we should disseminate whatever materials anyone wants to produce regardless of content. But I still flinch when I hear the word *condom* on television.... We've got to call a spade a spade and a perverted human being a perverted human being, not in anger but in realism ... I just want the American taxpayer's dollars to be spent in a moral way."

When Congress next considered AIDS funding, Helms pounced. The Labor-HHS-Education fiscal 1988 appropriations bill earmarked more than $946 million, including the CDC money, for AIDS research, prevention, information, and education to curb and cure the fatal illness. Helms attached an amendment designed to prevent the federal government from paying for any AIDS education or prevention materials that would "promote or encourage, directly or indirectly, homosexual activities."

"The subject matter is so obscene, so revolting, that I'm embarrassed to discuss it in sufficient detail for other senators to know that we have a problem here," Helms said. "Every Christian ethic cries out for me to do something."

The amendment rolled through the Senate with a 94-2 majority, carried the House 358-47, and became the law of the land. Two senators had the courage to vote against the amendment: Daniel Patrick Moynihan and Lowell Weicker. Only forty-seven House members resisted the homophobic hysteria and opposed the amendment.

This vote was just the first of a series of homophobic amendments Senator Jesse Helms would offer when the Senate appropriated money to fight AIDS. These spending restrictions, preventing gay sex from being "promoted or encouraged'" in federally funded AIDS education, were damaging. They effectively censored publicly funded AIDS prevention literature throughout the United States. No money could be spent on AIDS education or safe sex education. Simply a mention of anal intercourse, for example, could be seen as violating the federal mandate, even though anal intercourse was one of the primary routes of transmission for HIV.

These limitations contradicted the AIDS prevention principles and recommendations by public health authorities. According to the National Academy of Sciences, AIDS prevention materials should contain "explicit, practical, and perhaps graphic advice targeted at specific audiences." Failure to follow these principles carried grave risks, authorities warned, noting that "efforts to stifle candid materials may take a toll on human lives."

To comply with the restrictions, the CDC applied strict

guidelines to every pamphlet, flier, and poster it printed or paid for, making sure that they advocated the benefits of abstinence and warned against promiscuity and IV drug use.

As devastating to our fight for AIDS funding as the Helms amendments were, at HRCF, we found a way to capitalize on the setbacks. We took on Senator Helms in the national media, raising a whole lot of money and mobilizing our constituents to speak out.

The Human Rights Campaign Fund launched a series of full-page ads in newspapers of record across the country: *The New York Times*, *The Washington Post*, *The Los Angeles Times*, *The Boston Globe*, *The Dallas Morning News*, *The Providence Journal-Bulletin*, and *The Columbus Dispatch*.

JESSE HELMS IS OPPOSED TO THE ONLY WAY TO STOP AIDS...

AND HE'S WINNING WHILE MORE ARE DYING

Education is our only answer.

Yet Jesse Helms said no, and Congress went along.

The only known way to stop the relentless spread of AIDS is education—straightforward education about safe sex and about bad needles. But on October 14, Sen. Jesse Helms snuck an amendment through the U.S. Senate that could cripple educational programs now working desperately to stop this killer. On October 20, Rep. William Dannemeyer snookered a House endorsement of Helms's language. They did it by playing on people's bigotry.

The Helms amendment orders the federal government not to pay for AIDS educational programs that discuss sex outside of monogamous marriage ... If the Helms amendment doesn't die, more people will. Write or call your Representative and Senators and tell them we must have AIDS educational efforts that provide facts, not rhetoric.

We are working to save lives. We need education, not lectures.

HUMAN RIGHTS CAMPAIGN FUND

THE NATIONAL POLITICAL ACTION COMMITTEE of the LESBIAN and GAY COMMUNITY

(Excerpted from an ad that ran in The Washington Post *on Thursday, October 29, 1987)*

Board co-chair Vivian Shapiro spearheaded the ad campaign, striking a significant coup when she called on friends at *The New York Times* and other national newspapers and managed to procure deeply discounted "remnant rates" and preferred placement. It demanded some shrewd negotiating on Vivian's part, and she did it.

Especially significant was the standing those ads gave HRCF, the only gay and lesbian organization running full-page ads across the country. The ads generated thousands of phone calls, letters, and mailgrams to members of Congress.

As Vivian reflected, they gave our small organization a newfound legitimacy with an authentic national stature. We had joined the "big leagues" of other national organizations that frequently pressed their positions in newspapers around the country. The symbolism made us proud and generated massive support as we grew our constituent base.

Senator Helms wasn't happy, and he told me so in a letter.

"If I were asked to choose the one organization in America, I would prefer to attack me, the Human Rights Campaign Fund would win in a walk."

At last, the lesbian and gay community could see someone was doing something in Washington, D.C., to counter Helms's ugliness and his hate. We said "enough," and we were fighting back. Lesbians and gays all over the country learned about our work, even in communities that never saw our ads. It encouraged folks to come out and support us.

Each ad explained how people could easily participate by sending a mailgram that expressed their opinion. This way, we effectively harnessed the power of constituent mobilization to augment our lobbying efforts on Capitol Hill. By calling a special toll-free number, members would authorize Western Union to send letters to legislators in response to a particular matter or legislation. These letters were modeled after telegrams but delivered the next day. Steve Endean had capitalized on the process for it in a program first called the Fairness Fund and later Speak Out when we brought Steve back on staff and the program in-house.

Two high-level government medical professionals would become pivotal champions in our effort to enlist federal support.

The first was the U.S. surgeon general, C. Everett Koop. The second was Anthony Fauci, then the young director of the National Institute for Allergies and Infectious Diseases.

When Republicans insisted AIDS was a lifestyle issue for which its victims were to blame, Dr. Koop maintained that it would not restrict itself to the gay community, and AIDS shouldn't be ignored even if it did.

The Surgeon General's Report on Acquired Immune Deficiency Syndrome was released in October 1986 to great acclaim and instant criticism. Rather than delegate the report's preparation, as is often done, Koop wrote the report himself. It reassured Americans that AIDS could not be spread casually, so public schools and facilities were safe. It called for a nationwide education campaign for early sex education in schools, increased use of condoms, and voluntary testing, arguing that mandatory testing would drive AIDS sufferers underground, to the detriment of their rights and the public's health.

In the introduction, Dr. Koop wrote: "We are fighting a disease, not people. Those who are already afflicted are sick people and need our care, as do all sick patients. The country must face this epidemic as a unified society. We must prevent the spread of AIDS while at the same time preserving our humanity and intimacy."

In May 1988, Koop made sure the whole country had access to this information by mailing a booklet, "Understanding AIDS," to all 107 million households in the U.S. The booklet summarized his initial report, calling for education and condom use in the United States. It remains the largest public health mailing ever done.

Koop's work on AIDS helped change public understanding of the disease, explaining that AIDS is a chronic disease, treatable and survivable, and one that should not exclude a person with AIDS from full participation in society.

Dr. Anthony Fauci—known in the COVID-19 epidemic as "America's Doctor"—was perhaps the lesbian and gay community's greatest champion in civil service. Committed to fostering positive relationships with everyone impacted by AIDS, he maintained strong communication with me and the leaders of other LGBTQ and AIDS organizations like the National Gay and Lesbian Task Force and the AIDS Action Council. He supported our community when the rest of the Reagan administration was laughing at us.

Well known are the frequent clashes between Fauci and the ACT-UP activists, who protested outside Fauci's office in Maryland until he agreed to talk to them. That interaction made headlines.

In a letter published on the front page of the *San Francisco Examiner*, Kramer called Fauci a murderer and an incompetent idiot.

"If somebody is that angry to be able to print that in a national newspaper," Fauci later said in an interview with NPR, "I've got to find out, what is it that has stimulated him to do that? No one was really able to listen to their [ACT UP's] message because they were too put off by the tactics. I was able to separate the attacks on me as a symbolic representative of the federal government that they felt was ignoring their needs."

Fauci had a personal interest in the AIDS epidemic. His deputy director, Jim Hill, had AIDS and died in the late 1980s. Jim would hold frequent evening meetings at his home, where we could meet privately with Fauci and receive background information. Later, Fauci gave briefings at HRC dinners and Federal Club events around the country.

But few know how he quietly made himself available to me, other national lesbian and gay organizations, and AIDS organizations, including ACT UP, throughout the time I served as executive director. The meetings were held quietly and off the record to avoid unwanted political attention.

Our quiet activism of lobbying, financial support, and constituent mobilization was more readily received and generated more specific, measurable results in Congress than the actions of those activists who made a lot of noise but could claim few friends in high places. Our efforts enabled the Human Rights Campaign Fund to enlist champions in Congress that led to a significant, difference-making appropriation of funds to the fight against AIDS—specifically $47 million to finance the distribution of AZT to people with HIV.

Vivian Shapiro
By Andrea Sharrin,
former HRC Foundation board member

I remember sitting on the floor of my cousin's office with as many people as we could cram into the space, stuffing invitations to the Human Rights Campaign Fund's big gala. Or was it for the Night of a Thousand Gowns or An Uncommon Legacy Foundation or a political campaign or a Jewish cause ... ? It was the 1980s, and it was definitely for HRCF. Still, it could easily have been for any number of organizations or causes that Vivian Shapiro created, spearheaded, or lent a helping hand. The night was fun, energizing, important, and, for me—a young adult at eighteen stuffing her first political envelope—life-changing. But that is Vivian—fun, inspiring, smart, and unstoppably committed to change. Fueled by her experience as a Jewish lesbian daughter of Russian immigrants only a generation away from the Holocaust where some of our family survived, and some didn't, and the relentless AIDS crisis from which so many of our gay brothers were dying, her energy, passion, and commitment were compelling, and you couldn't help but want to be a part of it. Through Vivian, I learned the importance of being involved in something bigger than myself. I discovered the power of a collective voice and the power of money. I was proud, I was in awe, and I had to get a ball gown.

Vivian became co-chair of HRCF when it was teetering between success and failure as a new organization with a modest staff of maybe five people. In addition to her fundraising prowess, she helped transform the organization by reaching the political and financial middle across the country.

"We are here because we are gay and lesbian," she would say, "not because we support or oppose abortion or religion." An important message for such a diverse audience in liberal and conservative states.

"If each one of us gave a thousand dollars (or five thousand for some and five dollars for others), we can raise half a million dollars in one night." Motivated by her inspired words, the excitement of the evening, and perhaps by a few cocktails at HRCF's premier New York event, hands would inevitably and happily rise to make another donation. Raising funds was critical during the AIDS crisis to fill the monstrous gap left by the government. Tens of thousands of gay men were dying, and the president refused even to utter the word AIDS, let alone seek a cure or provide medical care. This crisis brought the gay and lesbian community together. The cross-pollination of lesbians skilled at building community and support with bankrolling by gay men allowed the movement to grow as never before. HRCF members were not just fighting for a cause; we were fighting for our lives. As a leader in the movement, Vivian worked tirelessly throughout the eighties and well into the nineties, with so many others, to keep our brothers alive and hold the government accountable for those who didn't survive.

Vivian's work during HRCF's young and critical days pushed the teetering organization toward success. It allowed it to grow into one of the largest and most influential LGBTQ organizations in the country.

When a light at the end of the very long AIDS tunnel began to flicker through the strength of a growing movement, Vivian turned her attention back to the lesbian community. Her desire to focus on women birthed An Uncommon Legacy Foundation, a national nonprofit founded on the idea that the lesbian community could make more meaningful change by pooling our resources to direct larger contributions to issues we cared about. In its relatively short history, Legacy awarded hundreds of thousands of dollars in grants to lesbian organizations and scholarships to lesbian students and honored countless talented sheroes.

Legacy was the first board I sat on. I was incredibly lucky to learn the ropes from this group of smart and powerful women led by Vivian and Lys Marigold. We traveled together, raised money together, and laughed together ... a lot. I learned from Vivian that humor is a much-needed antidote to some of the weightiness of activism. In the end, we made a difference and made lifelong friends.

Most impressive to me is who Vivian is in the world. Vivian's brand of activism is not mired in self-righteousness but rather in a deep wisdom that comes from making room for views other than one's own to create thoughtful and lasting change. This wisdom, buoyed by her vibrancy, intellect, and humor, invites us all one step closer to a better world.

Vivian continues to support many causes even today, but her proudest achievement was raising two wonderful children with her partner, Mary Nealon.

I'm grateful to call Vivian my family and mentor. Everyone could use a little Vivian in their life.

Chapter 17:
Dan Bradley Again Aligns the Stars

"The best way for Congress to handle an emerging epidemic is to begin by drawing attention to it. The next step is to provide money for research. Later on, when more information is available, the focus can shift to prevention and treatment. Each of these steps was made more difficult, and the public health consequences more dire, because Republicans in Congress and in the Reagan administration cast AIDS as a 'gay disease.'"
—Henry Waxman, "The Waxman Report"

Richmond Crinkley and Dr. Mathilde Krim continued to pursue money for AIDS from Congress. As I've mentioned, Richmond was an avid student of AIDS research who knew far more on the subject than most of us in the activist world. Picking up on Waxman's caution, he surmised that political progress could be enhanced by publicizing what he had learned. That is why we compiled his findings into the MedPac folder and which we distributed to opinion leaders, reporters, supportive elected officials, and researchers.

At the same time, Richmond was learning from officials at the National Institutes for Health that azidothymidine (AZT), an old drug originally designed to treat cancer, that was pulled off the shelf by researchers, showed promise as a treatment against HIV. The drug was in a double-blind trial at NIH, where neither the participants nor the researchers knew who was getting the drug or a placebo. It was apparent AZT prolonged life, albeit with a lot of side effects. It wasn't a miracle, but it was the first drug to show any ability to combat the virus.

Richmond argued to National Institute for Allergies and Infectious Diseases Director Dr. Anthony Fauci that if AZT was at least partially effective, the trial should be ended, and those on the placebo should be given the drug. It didn't require much persuasion since he and other researchers at NIH had come to the same conclusion. A primary ethical guideline for prematurely ending a trial was that, when there was overwhelming evidence of a drug's positive effect, the trial must be terminated, and the drug given to the placebo recipients.

Fauci was always our ally, keeping us informed on what the science was proving. And while he confessed that the researchers had confidence in AZT, he said there was no money to distribute the medicine to patients. He needed $47 million to make it available to those who needed it.

In a 2005 *Frontline* interview on PBS, Fauci recounted the days when money for AIDS was so very hard-won.

"Interacting with the constituencies was probably one of the most important things that I had done in my professional career," Fauci said on the program. "It really transformed the way we did things. You were trying to develop drugs and treatment protocols for a disease for which there was no treatment. At the same time that you had to do good science to get it right, you had to be sensitive to the fact that these people had nothing else and no other option. In a pristine world, you do the science first, and then you worry about everything else. You couldn't do that. That's how we came about with expanded access to drugs, how we came about with accelerating greatly the approval process. ...That went a long way to getting access to drugs for people who needed it at the same time as we had the integrity of the scientific process...."

Now that the trial was ended and AZT, with FDA approval, could be released for general distribution, Richmond set out to get the money Fauci needed to distribute the drug to those who desperately needed it, and that required an appropriation from Congress. When Richmond shared the great news about AZT, he let me know about the money problem, but he said he had a plan to deal with it.

In the grand scheme of federal appropriations, $47 million wasn't much. But no private group like ours had made a specific request like this one to administer AZT distribution—until Richmond persuaded me to get HRCF involved.

One of our champions, Senator Lowell Weicker, was the chairman of the Senate Appropriations Subcommittee on Health and Human Services—essentially the all-powerful bank for the giant federal health and social service agencies. Coincidentally, Weicker also was a Kennedy Center board member with Richmond. In another seeming coincidence, Senator Weicker's wife, Claudia, had worked for HRCF co-chair Dan Bradley when he was president of the Legal Services Corporation, and they enjoyed a long-standing friendship.

Richmond asked if we could schedule a meeting with Weicker to update him on the AZT development and to ask for his help in securing funding to distribute it.

"Use me," Richmond said. "I know all this stuff. And I know Senator Weicker."

I asked our lobbyist, Hilary Rosen, to arrange the meeting. We both agreed that Richmond was the right person to present the case.

We met soon after in the depths of the Capitol building, where committee chairs have rather expansive and ornate offices. Serendipitously, Claudia Weicker joined Richmond, Hilary, Senator Weicker, and me.

Richmond did a masterful job of presenting the facts to the senator. Toward the end of the meeting, he asked for money so that the drug could be accessible to the many thousands of people suffering with AIDS.

"Including Dan Bradley," Richmond noted, knowingly dropping an apparent bombshell. "Dan possibly could benefit from this drug, too."

Claudia Weicker's eyes widened in alarm.

"Dan?" she asked, looking from Richmond to me. "Dan Bradley?"

No one could speak for a moment. We thought she knew. She had worked with Dan for years, and they were dear friends.

Surely, he had told her, I thought. Apparently not.

"Dan has AIDS?" Mrs. Weicker asked.

"Yes," I acknowledged softly after a moment. "I'm sorry, Mrs. Weicker. I assumed you knew."

The news that Dan Bradley was dying—as was everyone diagnosed with AIDS in those days—clearly hit her hard. The emotion of the moment hit all of us hard.

Weicker responded by saying that while he would like to help, we were asking at the eleventh hour—the final vote on the full appropriations bill was scheduled for the next day. He was doubtful that there was enough time to add an amendment. We left hopeful but unsure about the outcome.

The next day—September 10, 1986—I joined Richmond, Hilary, and my staff at HRCF to watch with great anticipation as Weicker rose to speak on the Senate floor—and this I take directly from the Congressional Record.

"Yesterday," Weicker said, "I met with members of the Human Rights Campaign Fund. And they made the following request. They said, 'Would it be possible to supply additional moneys to make available to those suffering from AIDS—some ten thousand persons—with a new drug, AZT?' For apparently there is the possibility that this drug has some delaying effect as far as those suffering from AIDS are concerned."

He then offered an amendment to add $47 million to the appropriations bill to distribute AZT.

"At least ten thousand people can live six extra months, and I'm not coming off the floor of the United States Senate until I get the money to see that that happens."

Democratic Senator William Proxmire from Wisconsin rose to second the amendment. Support from Proxmire was particularly significant because he was the ranking Democrat on the committee, and he was notorious for his Golden Fleece Awards, which called attention to what he believed to be frivolous government spending.

Without debate, the amendment passed.

Weicker later shared how he pulled it off without a confrontation from Helms.

"So I went down to the floor," Weicker said, to present the bill at a time when few Senators were in the chamber. He then contacted Sen. Proxmire of Wisconsin.

"I told Proxmire that I'd like to put in a floor amendment for

$47 million for trials for AZT. 'I would appreciate it if we could get this amendment for AZT through on unanimous consent,' I told him. 'If we put this up for general debate, Jesse Helms is going to get down here and filibuster it, and nothing will happen.' Proxmire said, 'I'm glad to help out; I'm ready to go.' And the amendment became part of the bill."

With Proxmire's help, Weicker outmaneuvered Helms on yet another "no promo homo" amendment. That victory was almost as satisfying as winning the appropriation!

While my time at HRCF was filled with many highs and lows, this was, perhaps, the pinnacle. Never have I been so proud to have shepherded such a grand legislative victory for my community—a quintessential result of brilliant, effective lobbying. Achievements like this did not just happen in the U.S. Senate, especially around the then-unpopular issue of AIDS, without a lot of under-the-radar action. It takes a certain serendipity, an alignment of the stars, to evoke such an accomplishment.

Many who might otherwise have died had their lives prolonged, thanks to Lowell Weicker and his Senate allies, and to them, our community is deeply indebted.

But I want to extend my deepest gratitude to the two people who have never been acknowledged in cementing this win: Claudia Weicker and Dan Bradley. I believe Mrs. Weicker was the true inspiration for her husband's commitment to pushing this appropriation through at the very last minute. And while I do not know this for sure, I do not doubt that her love for Dan Bradley motivated whatever request she may have quietly made of Senator Weicker to offer the amendment and insist that his colleagues pass it.

Whether it was spearheading our White House protest, representing the growing strength of the lesbian and gay community on Ted Koppel's *Nightline* program, or being the inadvertent impetus for a miraculous appropriations bill to fight a plague, once again, just over a year before he died of the disease he fought so valiantly for so many, Dan Bradley aligned the stars.

Chapter 18:
A Call to Come Out

The War Conference
Because They're Making War against Us
A Call to Conference ... A Call to Action

This is a call to conference. A call to war because, indeed, we are at war.

This is a call to some 200 lesbian and gay Americans to meet, to share concerns and exchange ideas, to identify priorities, to brainstorm, to build trust and a sense of common purpose, and to organize ourselves to defend ourselves. This is a call to design some system by which our various organizations and institutions, nationally and locally, can work together toward strengthened national effectiveness of our movement.

This is a call to some 200 leaders within the gay and lesbian community. Leaders and leading people, as activists or supporters. Leaders in national organizations; leaders in local organizations; leaders of local organizations which exert a national influence. Leaders not involved in organizations at all, but who are leading, bright, resourceful people within their communities who happen to be gay or lesbian ...

This is a call to a national leadership conference of the gay and lesbian community of the United States. This is a call to mobilize gay America. Because for love and for life, we're not going back.

—December 15, 1987

Now that HRCF was getting traction in Congress, leading to fiscal appropriations to fight AIDS, we wanted to accelerate the effort. We required input from the lesbian and gay members of our community scattered in various organizations around the country, small, large, and disparate—if they were part of any organized group. The formal organizations did not necessarily work well together. The ambitions of HRCF and National Gay and Lesbian Task Force were too often at odds, and interactions between us could become contentious, for instance over whether to support S1220, the Federal AIDS Research and Information Act. The underlying cause of the contentiousness that NGLTF was politically more purist and HRCF believed in a more incremental and mainstream political ideology. ACT UP was always creating a ruckus somewhere, as it was designed to do.

HRCF board member Michael Shower called our attention to the lack of cohesion. Michael, a senior advisor to the executive director of UNICEF, the United Nations International Children's Emergency Fund, was HIV-positive and very frustrated with how slowly the government was moving on AIDS, which he and many of us believed was no accident. He was equally frustrated with the fractures in the lesbian and gay community and our inability to employ a strong, concerted front to Congress and the Reagan administration.

And he was frightened like the rest of us, in the depths of depression as the horrible disease took so many of our friends. On October 11, 1987, the second March on Washington for Lesbian and Gay Rights drew half a million people or more, according to organizers. Still, there was virtually no response from the Reagan administration.

Michael was an all-purpose fix-it guy. When big things needed to be done, we counted on Michael.

"What if we get together for a weekend for a conference," Michael suggested to the HRCF board. "We would call it a 'war conference' because, let's face it, we are facing a war—a war for our lives. We can invite everybody who is doing anything on behalf of gay rights. We would identify the most critical concerns. If we all come together, we could spend the weekend talking about the issues, talking everything out, and then together, we can figure out where to go from there. We can figure out where we want to go next and what's the best strategy. Let's find a path forward as a community."

Michael acknowledged our diverse community with multiple agendas and multiple commitments. Nobody wanted a single national gay organization—we were indeed too diverse for that. But people were dying, and we needed solutions—to that we all could commit. Michael wanted to bring leaders together to create a cohesive front that would address some of our most pressing concerns—especially AIDS.

The HRCF board agreed to back Michael in bringing together a leadership committee. Then we would step back to let them develop the conference. For it to be truly collaborative, it would not be an HRCF event. Michael represented HRCF, but he served as an independent coordinator, as would everyone on the committee.

He gathered thirty-four people representing more than a dozen organizations to form the organizing committee and plan the conference. (See the appendix for the committee members and the groups they represented.) They called it The War Conference and scheduled it for the last weekend in February 1988 at the Airlie House Conference Center in Warrenton, Virginia.

People from around the country, particularly on the coasts, expressed interest in attending. A bi-coastal bias on the part of the organizers was problematic. Most of those invited tended to be from the East and West Coasts. When Steve Shellabarger heard about it, he insisted on bringing a contingent from Columbus, Ohio, to be sure "flyover country," as he put it, was represented. His argument—and it was absolutely right—was that Columbus was an important community making groundbreaking progress that the whole country could model. Lesbians and gay men were successfully working together, which was not common at the time. Lesbians and gays held leadership positions in the Columbus community. Columbus city schools pioneered policies for AIDS. And the city and county governments provided money for AIDS when most local municipalities didn't even want to admit they had "homosexuals" among them, much less consider their needs. The Columbus contingent of five to the War Conference would bring plenty of experience and ideas to share.

Getting a couple of hundred participants to central Virginia demanded command of logistics and a masterful feat of coordination, which Michael oversaw. The lodging and meals at Airlie House weren't cheap. Travel from Washington was a thirty-five-mile trek into the Virginia countryside. He insisted that the conference be representative of our community and that everyone who wanted to come should attend, regardless of their ability to pay. In 1988, flights were still a luxury for HRC, and airfare was pricey. Michael took it on himself to raise money for scholarships.

Some two hundred lesbians and gays showed up at Airlie House on February 26, 1988, to forge a united community from disparate groups. You can't bring that many lesbians and gays together and expect it to be a kumbaya weekend. Grumbling before and during the conference was to be expected.

For example, the Houston community complained before the conference that while three white male board members of the Houston Gay and Lesbian Political Caucus were invited to attend, no lesbians or minorities from Houston were included in the invitation. The few black gay men who participated in the conference confirmed their experience of that bias.

It brought to light the institutional racism within the LGBTQ community, including the organizing committee when they sent invitations to the conference. Folks from the Columbus group, Stonewall, promptly took up that cause. When they went home, they implemented a policy requiring that the board include a certain percentage of people of color.

Fortunately, we had a decent balance of women and men, which tested the group at first. The women demanded an emphasis on collaboration as an organizing model during the formal discussions versus the traditional, hierarchical leadership models the men were used to practicing. They insisted on at least attempting to forge a consensus around decisions rather than reaching agreement strictly by majority vote. The process supported a solid grassroots organizing model, they argued. Discussions took longer because everyone who wanted to speak could. And, of course, emotions ran strong. Sometimes it seemed like nothing would ever get done.

Nevertheless, we developed a sense of camaraderie. We found ourselves talking *to* each other, not *at* each other. And it worked.

Participants joined breakout groups focused on various topics, including AIDS testing, our relationship with the Democratic Party, the public perception of lesbians and gays, and helping the closeted to come out. These topics generated a range of emotions and sparked heated debate.

But one issue we accepted universally: the closet was our biggest enemy. In it, we were invisible. Coming out could have the greatest positive impact on our lives. We had learned from experience that once our straight family members and friends realized they knew and even loved someone who was gay—maybe a brother or a cousin or an aunt—we became ordinary people to them, living ordinary lives. "To know us is to love us" was an expression so common that it has become an axiom in the community.

AIDS was forcing us out of the closet, and it demanded that our straight family and friends see us—and come to love us—for who we were. This newfound respect, as I have noted, was an unintended benefit from the tragedy of AIDS.

Phil Ryan, an African American man from New York, rose to share his perspective on the importance of being out with all the conference attendees.

"If I were a very light-skinned black person," he said, "and I spend my life trying to pass as white, what would you think? You'd think I have a problem with my identity. And you'd be right.

"Well, if you are a gay person and passing as straight every day of your life, you have a problem. Every time you don't tell somebody you're gay, you let them assume you're straight."

Phil's perspective hit home. It sparked a radical conversation about *bringing* people out.

Until the War Conference, our most sacred commitment was that no one should "out" someone who was in the closet—not even a politician who worked against us. We discussed this at the War Conference for the first time, and a new radicalism sprang forth.

"We realized we were going to have to change the rules of the game," noted Joe Tom Easley, a law professor affiliated with Lambda Legal and HRCF. "There needed to be a rule that said . . .

if someone dedicated themselves to fighting the gay community in public while being gay themselves, then that was enough to take away the protection of the code, the code of silence."

I later defended this decision to "bring out" duplicitous politicians in an interview with *The Advocate*: "Those who participate in the community and then vote against it are guilty of hypocrisy—hypocrisy that causes harm to a whole class of people. Their duplicitous, devious, harmful behavior ought to be exposed."

Together, the participants of the War Conference agreed to pursue several initiatives:
- the need to create improved relations with the media
- demand a strong commitment to AIDS from the new administration that would be elected later in the year
- recruit more openly gay and lesbian candidates for public office
- get more lesbians and gays registered to vote
- support lesbian and gay adolescents, and
- organize regular networking and conference opportunities.

The War Conference launched something even more lasting: National Coming Out Day. This annual event supports an environment in which living openly and honestly is possible. LGBTQ communities around the world have observed it every year since 1988.

Inspired by their work at the War Conference, Jean O'Leary and Rob Eichberg organized the first National Coming Out Day on October 11, 1988, a year after the 1987 March on Washington for Lesbian and Gay Rights. Jean came to the conference representing National Gay Rights Advocates, and Rob was the creator, with David Goodstein, of the personal growth weekend called "The Experience," in which gays and lesbians deal with being gay, coming out, reconciling with family, and other similar issues.

Joe Tom Easley was sent off to accomplish a phenomenal task. He was asked to summarize the weekend and synthesize the outcomes from the various breakout groups that met throughout Airlie House and on its grounds. We all were left scratching our heads, wondering how he could present the consensus of the entire weekend in a single statement. But Joe Tom did indeed pull off the miracle we asked of him—and he stayed up all Saturday night to do it.

On Sunday morning, as we concluded the weekend, Joe Tom held us spellbound. The man was truly a great orator, and he delivered that final statement forcefully, with conviction and emotion. It was a deeply authentic expression in words of the love emanating from two hundred people who, for the most part, previously were strangers. As Joe Tom spoke, there wasn't a dry eye in the room.

His inspiring final statement masterfully summarized the accomplishments of the dozen working groups and earned him a standing ovation.

The conference may have been a first: I do not recall two hundred lesbians and gays gathering in a single location over three days and two nights before this weekend.

"If we did nothing but laugh and cry together," Vivian Shapiro later reflected, "it would have been successful. We were carrying a huge burden individually in our own cities and towns. And at the same time, we were experiencing the unbearable loss of friends and family members every week. The War Conference brought us together with people doing the same work."

All that laughing and crying certainly shook up the Airlie House staff. While most were accustomed to women demonstrating close personal contact in public, many were distressed to see gay men displaying affection to each other in the common areas—and the staff made their discomfort clear. We, of course, did not care. Someone had to explain to the management that when they accepted the contract to serve the conference, we expected top-notch service with no complaints from staff. (Today, Airlie House claims us as a contributor to their "Island of Thought era," in which "gay and lesbian leaders assembled for The War Conference to advance human rights.")

The weekend event was an idea-generator, bringing together members of the lesbian and gay community who otherwise would never have met. That was of great significance to all of us. As a result, many of the attendees went on to become strong leaders in their home communities. Finding your community can strengthen your desire to make a difference, we learned that weekend.

Most of all, we came away with a feeling of unity. For the first time, I dare say, we had begun to forge a national lesbian and gay community—at last.

Final Statement of The War Conference (Excerpt)
Airlie House, Warrenton, Virginia

Our community is facing unprecedented threats ... Not only do we totally face the homophobia that has cost lesbians and gay men their jobs or housing, the love of their families, their children, their sense of dignity and self-worth, and—all too often—their lives, but we now have seen our community decimated by the scourge of AIDS.

We have seen political bigots of the far right attack us, while many politicians who profess to support us remain silent or even acquiesce.

We have suffered at the hands of a national administration inhospitable to the cause of lesbian and gay rights and cruelly indifferent to the catastrophe of AIDS. Confronted by these threats to our integrity, our humanity and our lives, we have met this weekend with several objectives in mind:

First to understand the nature and complexity of the threats we face. Second, to assess the strengths and weaknesses in our movement to help build the strong national force we must become if we are to secure our rightful place in this society. Finally, we have tried to consider a wide range of strategies to build our movement and defeat our enemies.

We recognize the many limitations of our conference.

We do not consider ourselves fully representative of our diverse community. Nor do we purport to speak for it.

While nearly one third of us are women we should be satisfied only when our conferences reflect their true strength in our community.

And our group is woefully underrepresented by people of color, and we are poorer for it.

In order to ensure full participation of all the members of our diverse community, we must commit to gender parity and to inclusion of at least twenty-five percent of people of color in all aspects of our organizing and political work. Future conferences of this kind should also reflect this level of representation.

We must be particularly sensitive to the needs of the physically challenged and make sure that all of our programs and facilities are fully accessible in order that they may participate in all of our activities.

In addition, we are not as geographically representative as we should be. And any future conference should reach out to those cities and states across the country, which have not been represented here. But we do span the continent. We're here from Portland, Maine, to Miami, from Los Angeles to Seattle, from Chicago, Tennessee, Arizona, Missouri, and many, many other places.

As we've looked at our movement, we have seen many strengths—our diversity perhaps most of all. We truly are everywhere. We have seen a movement of caring for each other, a movement of compassion, of talent, intelligence, passion and commitment. And we have seen remarkable strength in our community organizations, both national and local.

We are mindful of the invisibility of our community. As long as the overwhelming majority of our community remains closeted, we will continue to be dismissed. We must do a better job of encouraging people to begin the process of coming out and to support them when they do.

We recognize our failures to adequately deal with the media. We must fight for accurate and affirming treatment of lesbians and gay men and the press, on television, on radio, and in the movies and not settle for anything less.

We must acknowledge the extraordinary successes of our community-based efforts [to fight AIDS], while recognizing how woefully inadequate they are in the face of our twin threats: the disease itself and the callous and criminal response of our governments to it. We must immediately prepare a plan of action for demand of our new national administration and to support and extend our present efforts.

We must work to recruit more openly gay and lesbian candidates and to support them fully. And above all, we must get our community registered to vote, and we must make sure that they do vote.

We must recognize our special obligation to gay and lesbian youth. Adolescence is a trying time for everyone, but it is much more difficult for lesbians and gays. And their problems are even greater in the age of AIDS.

To make the movement what it should be and to advance the cause in this society, we recommend the following four steps as matters of highest priority:

First, we recommend a nationwide media campaign to promote a positive image of gays and lesbians.

Second, we need to establish a national emergency response network that will link all organizations—local, state and national—to provide the means for generating the calls, telegrams, letters, and mailgrams we need to pressure elected officials.

Third, we must have an annual conference of gay and lesbian activists, open to all.

Finally, we must have a National Coming Out Day, or week, to be held in the fall. We recognized that coming out is a process, not a single event. On the coming-out event, we can encourage everyone in our community to take the next step—it may be coming out to a friend, to a sister or brother, to parents to coworkers, or even in the media.

These then are our recommendations. We offer them not as the definitive agenda for our community, for we fully recognize our inability to speak for our vast and diverse movement. But they are the consensus judgment of nearly two hundred of us who have come and tried, with goodwill and good cheer and a sense of compassion and love, to help this movement to which we are all dedicated.

We have no illusions that these recommendations will be implemented tomorrow. But we dedicate ourselves that we will do our very best to see that they come to pass. It will be our strength, our resolve, our commitment, and our hard work that will make the difference.

We leave our conference fully aware of the challenges ahead. But we know that with energy and effort, with money and leaders, with warmth and respect for one another, and with love, laughter, and the determination of steel, we shall overcome.

—Joe Tom Easley, February 28, 1988

Chapter 19:
A Tipping Point

Senator Ted Kennedy exited the Senate cloakroom grumbling about the erotic comic books and explicit videos he found there. Senator Jesse Helms had left the material produced by the Gay Men's Health Crisis in anticipation of the upcoming consideration of the Acquired Immunodeficiency Syndrome Research, Information, and Care Act of 1988. The Senate and House cloakrooms, located just off the floor of each chamber, are the equivalent of breakrooms in an office, where members of Congress go to relax and discuss business. Each party has its own, so the fact that Republican Helms had infiltrated the Senate Democratic cloakroom to leave the material bordered on invasive. But such a concern for propriety would never deter this so-called gentleman from North Carolina in his ruthless attempts to intimidate his colleagues into voting for homophobic amendments.

"If the American people saw these books, they would be on the verge of revolt," Helms said on the Senate floor. He said the books show "graphic detail of a sexual encounter between two homosexual men. The comic books do not encourage a change in that perverted behavior. In fact, the comic books promote sodomy."

Kennedy's bill, identified on the Senate docket as S. 1220, proposed to fund testing, counseling, research, education, and patient access to experimental drugs to combat the virus that was decimating the gay men's community. Helms was, yet again, attempting to shame those who voted for it. His tactic had worked on President Reagan; he was betting it would work on his colleagues in the United States Senate. Helms put his colleagues on record by demanding roll-call votes on amendments otherwise certain to fail by voice vote. Any senator who voted against these amendments was, by his reckoning, promoting homosexuality or condoning pornography. He threatened to use his conservative political action committee to intimidate senators into voting for his "hateful" amendments. His National Congressional Club, a political action committee primarily funded by evangelical Christians, just might retaliate with campaign ads against senators supporting responsible AIDS policy before the next election.

The threats worked all too often. One of Helms's "no promo homo" amendments, passed with an overwhelming majority in October 1987, dictated that federally financed educational materials about AIDS stress sexual abstinence. They could not promote or encourage homosexuality or drug use.

S. 1220, the first comprehensive AIDS legislation to reach the Senate floor since the epidemic began, represented a first step toward the establishment of an overall federal AIDS policy. The bill would increase staff at federal health agencies, create a national AIDS research program, engage in greater international outreach, fund informational programs on AIDS at the national, state, and local levels, provide training programs for health care workers, and establish care and treatment programs for people with AIDS. For fiscal 1988, the bill authorized almost $700 million in research and education funds. The Centers for Disease Control and the National Institutes of Health would channel the money to a mix of national and international organizations, state and local governments, and community-based groups.

Finally, we were getting traction, and we needed S. 1220 to pass. Senator Helms was pulling out all the stops to make sure it didn't.

In 1987, Democratic Senator Kennedy became chair of the Senate Labor and Human Resources Committee (now called the Health, Education, Labor, and Pensions Committee) when the Democrats won control of the Senate. Republican Senator Orrin Hatch had chaired the committee before him from 1981 to 1987.

What few people remember today was the deep friendship

Kennedy and Hatch shared. They both served on the Judiciary committee, where they were constantly at odds. But they joined forces on the Health committee. They were called "the odd couple" for their politically mismatched friendship.

Even though he was a fiscal and social conservative, Hatch was firmly committed to public health and comforting the dying. Kennedy, deeply committed to civil rights and championing the underdog, saw the great injustice of the AIDS epidemic and wanted to address it. In what today would be considered a remarkable collaboration, the two came together to sponsor S. 1220. (Hatch's conservative, predominantly Mormon Utah voters hit him with considerable pushback.) This alliance forged trust among their Senate colleagues. Together, these two powerful senators managed to unite both sides of the Senate in what would eventually be the passage of significant legislation.

Kennedy, known as the "lion of the Senate," was a powerful persuader. Because the fear around supporting S. 1220 was so great, his staff, led by Michael Iskowitz, organized weekly private dinners at Kennedy's house for three or four senators at a time. They would invite AIDS experts like Dr. Fauci at NIH and Dr. Koop, the surgeon general, to answer every single question the senators had, even the stupid ones, so that the senators could educate themselves without embarrassment.

The Human Rights Campaign Fund helped Michael and his team compile an AIDS fact book of information consisting of every imaginable, factual document that scientists at that time had put out. The binders were enormous— about a thousand pages—and they soon became known as the "Fat Book."

Every senator got one, and they would bring them to the dinners, where Kennedy's staff would review essential points. The senators would mark up their copies, fold down corners, and annotate them, so they had specifics readily at hand when they needed them. The dinners helped them resolve any fears about AIDS they might have, so they could speak from their hearts about the disease to anyone who asked.

When we learned S. 1220 would be scheduled for a vote soon, HRCF pulled out all the stops. With solid support from the board, I decided we would put every effort into passing the legislation. We called on our lobbying firm, Wexler Reynolds, which required a considerable investment of some $10,000 a month. We ran our "no promo homo" anti-Helms ads in major newspapers around the country at a cost of $66,000. We sent twenty-seven thousand letters to people known to be "letter writers" who had never had a connection with HRCF before, asking them to write their senators in support of S. 1220 without hostile amendments. Some twenty-seven hundred people responded—a phenomenal ten percent response rate. We sent fifteen thousand letters to our donors with a similar request, and, again, ten percent responded. All PFLAG chapters (Parents, Families, and Friends of Lesbians and Gays) were asked to support the effort, and Reverend Troy Perry sent a letter to all Metropolitan Council of Churches congregations. We placed ads in the gay print media—twenty-five papers in eleven states—asking readers to lobby their senators to support the bill. Those ads generated an explosion of articles in the press. And we ran an ad in the *Washington Post* directed at members of the Senate, urging them to pass the bill intact, without hostile amendments.

I asked Steve Endean to power up the Fairness Fund and prepare our constituents to call or write their senators and ask them to support the bill and oppose any amendments offered by Helms. Senators received more than twenty-five hundred mailgrams in a single day.

Surprisingly, several lesbian and gay organizations, including the National Gay and Lesbian Task Force, objected to S.1220. Most were disappointed that the bill was not specific enough about how the money would be spent. But passing a law in the United States Congress is a precarious undertaking, and sometimes a lack of specificity is warranted to overcome objections from members of Congress. At the time, for example, we could generate greater agreement on research for AIDS than for prevention strategies. Kennedy's team started with reasonably strong language to implement AIDS prevention strategies. But as the bill moved through the legislative process, some specifics had to be weakened to assure final passage.

"We may have to change our strategy, but we never change our vision," Kennedy would say throughout the process.

As expected, Helms proposed a "killer amendment" to prohibit the use of federal AIDS education funds for activities that "promote or encourage, directly or indirectly, homosexual sexual activity." Such amendments were called killer amendments because they could become a "killer" for the whole bill.

Senator Lowell Weicker stood up in opposition to the amendment, urging the Senate to put science before homophobia.

"I hope that during the course of the voting on this bill," Weicker said, "that the voices which would most influence the votes of my colleagues would be those experts in medicine and science rather than those expert in philosophy.

"We are not dealing with anything other than a scientific mystery, a deadly mystery, but a scientific mystery that will be solved by science and education. Fear and ignorance will only compound the problems we face, only exacerbate the cycle of death that associates with this disease ... It is time to get fear and ignorance out of the arguments because we cannot move on the scientific and education fronts so long as fear and ignorance drive our responses to AIDS.

"In this legislation, we finally are setting policy. Policy not based on philosophy, religious beliefs, or partisanship, but policy encompassing compassion and knowledge that one day will bring an end to tragedy."

Still, the Helms killer amendment passed by an overwhelming margin.

Then Kennedy and Hatch proposed a counter amendment to salvage S. 1220. The amendment, called a second-degree amendment, required that AIDS education programs "stress the public health benefits of abstinence and a single monogamous relationship and the avoidance of illegal intravenous drug use."

Helms tried to thwart it on the Senate floor by calling out "the homosexual crowd."

That was a strong accusation for Senator Hatch, who was deeply committed to public health for everyone, including the "homosexual crowd." He took the floor and addressed Helms directly.

"I don't think this should involve a moral or ethical argument," Hatch said. "We're talking about public health. I'm not sure I should stand here on the floor of the United States Senate and pass judgment on anybody."

The killer amendment, the same "no promo homo" amendment

that passed in 1987 by a vote of 94 to 2, was put to rest, in essence, when the Senate adopted by a 62 to 29 vote the Kennedy/Hatch amendment. S. 1220 passed on April 28, 1988, by a vote of 87 to 4. We had won!

Representative Henry Waxman introduced the companion bill, H.R. 5142, into the 100th Congress, and the House of Representatives passed it on September 23, 1988. On November 4, 1988, President Reagan signed the Federal AIDS Research, Information, and Care Act into law.

At last, there was substantially more money for research, education, testing, counseling, and treatment. The money enabled the National Institutes of Health to establish an office of AIDS research and for the FDA to expedite promising new drugs. NIH, CDC, and FDA hired seven hundred fifty staffers to administer the new legislation. For the first time, states and local communities received money to provide AIDS education, counseling, and testing. Before, they had been attempting to raise funds themselves. Senator Hatch added a provision to the bill that provided home care and hospice services.

The passage of S. 1220 turbocharged the effort to reduce the impact of AIDS on everyone, gay or straight.

All our hard work—at HRCF and among the lesbian and gay organizations around the country—paid off. Thanks to the efforts of Steve Endean and the Fairness Fund, constituent mail and pressure played an important role in the passage of a bill favorable to the gay and lesbian community. Senator Kennedy acknowledged the impact of our proxy mailgram program, proclaiming that "The [Human Rights Campaign] Fund's mailgrams were an extremely effective signal that the American people were urging prompt congressional action in the face of this public health epidemic."

With the allocation of $47 million for the distribution of AZT shepherded by Senator Weicker and now the passage of S. 1220, I felt as if we in the lesbian and gay community and HRCF, in particular, had finally turned a corner. We had reached a tipping point. Those are a lot of cliches to say that, at last, we had learned how to beat the homophobes, and in the process, some hearts and minds were changed.

So, it was now possible to set a herculean agenda for the Human Rights Campaign Fund, and we set out to accomplish it:

- Legislative protection of lesbians and gay men from discrimination in employment, housing, and public accommodations
- Recognition of the legitimacy of our families in such matters as custody, parenting, and domestic partnerships
- Adequate federal funding for AIDS research, education, and treatment programs along with reasonable, responsible public policy
- Reform of immigration laws that prohibit lesbians and gay men from entering the country
- An end to the exclusion of lesbians and gay men from military service

Achieving our goals required legislators willing to support our agenda, and to get those, we needed to elect supportive candidates to the U.S. Senate and House of Representatives. By the 1986 election cycle, we significantly ramped up our contributions to friendly candidates. We began sending staff members to work in particularly viable campaigns, where we would organize the local lesbian and gay communities and offer staffing support to a few key races.

HRCF had the resources to promote Eric Rosenthal from "jack-of-all-trades" to political director. Many candidates came to Washington every year in search of our support. Eric met with them privately and in groups. He streamlined our political action committee process, figuring out how to identify those prospective winners. He also met with labor unions, progressive PACs, and organizations like the NAACP and the Anti-Defamation League, sharing information about candidates and discussing which races were most viable.

How times were changing. It had only been a few years since GRNL had been accepted quietly into progressive organizations like the Leadership Conference on Civil Rights as long as we agreed not to raise the "gay" issue inside the conference. Now candidates and organizations were actively soliciting our participation and support.

Eric walked a tightrope when recommending candidates for HRCF financial and campaign support. We gave the most where it could make the biggest strategic difference, naturally, regardless of the candidates' party affiliation.

In 1986, we raised $886,000, making us the largest national lesbian and gay organization in the country. By 1989, with a budget of $2,290,000, the Human Rights Campaign Fund was ranked ninth in the country among "non-connected" PACs, meaning those not connected to an organization, business, or association.

After we brought the Fairness Fund and Steve Endean into the fold in March 1988, HRCF also supercharged constituent mobilization in national legislative matters. Steve grew the National Mailgram Campaign, which enabled people to authorize communication to their congressional representatives. He set up "action hotlines" to counteract the radical right's efforts to derail legislation supporting gay-affirming issues.

"We'll use the hotlines to combat and offset the radical right's extremely effective grassroots mail machine," Steve said. "We still lose too often because members of Congress are flooded by mail from our opponents. Congress doesn't hear from the majority on our side."

He continued to grow the grassroots network of state coordinators, congressional district field associates, and local organizing committees. He also oversaw a "Congressional Action Alert" system to inform leaders and organizations around the country about legislative developments.

Personal computers were precious commodities in the late 1980s, but they enabled us to develop new ways to communicate with our community. We built a computerized bulletin board called HRCF NET to provide political, media, and legislative information. Lesbian and gay computer users could access it for legislative updates and congressional voting records on the most recent gay-related legislation. They could receive our news releases and my monthly editorial at the same time the media did.

After HRCF lost Hilary Rosen to the recording industry, I hired Carlton Lee and Steve Smith as lobbyists. I also hired Tim Furlong on retainer. The three joined forces to become dynamos on Capitol Hill.

Our increased efforts demanded hiring new staff members and finding a larger office to hold all of us. We tripled our space by moving from Eastern Market to a downtown office building. Eventually, we took over the whole floor, giving us a whopping six thousand square feet of offices and meeting rooms. The new location enabled us to work much more efficiently and raised HRCF to a new level of legitimacy.

We hadn't slowed our efforts to fight the epidemic, but we finally could breathe a little. With additional staff and office space and the momentum we gained in the AIDS fight after S. 1220 passed, I felt we could finally turn some of our attention back to civil rights. The Lesbian and Gay Civil Rights Bill was reintroduced into Congress in 1989 by Congressmen Ted Weiss and Henry Waxman.

"Discrimination in any form, against any class of persons, should be abhorrent to all those who live in a civilized society," Weiss said when he introduced the bill. "Gay men and lesbians are in every occupation and institution in our nation, be they doctors or nurses, lawyers or clerks, writers, union members, and managers. They are rich and poor, black and white, rural and urban, and number perhaps twenty million of the hard-working, law-abiding citizens among us. But this minority is different from others in that they do not now have legal recourse when they encounter discrimination."

"We will seek opportunities to move lesbian and gay civil rights issues wherever we can," commented Eric Rosenthal, HRCF pollical director, when the legislation was reintroduced.

The iconic black-tie dinners continued to grow in popularity around the country. I hired Philip Dufour as our field director, and he helped launch dinners in Seattle, Atlanta, and Chicago. We soon began drawing members from around the country to the annual dinners in New York and Washington, D.C., perhaps because we could attract popular notables like Coretta Scott King, Gloria Steinem, Abigail Van Buren (the advice columnist known as Dear Abby), and Phil Donahue.

One particularly memorable Washington dinner in 1985 offered a tribute to Broadway composer Jerry Herman, a friend of Bob Alfandre. Dr. Ruth Westheimer, the noted sex therapist, served as the emcee.

Dr. Ruth, as she is known, gained popularity with a candid, nationally syndicated radio show called *Sexually Speaking*, various newspaper columns, a column in *Playgirl* magazine, and a television series: *Good Sex! With Dr. Ruth Westheimer*. She is noted for her frank and often humorous advice delightfully delivered in her distinctive German accent.

Dr. Ruth asked me to call her at home the night before the dinner to brief her on the evening and what we expected of her. So there I was, talking to Dr. Ruth Westheimer, the famous sex therapist. I am, by nature, an introvert, and I was just a little bit intimidated. Well, maybe a lot.

"Now, Victor, you sound nervous," Dr. Ruth said. "Are you nervous?"

"Well, I'm a bit nervous," I replied, thinking, *I'm talking to Dr. Ruth! Of course, I'm nervous!* Also, the weather report threatened Washington with a hurricane that night, which gave me some concern she might have trouble flying in from New York.

"Don't be nervous," she said, thinking I was unsettled about the upcoming event and her appearance. "I'll be there tomorrow. Don't worry, Victor—everything is going to be okay."

And it was. I picked Dr. Ruth up at Washington National Airport the next day. In those days, the airport was small, and you could meet passengers at the gate, so I did. There was no mistaking the diminutive powerhouse walking off the plane—all four feet seven inches of her.

I smiled and waved to catch her attention.

"Are you Victor?" she asked. I nodded and reached out to shake her hand and take her bag. "You see, I'm here. Don't be nervous."

And I had no reason to be nervous after she declared to our guests at the Shoreham that "good sex is good sex, whether practiced by heterosexuals or homosexuals."

A thousand men and women paid a hundred twenty-five dollars to attend the second Washington HRCF dinner that night, tripling the attendance from the first Washington dinner a year earlier. No doubt Jerry Herman was the draw—what gay man doesn't love a Broadway musical? Herman accompanied singer Patrick Quinn as he sang Herman's "I Am What I Am" from *La Cage aux Folles*.

"Everyone I know has lost someone [to AIDS]," Herman said. "People who were in shows of mine, people I worked with—I don't know anyone who hasn't been touched by this."

"There are people out there with the misguided notion that gay sex is different from straight sex. Well, I guess it is a little different...," Dr. Ruth said, displaying her trademark wit. "People who would spread the idea that homosexual sex is not as good or important as heterosexual sex are themselves spreading a disease as threatening to society as AIDS itself.

"Instead of spreading fear and hysteria, you have been spreading guidelines and facts."

We raised $130,000 for the AIDS Campaign Trust that night, announcing that the first two contributions of a thousand dollars would go to Congressmen Henry Waxman and Ted Weiss, both of whom were in attendance.

Perhaps HRCF's ultimate acknowledgment came from ACT UP's Larry Kramer, who managed to alienate just about everyone, including many allies.

"I think New York has lost the lead with political gay activism," said Kramer, who rarely exhibited such generosity of spirit to other gay organizations. "Tonight, Washington has it."

His magnanimity stunned me.

A private dinner one night with my partner proved even more stunning.

George Graupera and I were enjoying dinner at a gay restaurant when another patron came up to our table to talk to me. I did not recognize the man, and, surprisingly, it unnerved me.

Is this someone I have met? I wondered. *Should I know him? Is he from the press? Is he from an organization we work with?*

He seemed to be a nice person, and he was sharing his great admiration for me, but I found it upsetting, probably because I am an introvert, and uncomfortable with any level of celebrity. I realized that night how uncomfortable I was in such a public role—one that would only shine an even brighter spotlight on me as time went on and HRCF continued to grow.

I gave it a great deal of thought and reflection. The Human Rights Campaign Fund had grown significantly in my six years as executive director. We were giving away lots of money—our budget had grown to more than two million dollars from a debt of five thousand dollars when I arrived. The Federal Elections Commission ranked HRCF twenty-fourth largest PAC overall (of more than four thousand). I helped transform it into the largest and most powerful lesbian and gay political action committee and lobbying force in the country.

I also knew that organizations have lifecycles, and particular leaders serve them best at specific times. Some leaders are best at starting organizations and getting them launched. Others are better suited to growing the organization. I was best at the former. Someone else might be better suited to growing HRCF into the national powerhouse it was destined to become.

Even after a few weeks of deep consideration, I came to the conclusion I had that evening at the restaurant with George. I knew I worked best on the ground and behind the scenes. It was time to turn HRCF over to leaders who could assume a more visible national role and take HRCF to the next level. Those leaders would be Tim McFeeley and later Elizabeth Birch.

Chapter 20:
Progress—A Lot of It. And, Still, AIDS ...

President Bill Clinton stood backstage with the Human Rights Campaign's third executive director, Elizabeth Birch, at the first Human Rights Campaign National Dinner in 1997. They looked out at fifteen hundred elegantly dressed women and men in the ballroom of the Grand Hyatt in Washington, D.C., just blocks from the White House. Never before had a sitting president addressed an LBGTQ audience. As Clinton approached the podium following Elizabeth's introduction, the crowd jumped from their seats, erupting in a riotous, celebratory round of applause.

Showing he fully understood the historical significance of his presence at the dinner, Clinton focused on Harry Truman's speech to the NAACP at the Lincoln Memorial fifty years earlier. It was the first time a sitting president spoke before the nation's leading Black civil rights group.

"It is more important today than ever before to ensure that all Americans enjoy the rights [of freedom and equality]," Truman had said. "And when I say all Americans, I mean all Americans."

Clinton looked out at the crowd and echoed Truman. "Well, my friends, all Americans still means *all Americans!*"

A bolt of electricity raced through the crowd as they leaped to their feet to give the president a second round of thunderous applause.

The emotions Clinton's remarks touched in the audience likely were the same as those touched by Truman in his audience in 1947. No less a personage than the president of the United States, at last, addressed each group, acknowledging their long quest for the equality every American expects and to which each is entitled. But beyond that was something much deeper, an unspoken yearning for basic dignity and validation, things so easily taken for granted by those who have never had them denied from birth or stripped away.

Change was in the air, and this crowd wanted action. (Nothing new there with our community!) A smattering of attendees called out their displeasure with what they saw as slow progress in the battle against AIDS. One man shouted, "People are still dying of AIDS!" while holding a sign above his head that read, "End the ban on AIDS funding." Clinton was prepared for the interruption, responding that he agreed with the protester but adding that his administration was spending many more times the amount on AIDS than on people with breast or prostate cancer.

I suspect many shared a willingness to take the long view. We finally had an ally in the White House who had delivered far more for the LGBTQ community than all his predecessors combined. Accomplishing all of our goals would take time, perhaps more years than Bill Clinton had remaining in his presidency.

Still, others, and I include myself, had been around politics long enough to become a bit cynical, believing that we would win equality when *we* could make the stars align, i.e., accomplish the impossible and make it safe for lawmakers to do the right thing. They would do it only when supporting us did not make them feel vulnerable to defeat in the next election. Profiles in courage they overwhelmingly are not. No one was going to give us anything because it was the right thing to do. That is the reality of politics, and it meant that we could successfully navigate the road ahead only with a lot of hard work and a great deal of money. A president may be powerful—but not all-powerful.

Regardless of the individual attendees' personal politics, whether they were avid Clinton supporters or angry protesters, everyone noted the significance of his appearance that night. No one could deny how far the movement had come since Stonewall. There was a growing respect for the gay community, and politicians were taking note. The Human Rights Campaign Fund over nearly two decades contributed significantly to that respect.

When I started work at HRCF, I was only the third paid

employee. We had bills that equaled the amount in the bank account. By the time I left in 1989, HRCF had seventeen employees and an annual budget of more than $2 million. When we merged with the Gay Rights National Lobby and the Fairness Fund, we added lobbying and constituent mobilization to campaign contributions, making us the largest national gay and lesbian political organization in the country.

Since organizations have life cycles, the best leaders have specific qualities that enable them to guide the organization to the next stage, be it five or ten years in the future. Steve Endean brought sheer grit and an unrelenting commitment to launch a nascent gay rights organization, even in a hostile environment—when members of our community were misunderstood and even despised.

I was a community organizer—I brought the ability to take that scrappy organization and build it. I had a vision of what gay political action could look like, and I could engage people—be they staff, board members, donors, or prospective donors—and inspire them to take on challenges they perhaps never thought they could do. I involved people who were not necessarily traditional activists.

I also had the chutzpah to ask wealthy people to support my vision with their money. (I had to muster up that nerve with every request, but I managed to do it for six years.)

What I did not have was the extroverted nature to represent HRCF on the national stage. But Tim McFeeley did.

In five years, Tim McFeeley grew HRCF to become recognized as an even more powerful political force in Washington. He expanded HRCF to address women's issues and resumed Steve Endean's fight for legislation protecting civil rights for lesbians and gays and against workplace discrimination.

But always, AIDS haunted us. By the time Tim took over my job, a hundred thousand cases had been reported to the CDC—fifty thousand between December 1987 and July 1989. The CDC says those numbers are low because too many cases were underdiagnosed and underreported. By the end of 1989, AIDS had killed some ninety-thousand people. Still, federal support was inadequate, and a cure was nowhere in sight.

Tim brought to HRCF a strong record of political leadership

in Boston, where he served on the boards of directors of Gay & Lesbian Advocates and Defenders and Boston Aging Concerns. He was a founder of the Boston Lesbian and Gay Political Alliance and the Baystate Democrats. He served as the chairman of Boston's Ward Five Democratic Committee from 1984 to 1988. A lawyer, Tim was the principal draftsman of Boston's Human Rights Ordinance, which provided lesbian and gay Bostonians protection from discrimination.

Tim continued HRCF's commitment to increasing government involvement with HIV/AIDS and to fight discrimination against people with AIDS. He began to gain traction when George H.W. Bush became president in 1989. Alarmed to see increasing numbers of their workers become ill, U.S. companies urged Bush and the Republican leadership to do something about AIDS. There was a shift in the expression of concern but little increase in resources. So, Tim turned HRCF toward Congress again and successfully lobbied for passage of several important pieces of legislation.

In 1990, Congress debated The Americans with Disabilities Act, which included a provision protecting people with HIV/AIDS from employment and other forms of discrimination. At the last minute, the National Restaurant Association fought for an amendment offered by Congressman Jim Chapman, a Democrat from Texas that would allow employers to deny jobs with food-handling duties to people with "communicable diseases." Association members feared restaurant customers would refuse to eat at restaurants if gay workers could pass the virus through food or casual contact. Of course, supporters of the amendement knew no established medical evidence demonstrated that AIDS could be transmitted through food handling. Still, they perpetuated the stigma, arguing that the amendment could guard against public hysteria against AIDS.

The disability community had worked for a decade to get a bill that would prohibit discrimination against people on the basis of disability. But they were willing to walk away from it if an exception was made that did not protect food handlers with HIV. Tim attended a meeting at the White House at which disability activists asserted that they would not support the bill unless it covered all people with AIDS. Tim listened as an activist named Bob Williams shared that, when he was a child in a wheelchair, his family was often asked to leave restaurants because the management feared that other patrons would be "uncomfortable." Williams noted that if the Chapman amendment passed, nothing in that so-called civil rights bill could be considered "c-i-v-i-l" or "r-i-g-h-t."

The Chapman amendment passed. But Senator Orrin Hatch, ever the champion of those with disabilities, offered a substitute amendment that effectively nullified it, much as he and Senator Kennedy did when fighting Senator Helms's homophobic amendments. This seemingly small piece of legislation did more than protect workers—it educated people that they would not get HIV through casual contact.

In 1990, Bush signed two more significant pieces of legislation. The Ryan White CARE Act and the Federal Hate Crime Statistics Act were made possible, in part, by the efforts of HRCF.

On March 6, 1990, Senator Kennedy introduced S. 2240, The Ryan White Comprehensive AIDS Resource Emergency (CARE) Act, named after a child who contracted HIV from a blood transfusion. It passed in just two months with bipartisan support—a great victory. The bill provided federal funds to cities that AIDS had severely impacted, including New York, San Francisco, and Los Angeles. Finally, money was available to provide services to those who had not been able to afford them, had no insurance, or were underinsured. Finally, the nation responded to the AIDS crisis, providing comfort and treatment to people who had had nowhere to turn.

Few people know of Senator Kennedy's secret weapon that helped secure the rapid, bipartisan passage of the largest federally funded program in the United States for people living with AIDS. Perhaps the influence of the "Girls in Pearls," led by Sandra Thurman, was why the bill passed swiftly and with bipartisan support.

Sandy comes from a family of activists. Her maternal grandmother worked for civil rights and prison reform. Her great-grandmother had the audacity, as Sandy put it, to think that all children, black and white, should have access to equal education—a radical thought in North Georgia for the time. She grew up in a family that was very involved in the gay community. Her father was a fashion designer. Her mother was a lawyer—

one of only a few female lawyers at the time—and a civil rights activist who was also active in the Atlanta arts community.

Sandy says her mother laughed when, as a teenager, Sandy told her how surprised she was to learn the majority of the population was straight. She and her former husband owned gay bars in Atlanta. Their business partner was one of the first to die of AIDS. When AIDS began to race through the community, Sandy provided respite care to friends whose partners were sick before raising money to fight the impact of the virus. Soon much of her time was given to advocacy and public policy as the director of AID Atlanta in the late eighties. And this is what brought her to the attention of Senator Kennedy.

Kennedy's point person on the legislative effort was Michael Iskowitz, who asked Sandy to lobby for S. 2240, the Ryan White CARE Act. Sandy responded affirmatively and with alacrity. She rounded up two dear friends. Dr. Mathilde Krim,. Mary Fisher, who had contracted HIV, came from a prominent Republican family and in 1992 addressed the Republican National Convention about AIDS. The three women donned their "nice little black suits, some damn good pearls, lots of blonde hair, and black high heels—no sensible flats" and headed to Capitol Hill.

"'You can't raise any fucking money in sensible shoes,' my mother used to tell me," Sandy said. "'Do not look poor when you go in to ask somebody for money. They're never going to give it to you.'"

The Girls in Pearls set out in those heels set out to educate key members of Congress. Their presence was far from what most legislators would expect of AIDS activists, and the doors of Southern congressmen and senators opened easily to them.

The trio paid special attention, Sandy told me, to the "good old boys who were not being cooperative," but who could be at ease with a woman who spoke with the requisite Southern drawl and was dressed the part. The Girls in Pearls befriended congressional staff and were welcomed into the inner sanctums to meet with the members themselves.

Mississippi Republican Senator Thad Cochran grew comfortable enough that he asked Sandy the question that likely was on the minds of all the "good old boys."

"How does a nice girl like you get involved in an issue like this?"

So, she told him of her experience as a community volunteer and her work in a hospice. When AIDS came along, she said, it was natural for her to want to use her skills to alleviate the suffering of those she cared about. Cochran understood volunteerism and support for a cause. He understood Sandy.

"It's usually not hard to change someone's opinion or at least get them to hear what you have to say if you create the right environment," Sandy told me.

And perhaps that is just what happened when Senator Jesse Helms demonstrated a sliver of a heart around the AIDS crisis in Africa. Over the next decade, Sandy was able to develop a relationship with him. When her work turned to the plight of children in Africa with AIDS, Helms pushed for much more federal spending on the problem around the world. In 2002, he called for putting $500 million in the pending $27 billion supplemental appropriations bills to eliminate mother-to-child transmission of the AIDS virus in Africa. Helms confessed in *The Washington Post* that fear of heavenly retribution changed his mind. Helms wrote that his conscience was "answerable to God," adding, "Perhaps, in my 81st year, I am too mindful of soon meeting Him."

"I have been too lax too long in doing something really significant about AIDS," he announced at a Christian conference, adding that he was "so ashamed that I have done so little."

Nevertheless, he never repented for his conviction that the "homosexual lifestyle" was the cause of the spread of AIDS in this country and that spending on AIDS research took necessary money away from more worthy areas of study like "heart problems and other medical defects of humanity."

Maybe Sandy Thurman can lobby him in heaven. Who knows? A cleansing of that man's conscience would take a miracle only the Girls in Pearls could evoke.

Today, the FBI defines a hate crime as a "criminal offense against a person or property motivated in whole or in part by an offender's bias against a race, religion, disability, sexual orientation, ethnicity, gender, or gender identity." But until the 1980s, too many members of straight society generally regarded acts of violence as "natural" reactions to lesbians and gays—anyone who did not conform to traditional gender norms. In April 1990, at the invitation of President George H.W. Bush, HRCF representatives attended the signing ceremony of the Hate Crimes Statistics Act, the first federal law to directly address problems faced by sexual minorities and to include a *sexual orientation* provision. It required the Attorney General to collect data on crimes committed because of the victim's sexual orientation, as well as race, religion, disability, or ethnicity.

HRCF continued to help shape gay-friendly legislation in 1990. Congress passed the Breast and Cervical Cancer Mortality Prevention Act to provide screenings and diagnostic services to low-income, uninsured women. Lesbians are at increased risk for these cancers because they are more likely never to have had a baby, so HRCF worked to pass this bill.

Until 1990, immigrants could be excluded from entering the United States because they were gay or had AIDS. Congressman Barney Frank made sure the Immigration Act of 1990 removed the exclusion of "sexual deviants," as gays were called in previous legislation, removing homosexuality as a ground for prohibiting immigration to the U.S. Those pieces of legislation laid the foundation for the federal government's involvement and support of lesbian and gay rights—well, at least a glimpse into recognizing the need for such support.

And always, there was AIDS. By the end of 1991, 156,143 people had died of AIDS in the United States. While we were making progress in getting support from the government, it still wasn't enough. Tim felt the crisis should be treated like a natural disaster and given every bit of federal support possible. Only clear, dedicated, unwavering leadership from the Oval Office could make that happen, Tim figured. HRCF was growing its membership, increasing its financial resources, and building its lobbying and campaign support staff. By 1992, Tim and HRCF threw their efforts and resources to electing a Democrat to the White House.

In the 1992 Democratic primary, Massachusetts Senator Paul Tsongas, Arkansas Governor Bill Clinton, California Governor Jerry Brown, Nebraska Governor Bob Kerrey, Iowa Senator Tom Harkin, and Virginia Governor Douglas Wilder announced plans to run against George H.W. Bush. Clinton was a relative unknown early in the race.

Paul Tsongas introduced Steve Endean's civil rights bill into the United States Senate in 1979. He continued to support the bill, which had yet to come to a Senate vote thirteen years after he introduced it. He had fought for a gay rights plank at the 1980 Democratic convention. He hired openly gay people to serve on his staff and worked for a more enlightened federal AIDS policy "whose goal," he said, "is to save lives, not appease the homophobic right."

Tsongas received enormous support from the lesbian and gay community, and he became the early frontrunner in the Democratic primary. Then the presidential primary campaign moved to the South, where voters found politicians who supported the lesbian and gay community less appealing.

"Unfortunately, it would probably be a political negative for Senator Tsongas to be closely identified with gay and lesbian support," said Dwight Drake, a longtime Democratic activist from South Carolina and a member of Clinton's presidential campaign steering committee.

"People's memories are short; they don't know what Paul Tsongas did," Steve Endean said, who had abandoned his hopes to be a Tsongas delegate at the Democratic convention when Steve was diagnosed with AIDS. "You can simply introduce a bill and never do anything on it, never pursue it, never hold hearings, never take the steps to do the nitty-gritty grunt work. Tsongas did all that and worked hard on the legislation, although he knew it was going to be painstaking and slow."

Clinton earned the nickname "the Comeback Kid" for his second-place finish after Tsongas in the New Hampshire primary in 1992. As the campaign moved into the southern states, Clinton began to pull ahead of the primary pack, winning every state after April 2. Tsongas dropped out, Clinton caught the eye of the lesbian and gay community, and HRCF threw all their efforts into electing him.

"After twelve years of ignorance, inaction, and indifference, the choice in 1992 is too important for our community to stand on the sidelines," said HRCF co-chair Laura Altschul.

"The crucial decisions affecting the lives of lesbians and gay men during the next four years will be made by the president of the United States," added co-chair Randy Klose.

Tim called Clinton "far and away the best candidate our community has ever had as a national party nominee."

In the final weeks of the campaign, HRCF deployed much of its staff around the country to mobilize volunteers in the Clinton-Gore campaign and critical congressional races. Lesbian and gay voters contributed an estimated $3 million to the campaign and "clearly voted in a bloc this year for the first time," helping to push Clinton over the top on election day.

HRCF hailed Clinton's election as "the most significant day in the history of the lesbian and gay civil rights struggle since the Stonewall Riots of 1969."

Clinton appointed more than one hundred fifty openly gay men and lesbians to all levels of government, including judicial appointments and top executive branch positions requiring Senate confirmation. He nominated James C. Hormel to be U.S. Ambassador to Luxembourg, making him the first openly gay United States Ambassador.

Before Vice President Al Gore first spoke to a Human Rights Campaign dinner, Philip Dufour briefed him as he reviewed his speech. Gore questioned Philip about a line in his prepared remarks.

"This says that Bill Clinton and I are proud to have more openly gay and lesbian staff members in our administration than all the previous administrations combined," the vice president said. "*Combined?* Is that right? You just mean more than in the Bush administration, right?"

"No," Philip replied. "We mean more than all the administrations that have come before you. Until the Clinton administration, no lesbian or gay person was ever allowed to serve openly."

Tim expertly led HRCF through the many demands of the ongoing AIDS crisis, expanded HRCF's focus to address women's issues, and resumed the fight for civil rights and against workplace discrimination. But his greatest challenge came just days after Clinton was elected, and he faced what he called an existential crisis for HRCF.

HRCF found itself mired in an unwanted fight against military leadership and veterans groups, most Republicans, and the religious right. On November 11, 1992—Veterans Day— U.S. District Judge Terry J. Hatter Jr. ordered the Navy to restore Keith Meinhold, a Navy sailor discharged for homosexuality, to his former position. When Clinton, who had explicitly promised to rescind the gay ban after his inauguration, was asked his opinion of the judge's decision, he said he supported it. Less than a year later, the notorious and despised "Don't Ask, Don't Tell" policy became the government's "solution."

This unjust policy was particularly painful because, in a meeting in the Oval Office, President Clinton had personally assured leaders of the gay community, including Tim McFeeley, that he believed we could lift the exclusion of gays from military service.

Gay organizers never before had experienced a president say a kind word about lesbians and gays, Tim later said. Clinton encouraged us, so we couldn't see how we could lose. That may be, in large measure, why we did.

"No gay or lesbian leaders had ever before in history met with any president of the United States to discuss issues of importance to the gay community," noted Tim, "and here we were being treated like comrades in the fight against the forces of darkness. It was inspiring, heady, romantic, and sad to say, totally unrealistic."

"We elected a president and got a barometer."

We were blinded in this fight by a naïve belief that fairness could overcome fear, that principal trumps politics. Our gullibility was not unfounded. When he was secretary of defense, Dick Cheney told Congress that to exclude gays because they could be security risks was an "old chestnut." Virginia Senator Chuck Robb, a former U.S. Marine, told General Colin Powell in 1992, "The military ... should not bar individuals from service based on who they are ... Like racial or ethnic origin or gender, sexual preference has no bearing on how great a contribution an individual can make to the United States."

In 1991, HRCF had commissioned a national poll on the military's anti-gay ban. It found that 65 percent of Americans supported admitting openly lesbian and gay men into the armed forces. An even larger proportion—81 percent—opposed the Pentagon policy of discharging gays and lesbians when their sexual orientation became known. Fully 90 percent opposed the discharge of any gays and lesbians who had served in the Persian Gulf War. The poll was later cited in a 1992 study by the General Accounting Office, which concluded that the military's anti-gay ban cost the Pentagon $27 million annually.

The question was never a defining issue in the 1992 campaign for president. HRCF asked the candidates if they favored a change in the anti-gay policy. Bob Kerrey, Tom Harkin, Jerry Brown, Paul Tsongas, and Clinton all expressed their support. Clinton, the most conservative of the Democrats, declared in an address to the lesbian and gay community in Los Angeles that the policy of keeping homosexuals from serving the U.S. in uniform would end. Even the Republicans declined to make it an issue.

A cavalier attitude led us to assume that Clinton would act on the issue in his first hundred days. After Clinton was elected, the HRCF board met to discuss the issue, with some members expressing concern about the growing opposition. David Mixner, a friend of Clinton and a well-known member of our community, attended the meeting and assured us that the president would lift the ban on gays serving openly in the armed forces, and he would do it by executive order.

"This is a done deal!" Mixner proclaimed to the HRCF board, pounding the table for emphasis. "Let's move on!"

We did not count on the inexperience (and early missteps) of the new administration. We did not expect Secretary of Defense Les Aspin to surrender the fight just four days after Clinton's inauguration. We never suspected that the Democratic chairman of the Senate Armed Services Committee, Senator Sam Nunn (who was known for his homophobia and opposition to gays in the military), would actively block lifting the ban. We did not anticipate the vitriolic aggression of Republican voters who flooded every congressional office with letters and phone calls opposing lifting the ban.

We were overconfident and preoccupied with working for protection from employment discrimination and fighting hate crimes. And, of course, always AIDS demanded everything HRCF could give—and more.

A group of prominent gay activists closely aligned with President Clinton, including Mixner, organized the Campaign for Military Service and appointed Tom Stoddard as executive director. Although Tom was a good lawyer and the former executive director of Lambda Legal, he was not a campaign manager, which is what such an operation required.

While HRCF was included in meetings, organizers made it

clear to Tim that they considered HRCF unable to manage such a high-level national operation.

But they were wrong. HRCF spent more than $1 million on "Operation Lift the Ban." We ran full-page ads in major newspapers and held public forums and media events. We organized town meetings, conducted Speak Out canvassing, hosted bar nights, organized Federal Club functions, and held press conferences. Speak Out delivered more than half a million mailgrams.

But we failed to effectively implement the most powerful tactic we had—communicating directly with members of Congress. That spring, hundreds of thousands of lesbians and gay men marched in Washington. Tim called on those assembled on the Mall to contact Congress.

"Without this kind of legislative action on our part," he said, "this is but sound and fury, signifying nothing."

But only a few hundred bothered to lobby their members of Congress, once again supporting my claim that slow-but-steady lobbying changes policy, not the antics of angry activists. As Tim said, "More people donned their trendy 'Lift-the-Ban' dog tags and danced until dawn than ever lifted a pen to write their congressmen."

He later shared his astute assessment of the demoralizing loss:

"Engaging in the political process to change public policies involves more than idealism and principles. It requires tough, honest appraisals of political strengths and weaknesses and realistic strategies that can favorably shift the balance. It mandates retreat in the face of devastating losses, especially where *people's* lives are in jeopardy, and aggressive advances when the opposition stumbles. Finally, politics often requires compromise to effect incremental change and prevent permanent marginalization. The 1993 experience in attempting to lift the ban on military service by gay and lesbian Americans provides an example that we ignore at our peril."[1]

---

[1] *Creating Change: Sexuality, Public Policy, and Civil Rights*. Ed: John D'Emilio, William B. Turner, Urvashi Vaid, pg. 236, St. Martin's Press.

In October 1993, Clinton signed the law directing that military personnel "don't ask, don't tell, don't pursue, and don't harass" its servicemembers, denying protection to lesbians and gays in the armed services from harassment for their sexual orientation. The policy continued until September 20, 2011.

Tim regretted HRCF's involvement in the Campaign for Military Service, an opinion I shared, believing they had wasted any political capital HRCF may have had with the Clinton administration in tilting at that windmill. Those six months would have been better spent working with the new Democratic president to reverse negative government AIDS policies. As always, of course, there was AIDS.

"So, what are we going to do next?" Tim asked the board. The answer was obvious: end discrimination in employment. It was obvious because it was a response to a frequent question from our community during the military debate. "Why are you asking the federal government to ban discrimination when private employers can discriminate against us?"

Shortly after I left, HRCF took on Western Union—the company that had for years delivered Speak Out mailgrams to Congress—when the company challenged the constitutionality of San Francisco's human rights ordinance outlawing discrimination based on sexual orientation. The company had chosen the drastic tactic to defend itself from a case of anti-gay discrimination. The company rep who managed our $350,000 annual account tried to argue our case without success. Even Tim, a corporate lawyer and skilled negotiator, could not persuade the company to back down from their lawsuit. To continue to use Western Union as our vendor was untenable to HRCF and the lesbian and gay communities in California. So, he fired them.

"We want to send a clear message to Western Union," Tim said. "Lesbian and gay Americans do not intend to spend their money with an organization that is fighting to deny our rights to live free from discrimination."

In April 1990, a San Francisco court ruled against Western Union and upheld the ordinance. The decision made national news, and the company came back begging to get the HRCF account back. As a gesture of apology—a sort of peace offering—they handed over a gift of a hundred thousand dollars, which

Steve Endean accepted gladly. But he had found another company to deliver mailgrams for less money, and HRCF never went back to Western Union.

In 1991, only two states, Massachusetts and Wisconsin, and about eighty cities and counties specifically prohibited discrimination in hiring based on sexual orientation. That year, the Cracker Barrel chain of restaurants, based in the very Southern state of Tennessee, fired nine gay employees, and stated that the company would no longer employ lesbians or gays. In a national announcement, the company declared that Cracker Barrel was founded on a "concept of traditional American values." Continued employment of those "whose sexual preference fails to demonstrate normal heterosexual values which have been the foundation of families in our society" appears inconsistent with those values and the "perceived values of our customer base."

Cheryl Summerville, a thirty-two-year-old lesbian who for more than three years had worked as a cook at a Cracker Barrel in Douglasville, Georgia, said her managers wanted her to be quiet and wait for everything to calm down. But Summerville would not stay at a job from which her gay coworkers were fired because of their sexual orientation.

Tim invited her to speak at Atlanta's black-tie dinner.

"Speaking of heroes," Tim said as he introduced Summerville, "what about the Cracker Barrel employee who went to her boss after management had fired her gay coworkers and told them that she was a lesbian and they'd have to fire her, which they did? And when Cracker Barrel tried to hire her back, she refused unless they hired the gay men back as well. She put her job on the line—not once but twice. She's a real hero, and she's with us tonight with her lover of ten years and her mother as well."

News outlets around the country told Cheryl's story. As a result, Cracker Barrel quickly ditched the new company policy that required employees to "demonstrate normal heterosexual values." Still, no federal employment non-discrimination law covers the LGBT community.

Until 1994, HRCF focused its anti-discrimination efforts on passage of the civil rights bill Bella Abzug had introduced twenty years earlier that would have amended existing civil rights statutes to protect gays and lesbians from discrimination in employment, housing, credit, and public accommodations. In twenty years, the bill had not passed. We tried a new strategy—passing independent legislation focused solely on banning discrimination against lesbians and gays in the civilian workforce.

Tim turned to the Leadership Conference on Civil Rights to draft the Employment Non-Discrimination Act (ENDA). The LCCR agreed to champion the bill, and within the first six months, it picked up a hundred and fifty cosponsors. Senator Kennedy guided it through his committee, holding the first Senate hearings ever on gay civil rights.

"This is about real Americans whose lives are being shattered and whose potential is being wasted," Kennedy said in his opening remarks.

Congressman Barney Frank delivered the speech of his career, which earned him a standing ovation from his colleagues.

> Mr. Speaker, we say here that we don't take things personally, and usually that is true. Members, Mr. Speaker, will have to forgive me. I take it a little personally.
>
> Thirty-five years ago, I filed a bill that tried to get rid of discrimination based on sexual orientation. As we sit here today, there are millions of Americans in states where this is not the law ...
>
> I used to be someone subject to this prejudice, and, through luck, circumstance, I got to be a big shot. I am now above that prejudice. But I feel an obligation to fifteen-year-olds dreading to go to school because of the torments, to people afraid they will lose their job in a gas station if someone finds out who they love. I feel an obligation to use the status I have been lucky enough to get to help them.
>
> I want to ask my colleagues here, Mr. Speaker, on a personal basis, please, don't fall for this sham ... Don't send me out of here having failed to help those people ...
>
> Yes, this is personal. There are people who are your fellow citizens being discriminated against. We have a simple bill that says you can go to work and be judged on how you work and not be penalized. Please don't turn your back on them.

ENDA never became law. While the bill passed in the House of Representatives, it died in the Senate. It was replaced by the Equality Act, a far more comprehensive bill—more similar to Bella Abzug's original bill—that would amend the 1964 Civil Rights Act to explicitly prevent discrimination based on sexual orientation and gender identity. As of this writing, the Equality Act, which passed the House in the last Congress, but died in the Senate. It has not yet been reintroduced in the current Congress. Despite the 2020 U.S. Supreme Court decision in *Bostock v Clayton County* prohibiting discrimination against LGBTQ people, explicit and comprehensive civil rights protections still do not exist for us at the federal level. The need for federal protection is growing alarmingly evident as conservative states pass laws that discriminate against us.

In Tim McFeeley's five-year tenure as executive director, HRCF tripled the size of its staff and membership and quadrupled the size of its annual budget from $2 to $8 million, enabling the organization to come within one vote of passing a nondiscrimination bill in the Senate. This incredible growth opened the way for Elizabeth Birch to shepherd a massive transformation of the organization into one that was virtually unrecognizable from the dream Steve Endean launched from a tiny office in a seedy part of Washington, D.C.

Chapter 21:
So Much More Than a Fund

Elizabeth Birch was the clear choice to become the next executive director of the Human Rights Campaign Fund and lead it into the twenty-first century.

"I was born for this job," Elizabeth said. "It was like a calling. It was the clearest career choice I ever made."

Elizabeth left a top position at Apple, the bastion of forward-thinking U.S. corporations, to come to HRCF and upgrade the reputation of what many considered an exclusive group of rich, gay, white guys hanging out on Capitol Hill and dressing up for fancy dinner parties. Elizabeth's avowed personal commitment was to make sure every LGBTQ person in the country felt they belonged; the Human Rights Campaign Fund would welcome them. She brought a vision of transformation that few others could see at first, including me. That vision dramatically expanded the scope of the organization and its outreach into the community. At the time, I thought it bordered on revolution. It was heresy… mission creep… totally inappropriate. I was wrong. In hindsight, I saw that what Elizabeth came to do was exactly what we needed at the time to move HRCF out of the nineties and into the next millennium. We needed a vibrant community that reached beyond the halls of Congress into every home in the country with young people who needed to know they were not alone. And that is just what Elizabeth set out to do.

The first distinction the new head brought to the largest lesbian and gay political organization in the United States was obvious—Elizabeth Birch is a woman. Since Steve Endean first insisted on a balance of men and women on the board, we strove to include lesbians on a par with gay men, but only somewhat successfully. Elizabeth's leadership represented a powerful shift from the first day she showed up to work. But there had been other blind spots as well, particularly when it came to the transgender community. Trans people had been at Stonewall, and yet national organizations, including HRCF, were often unaware of issues central to the transgender community. That began to change.

Launching a "corporate repositioning," Elizabeth reconfigured the face HRCF proclaimed to the world, from its graphics to every message it disseminated. Noting that "We're so much more than a fund," she changed the name to the Human Rights Campaign, tucking the previously dominant fundraising function to a subset of its mission. She vowed to make HRC more inclusive and accessible to everyone, regardless of their willingness or ability to give money. She expanded the focus, reducing the emphasis on politics and legislation and creating programs and messages that would appeal to every LGBTQ person in the country.

"I wanted to make HRC an organization I would want to belong to," Elizabeth told me. "I wanted to open it up, make it welcoming to everybody. I wanted our members to know they fit in, that they could become whole, respected people making full-blown contributions in the world. These messages were important to help people get out of the closet."

Under her leadership, HRC implemented a new slogan—EQUALITY—and commissioned a simple, bold logo of a yellow equal sign in a blue square. Today, "equality" has superseded the term "gay rights," and nearly three decades later, the logo continues to symbolize the fight for equal rights for LGBTQ Americans.

HRC continued its lobbying, field organizing, and political action committee activities while expanding its education, research, communications, marketing, and public relations functions. HRC grew into an organization as effective in serving its members as it had been in influencing Congress.

Reflecting a new, expanded mission of inclusion, HRC launched two programs. One provided broad support and information on resources available to same-sex couples who wanted to have families. The other was designed to transform the workplace into a more LGBTQ-friendly environment.

WorkNet—now including a rating system called the Corporate Equality Index—gathered news and information on companies with non-discrimination policies, domestic partnership benefits, and employee support groups. It shared advice and resources for LGBTQ people interested in convincing their companies to add sexual orientation and later gender identity to the corporate non-discrimination policy or forming an employee resource group. It also provided a referral service for legal assistance regarding job discrimination.

Elizabeth was determined to demystify gay life for straight Americans, and particularly for parents. HRC created programs that used non-threatening language parents could understand—and maybe even accept. Elizabeth insisted that nothing alienate the dad in Idaho or the mom in Kentucky.

The organization also worked with Hollywood to hold gay-friendly conversations in popular television shows. This tactic emulated the common practice of "product placement," in which a television show or movie displays a particular product. Remember, Elizabeth came from Apple, and she knew the effectiveness of showing Apple computers and phones on TV.

High-profile lesbians and gays became emissaries. To deliver a gay-friendly message, HRC enlisted celebrities like Cher, whose child Chaz first came out as a lesbian in 1995 and then made history when coming out as a trans man in 2009. Amanda Bearse of Fox-TV's *Married ... With Children* was the first working TV actress on network television to come out. HRC recruited her to appear in a public service announcement. "I'm not a straight woman," she said, "but I play one on TV. And that's where acting belongs—on television or in the movies, not in real life. That's why I stopped acting and came out."

Of course, Ellen DeGeneres's hit TV series *Ellen* is best known for its coming-out episode in 1997 when Ellen DeGeneres came out as a lesbian. HRC tried to buy an ad on the program, but ABC turned it down. So, Cathy Nelson, the HRC development director, created "Ellen Coming Out House Party" kits with invitations, posters, an *Ellen* trivia game, and a videotape of the HRC ad, along with a membership appeal from Elizabeth. HRC expected to send around three hundred kits. Deluged with requests, Cathy mailed some two thousand kits. Another thousand were downloaded from the website.

Ellen's mom, Betty DeGeneres, became a role model for parents of lesbians and gay men after she described her challenge in coming to terms with her daughter's sexuality on national television. She came to Washington, D.C., to meet with HRC staff, and Elizabeth invited her to be the first straight spokesperson for the National Coming Out Project. In that role, Betty DeGeneres shared the importance of parents of lesbians and gays supporting their children. "Ending discrimination based on sexual orientation is not just important to gay people. It's important to their families," she said.

At last, pride began to permeate the LGBTQ community and the straight world, thanks, in part, to the increasing influence of the HRC campaigns. Next, HRC would take on the most ambitious campaign in its history—owning an office building in downtown Washington, D.C. Over eight years, Elizabeth had quadrupled the HRC staff, which enabled the organization to execute and expand its broader mission. Frequent moves to garner more office space proved tedious and costly in time and money. Owning a building would eliminate those expenses. The greater benefit would be the visibility a permanent headquarters in the nation's capital would bring.

Elizabeth tapped Terry Bean and Edie Cofrin to head up the capital campaign. Terry raised early money for the Gay Rights National Lobby, and his dedication to the movement had never wavered.

"I remember driving around Washington with Steve [Endean] early on," Terry told me. "We [GRNL] had a tiny office in a Capitol Hill rowhouse at the time. We saw buildings for unions and organizations like the Chamber of Commerce and even the NRA, God forbid. I said to Steve, 'Wouldn't it be cool if we had our own building someday? Imagine being a seventeen-year-old closeted kid and visiting D.C. on your field trip. You see a building for an organization that stands for the safety and protection of all gay, lesbian, bisexual, and transgender people. Imagine how you'd feel.' It was just this almost-ridiculous dream then. But I kept that in my mind from then on as a possibility."

Elizabeth's and Terry's leadership, combined with the lead gift from Edie Cofrin, helped make that almost-ridiculous dream come true. Aside from its very generous size, Edie's gift is particularly noteworthy because she placed just one stipulation on it: no individual's name should ever appear on the building. She wanted the building's identity to be HRC's alone.

The original plan was to build on a vacant parcel occupied by a parking lot. But an early excavation revealed issues beneath the surface that made it impossible to create an adequate foundation and underground parking without an unbudgeted investment of several million dollars.

That's when serendipity struck, and we learned that the building next door was for sale. It wasn't just any building. It was owned by the B'nai B'rith, the oldest and largest Jewish human rights organization, and it was just six blocks from the White House. HRC would carry on the civil rights tradition in B'nai B'rith's former home.

HRC had to commit to buying the building before they could raise all the money. Not wanting to lose it to another buyer, Elizabeth took the plunge and committed HRC to the purchase. This was a huge financial commitment. She tapped Jeff Sachse and Chris Speron to raise $28 million for the purchase and renovations. Each week Jeff and Chris reported to the board on their fundraising progress.

The capital campaign invited members to give as much as they could or as little as fifty dollars. Larger legacy gifts could be made in installments, a rare opportunity in such a fundraising endeavor. But HRC wanted to include as many people as possible. Hundreds of people made small donations, and they can see their names posted in the building.

Smoot Construction, a Black-owned company, conducted the renovation. They replaced the existing façade with floor-to-ceiling windows. Elizabeth wanted the building to communicate transparency—the opposite of the closet. Similarly, office spaces were framed in glass. The building included the first green roof in downtown Washington.

Before its dedication, HRC moved into the building, wrapped with a decal-like substance that enabled one to see out, but not in. The wrap declared "Coming Soon: The Human Rights Campaign," which made people eager to offer financial contributions.

"When you do a capital campaign for an organization, it actually changes the organization," Chris Speron told me. "More people want to invest. This building was a textbook example. We saw an increase in donations and an increase in support. Suddenly HRC, an organization many in Washington had hoped would disappear, showed up differently. We had a presence. That trajectory has continued to this day. The $28 million we raised was the largest amount raised for any LGBTQ civil rights project at that point. Now the HRC budget is almost $70 million a year!"

HRC dedicated the new space on National Coming Out Day, October 11, 2003. The street was closed to accommodate an enormous block party. It was a celebration of hope and opportunity. That morning, the organizers raised the American flag and the Equality flag. Just as the flags reached the top of the flagpole, giant blue and yellow ribbons cascaded down to reveal the building's exterior. I cannot adequately express how moving that day was for my fellow community members and me. After so many years of struggle and being marginalized, finally, there was a beautiful symbol denoting legitimacy and permanence. We were here, we were visible, and we were here to stay.

That building was just one of many bold ambitions Elizabeth brought to her job at HRC, but none was bolder than to have President Clinton speak at its first National Dinner. It was never far from her mind, and she made sure it was front of mind of everyone she knew who could influence the White House.

"I lobbied every one of his close advisors, from George Stephanopoulos to Craig Smith—all the handlers who were close to him," she told me. "I would say things like, 'Craig, every single morning, when you get up and look at yourself in the mirror, I want you to ask yourself: What have I done to get President Clinton to the HRC dinner? And then I want you to get some lipstick and write it on your mirror. Have you done that today?' I bugged them for a year.

"Erskine Bowles was Clinton's chief of staff. One night at an event, I literally followed him into a bathroom—I was that intent on locking in Clinton. I went in, and then I noticed the urinal, and it dawned on me where I was. 'Oh, my God,' I said. And he said, 'Elizabeth, I want you to be happy. I will do anything for you. But can I go to the bathroom, please?' So, I waited for him outside the bathroom."

Elizabeth's persistence paid off, and President Clinton

addressed the National Dinner on November 8, 1997. The president's presence was the supreme acknowledgment, bestowing a significance that most people today could not fathom unless they grew up gay in the last half of the twentieth century.

"To the men in the room that night—the women too, but mostly the men," Elizabeth told me, "Clinton represented the father who never heard them. Their country was symbolized by a human at the front of the room, basically saying, 'You're a part of this country, and you are important.' The men in that ballroom, dressed in tuxedos and black tie, had been despised for decades. They had lost so many loved ones to AIDS while a stony, horrible government ignored them and their plague. AIDS still was an ever-present, gripping fear because we still did not have a cure. We had been on edge our whole adult lives. We had buried so many people. Finally, here is the president of the United States seeing them, acknowledging them. It was extraordinary."

Indeed, it was extraordinary, as was Elizabeth's leadership taking the Human Rights Campaign from the nation's most powerful lesbian and gay political organization to one of the largest and most effective mainstream advocacy organizations in the country. Of course, she stood on a solid foundation built by countless dreamers—and activists and fundraisers and rabble-rousers and lobbyists and voters and lawmakers and letter-writers and all kinds of supporters—LGBTQ and allies—who gave their time and money to upend misunderstandings and plain old hate. I do not doubt that her vision—to see LGBTQ members welcomed in their homes and their communities and now recognized by the president of the United States—surpassed even Steve Endean's wildest dreams.

And it all happened in a little more than twenty years.

Chapter 22:
"In one night, everything seemed to change"

The AIDS epidemic would transform the conversation and eventually gain civil rights and public acceptance for our community in a way that a concerted political effort never would. Lesbians stepped up to care for their sick brothers. Straight people began to open their hearts. The government finally acknowledged some responsibility to care for all its citizens, including those with AIDS. The tide was turning, and HRCF had helped to turn it. Nothing demonstrated this shift so dramatically as when, on November 8, 1997, I had the tremendous pleasure to join fifteen hundred lesbians, gay men, and their supporters at the first Human Rights Campaign National Dinner—addressed by President Bill Clinton.

Had Steve Endean lived long enough to witness President Clinton's speech on that November night in 1997, perhaps he would have contemplated the moon-shot challenge it was to get a sitting president to speak to lesbians and gays in the nation's capital—and relished the sweet achievement. He might have recalled the days he sat in the Minnesota Capitol's House and Senate galleries listening as his bills were debated and how he cringed as lesbians and gay men were described in the vilest terms. He might have thought of an early fundraising workshop he attended with Kerry Woodward, HRCF's first co-chair, before he moved to Washington to jumpstart the Gay Rights National Lobby.

"In that workshop," Kerry told me, "we were asked if we believed that our cause was an important national cause, not just one important to a small community. I remember Steve and I looked at each other and asked, 'Huh. Is it?' Of course, we thought gay rights was an important issue. But would others see it the way we did? Was it a *national* concern? And we actually weren't sure. That's where the movement was then."

Steve was smart. And he was doggedly determined. When he moved to Washington, D.C., in September 1978, his top priorities were to raise enough money to keep the Gay Rights National Lobby's doors open and figure out how to advance a lesbian and gay civil rights bill. His strategy included the direct education of legislators, building coalitions, developing significant grassroots political pressure, creating an effective communications vehicle, and establishing political clout to raise money and mobilize volunteers. In doing so, he initiated the three components we needed to influence Congress: lobbying, the political contributions, and constituent mobilization, realized in the Gay Rights National Lobby, the Human Rights Campaign Fund, and the Fairness Fund.

When I came on as the Human Rights Campaign Fund executive director, AIDS dominated our lives and our work all too soon. But Steve refused to abandon the gay civil rights agenda to concentrate exclusively on AIDS issues. He believed that getting a job and keeping it was of utmost importance, that the opportunity to be judged on the merits of one's work over some irrelevant aspect of private life was worth protecting.

"I'm probably going to die of AIDS someday," he told Minnesota state senator Allan Spear, "but my heart is still with the civil rights struggle. I can't just think about AIDS all the time."

Stephen Endean, the nation's first professional lobbyist for the lesbian and gay community, died August 4, 1993, at his home in Washington two days before his forty-fifth birthday. In April, he had been canvassing attendees at the 1993 March on Washington.

"He was spending ten hours a day out there with his clipboard and petitions," Terry Bean noted. "He believed so strongly that this was the way to make change that he was willing to do whatever it took."

"Few individuals made as great a contribution toward ending discrimination than Steve Endean," said Tim McFeeley.

Congressman Barney Frank called him "one of a handful of Americans who deserve the hero's mantle" for moving the fight for gay rights from street corners to the halls of Congress. "He has also been a genuine, living, breathing human being—who jokes, swears, schemes, gets mad, gets even, enjoys himself and enjoys his friends ... It is precisely these human qualities that have made him one of the most effective fighters for gay and lesbian rights in the history of this country."

Steve Endean's inspiration and dogged determination more than forty years ago contributed enormously to the progress—from the privilege to serve in the military to the opportunity to marry—LGBTQ people experience today. (Of course, with no national law, these rights are always at risk, so our fight continues.)

Gay activism took hold in the 1960s, born of the era's political radicalism and counterculture. Steve was the antithesis of those who wanted to revolutionize the system. He wanted to work within it. He believed honoring the political process was as critical to our success as the commitment to the issue. He insisted on lobbying Congress with respect for the legislative process, and he knew that change would not come quickly. This approach wouldn't get the headlines the street activists did. But he knew that working within the system would generate greater results than angry activism could.

He was right. Those of us who have walked the halls of Congress know from experience that change at the national level is a slow process and largely a quiet one, but one we now know to be a sure one.

That evening, I also reflected on my contribution. While Steve was the catalyst for the three components of the Human Rights Campaign, it fell to me to execute them.

I arrived in 1983 to head up a political action committee with a nearly empty bank account. That meant raising money—and a lot of it. But a PAC could only take us so far. I wanted to model HRCF on other successful mainstream political entities, and that meant incorporating lobbying and constituent mobilization. Saving the Gay Rights National Lobby from dissolution gave us the foundation for our lobbying effort on Capitol Hill. Acquiring the Fairness Fund provided the grassroots component. Under my leadership, HRCF also created the foundation, which educated elected officials and the public about important issues to the LGBTQ community—and gave donors a tax deduction.

All this cost money, and it was my job to raise it. Campaign contributions cost money. Outreach to grow our membership base month after month demanded an investment. Supporting a top-notch staff required making a growing payroll every two weeks. The black-tie dinners and major gifts contributed much of the funding, and they also contributed to our reputation as an elitist organization. But in this case, the ends justified the means, and knowing HRCF was called "the Human Rights Champagne Fund" by some was sarcasm I was willing to bear to achieve our mission.

Another significant accomplishment on my watch was building the political muscle to get legislation passed. In the six years I served as executive director, HRCF helped transform how Congress responded to the lesbian and gay community. We went from being derided by the homophobes in the House and Senate every time the issue of homosexuality came up to passing legislation, specifically S. 1220, and finally defeating Senator Helms's nefarious "no promo homo" amendments. As a result, our legislative victories accelerated over the next decade.

As I listened to President Clinton, it occurred to me that I fulfilled my life's mission by the time I was forty-three years old. Oh, I continued to serve our community, including co-founding the LGBTQ Victory Fund, an organization dedicated to electing openly LGBTQ candidates, and working in the Clinton and Obama Administrations. But nothing compared to the sense of purpose I got from my work with the Human Rights Campaign Fund as we were pioneering change and working desperately to save lives.

Had Steve been at the National Dinner with me the night Clinton spoke, I like to think we would have reminisced about the first black-tie dinner at the Waldorf-Astoria Hotel in New York just fifteen years earlier. The guest speaker, of course, was former Vice President Walter Mondale. In 1982, it was risky for anyone seeking national office to attend such an event, but Mr. Mondale came, and hundreds paid to hear him.

"Nothing like that had ever happened before,'" said Vivian Shapiro, who was on the dinner committee. "In that one night, everything seemed to change."

"Whether you know it or not," Mondale later wrote Steve,

"you were a very important person in shaping my views toward the gay community in our country."

Had Steve been at that dinner with me, perhaps he would have taken a moment to reflect on his monumental contributions that launched a movement for equality that has changed the lives of two generations of LGBTQ people. And then, perhaps, he would have smiled at how far we have come in what seems to some of us like an eternity—but really has been just the blink of an eye.

Every time we take a step forward in the struggle for equal rights, we should pause to give thanks to Steve Endean. — Joan Mondale, wife of former Vice President Walter Mondale at the HRCF Minneapolis Dinner, 1992

Epilogue

Now, nearly fifty years later, much has changed, and so many are gone. In the words of my dear friend Joe Tom Easley, "They are the ones on the shoulders of whom this movement rests."

Of the major national LGBTQ organizations active in politics in the 1980s, only a few remain other than the Human Rights Campaign. The National Gay Task Force (now the National LGBTQ Task Force) is still influential, as is the LGBTQ Victory Fund.

The Task Force has worked to end discrimination for half a century. I attribute its longevity in part to the strong foundation laid by Virginia Apuzzo, a dynamic executive director and my colleague when I headed up the Human Rights Campaign Fund. In fact, I considered her a mentor of sorts when I was just getting started. Ginny was a charismatic and effective leader, and this benefited the Task Force while she was there. But she did not build the organization into the powerhouse it could have become.

The Victory Fund, of which I was the principal founder, was modeled after EMILY's List, giving early money to LGBTQ candidates to get their campaigns up and running and to prime the campaigns to raise more.

While statewide groups have proliferated and are active across the country, HRC is the only national organization actively lobbying in Washington, D.C., on Capitol Hill for LGBTQ equality.

Many organizations dedicated to fighting the AIDS virus and getting support (finally) from the federal government are nearly gone now, including ACT UP. Many were vocal, even angry, groups conducting confrontational activities that people often found extreme and intimidating, even offensive. Their expressions of rage generated a lot of media attention, and I know they offered a necessary catharsis to those taking part. But I contend that decision-makers found screaming in churches and throwing fake blood on government employees' computers more offensive than welcome.

HRC favored practicing mainstream activism and pragmatic politics. We educated legislators and their staffs, we built coalitions, we grew grassroots support around the country, and elected LGBTQ-friendly candidates to Congress.

I assert that angry confrontation isn't as successful as heartfelt dialogue. It's the difference between war and diplomacy. That's a reason HRC is still here.

HRC also had the foresight, under the visionary leadership of Elizabeth Birch, to expand the HRC Foundation, broadening the mission and scope of HRC beyond political action. Today, the foundation offers a rich collection of programs intended to improve every aspect of life in the LGBTQ community, including:

- Supporting teens and youth, including training educators to create an LGBTQ-inclusive atmosphere in schools
- Research and education addressing misconceptions about transgender and gender non-conforming people
- Outreach to child welfare professionals, with a special emphasis on inclusion in foster care and adoption agencies
- Helping communities of faith to support members of our community and the Equality Act
- Working with Historically Black Colleges and Universities to establish LGBTQ-inclusive climates on HBCU campuses.
- Supporting the transgender, non-binary, and gender-expansive communities through the foundation's Transgender Justice Initiative with a particular emphasis on Black, Indigenous, and People of Color (BIPOC) community leaders
- Expanding the popular Corporate Equality Index (CEI), started during Elizabeth Birch's tenure, HRC offers a "Best Places to Work" designation recognizing those superior companies that provide an exemplary

environment for LGBTQ employees, going beyond good human resources policies and offering inclusive benefits.

And of course, the HRC Foundation still focuses on health. Its HIV & Health Equity program supports marginalized communities and those that are disproportionately affected by HIV. HRC also supports the needs of older LGBTQ adults in healthcare facilities, including long-term care communities.

Jay Brown leads a team of professionals who manage the HRC Foundation programs. I reached out to him for a current update on the progress made and the ongoing prejudice we're still confronting.

As I write this in 2022, Jay told me some twenty million people identify openly as LGBTQ, including one in five members of Generation Z, born after 1997. Young people today identify with more fluid, nonbinary senses of gender and sexuality. Still, they face in 2022 the impact of an increasingly polarized society and a resurgence of the discrimination and attacks our community confronted in the 1980s. Transgender people are particularly at risk.

HRC and the foundation continue to work to combat this prejudice and generate support for equality in the general population. Sincere acceptance comes most deeply as it did at the height of the AIDS crisis—from knowing someone who is LGBTQ. "To know us is to love us" still holds true today—no more so than for members of our transgender community.

As long as there is a need to protest discrimination and drive inclusion, HRC will continue the work, Jay told me. "We are pushing for inclusive and diverse representation in a variety of platforms. But we are still protestors, and we will continue to march in the street and call out bad actors in ways that may look aggressive."

Sadly, much is still the same today. As I started writing this book, the world shut down to protect as many people as possible from contracting a deadly virus, getting sick, and dying. With the COVID-19 virus, it took a matter of weeks, not years, for the government to respond. (I certainly believe that the response was inadequate, under-funded, and without the full resources of the federal government, but that's not my point. The government *responded*.) In about a year, the FDA approved emergency use for a vaccine. But still there is no vaccine for AIDS.

And our community is once again fighting discrimination from fundamentalists and right-wing politicians. We need laws to deter discrimination in employment, foster care and adoption, housing, education, school sports, medical care, even public accommodations. The LGBTQ community still does not have full protection under federal law, and we cannot count on the Supreme Court of the United States, under the current political climate, to make sure we do.

Despite these threats to our freedom, the future for lesbians, gays, bisexuals, transgender, and queer people overall is bright. I hope the action in conservative states is a transitory setback.

Public opinion has clearly shifted in our favor, especially with young people. I share Joe Tom Easley's words of welcome to you personally and his encouragement to join us in our work: "There's so much more to be done. So, let's roll up our sleeves and let's get to work and make the lives of lesbians and gays of today what it ought to be."

Acknowledgments

Jim Hormel was of great support to me in preserving the early years of the Human Rights Campaign in this book. I'm sad to say he died before he could read it. Throughout my career, much of which required raising money, he always responded affirmatively to my requests, whether they were desperate pleas to make payroll or to support LGBTQ and AIDS causes. Jim will always be known as a philanthropist, an opportunity he told me he considered "a privilege." I will remember him as my friend.

Joe Tom Easley was also a friend, but he was so much more than that. What I think about most often is his loving, affectionate manner, his humility and loyalty to friends, his sense of humor and his unshakable political values. For over forty years, he supported, mentored, and encouraged me in nearly everything I did, including the writing of this book. He died unexpectedly, and I miss him now more than words can express.

Winston Johnson was as kind, attentive, and gentle a soul as I have ever known. He was also a fearless and fierce advocate for LGBT equality. I frequently called on him for help with these chapters, and even though his health was failing, he always found the energy to read them, make excellent suggestions, and cheer me on. He died, too, before he could see this book, but not before he declared that it would be a valuable contribution to recording LGBTQ history.

Jim, Edie Cofrin, and Terry Bean generously contributed to this work and for that, I am deeply grateful.

To my friend Chuck Middleton I owe enormous gratitude for his early encouragement and invaluable guidance.

Special thanks for Barney Frank for writing the foreword to this book and for his insightful comments on its contents.

Many thanks to Tom Bastow, Terry Bean, Kathryn Berenson, Michael Berman, Elizabeth Birch, Joe Blount, Jay Brown, Larry Bye, Joe Cantor, Edie Cofrin, Philip Dufour, Steven Dwyer, Joe Tom Easley, Joan Eisenstodt, Anthony Fauci, Peter Fenn, Elliot Fishman, Chuck Forester, Barney Frank, Mike Grossman, Jim Hormel, Andy Humm, Winston Johnson, Michael Iskowitz, Vic Kamber, Gregory King, Peter Kovar, Ellen Malcolm, Michael McConnell, Tim McFeeley, Kate McQueen, Cathy Nelson, Patricia Neubeller, Troy Perry, Don Randolph, Hilary Rosen, Eric Rosenthal, Bob Sass, John Scagliotti, Vivian Shapiro, Steve Shellabarger, Judy Shepard, Christopher Speron, Sean Strub, Sandy Thurman, Susi Walsh, Tim Westmoreland, and Kerry Woodward. They provided crucial support or gave freely of their time, sharing invaluable memories that made this story more accurate and complete.

I am especially grateful to Elizabeth Birch, Terry Bird, Joe Cantor, Steven Dwyer, Gregory King, and Andrea Sharrin for authoring profiles of some of the people who were instrumental in laying the foundation on which today's HRC is built.

Very special thanks to Fabrizio Claudio, Mary Ann Pryor, Noel McCaman, Edie Cofrin, Dennis Lonergan, Cathy Nelson, Chuck Forester, Judy Shepard, Ray Mulliner, Jeff Trammell, and Bob Witeck whose friendship, support, and encouragement made all the difference.

It took more years than I care to admit nurturing an idea into an actual book, and that never would have happened without the incredible help of my collaborator, Donna Mosher. But for her persistence, candor, great skill, and gentle prodding, the book would still be a work in progress. I am deeply indebted to her for making it a reality.

JEREMY LEÓN

About the Author

Vic Basile has dedicated his life in whatever way and however small to bending that long moral arc of the universe toward justice.

Vic has enjoyed the rare opportunity and extraordinary privilege of a career of public service and social justice advocacy. A widely recognized national leader in the LGBT community, he has committed his efforts to guaranteeing equality for this constituency.

His initial work as a VISTA Volunteer community organizer in the rural South set him on a course of public service and advocacy. During the Obama Administration, he served as the Senior Counselor to the director of the United States Office of Personnel Management. In that role, he was the director's principal lead on all LGBTQ issues affecting the civil service.

Throughout the 1970s and early eighties, he held positions at ACTION, the former umbrella agency for the Peace Corps and VISTA. While there, he became a labor activist on behalf of federal employees.

After coming out, he transferred his energy and experience to the struggle for gay, lesbian, bisexual, and transgender equality. He served as the first executive director of the Human Rights Campaign. He later co-founded the LGBTQ Victory Fund to help openly LGBTQ candidates get the money and support they need to win elective office.

In the mid-nineties, he did capacity-building consulting with many local and national nonprofits. During that time, he co-executive produced the award-winning documentary *After Stonewall* and the PBS series *In the Life*.

In 1998, Vic returned to his volunteer roots by accepting a Clinton Administration appointment as Director of Private Sector Cooperation and International Volunteerism at the Peace Corps.

Before returning to the federal government in 2009, he was the executive director of Moveable Feast, Inc., a Baltimore-based nonprofit serving the HIV/AIDS community. Now retired, he lives in Chevy Chase, Maryland, with his partner, Fabrizio Claudio.

Appendix

ORIGINAL BOARD OF DIRECTORS OF THE GAY RIGHTS NATIONAL LOBBY

Kate McQueen, Co-chair	South Portland, ME
Jerry Weller, Co-chair	Portland, OR
Paul Kuntzler, Treasurer	Washington, D.C.
Jean O'Leary, Exec. Comm.	Los Angeles, CA
Pokey Anderson	Houston, TX
Virginia Apuzzo	New York City, NY
Terry Bean	Eugene, OR
Dan Bradley	Miami, FL
Larry Bye	San Francisco, CA
Jack Campbell	Miami, FL
State Rep. Karen Clark	Minneapolis, MN
Gwen Craig	San Francisco, CA
R. Adam DeBaugh	Silver Spring, MD
Karen DeCrow	Syracuse, NY
Kathy Deitsch	San Antonio, TX
Meryl Friedman	Brooklyn, NY
Barbara Gittings	Philadelphia, PA
Mary Hartman	Minneapolis, MN
Cathie Hartnett	Washington, D.C.
Franklin Kameny	Washington, D.C.
Rev. Troy D. Perry	Los Angeles, CA
Chuck Renslow	Chicago, IL
Roz Richter	New York City, NY

Rev. Jim Sandmire — San Francisco, CA
Frank Scheuren — Atlanta, GA
Leanne Seibert — Coral Gables, FL
State Senator Allan Spear — Minneapolis, MN
Bruce Voeller — New York City, NY
Claude Winfield — New York City, NY
Louise Young — Dallas, TX

FIRST BOARD OF DIRECTORS OF THE HUMAN RIGHTS CAMPAIGN FUND

Kerry Woodward, Co-chair — Oakland, CA
Jerry Berg, Co-chair — San Francisco, CA
Steve Endean, Treasurer — Washington, D.C.
Virginia Apuzzo — New York City, NY
Jack Campbell — Miami, FL
Dallas Coors — Rhode Island
Gilberto Gerald — Washington, D.C.
Ethan Geto — New York City, NY
Rev. Elder Jeri Ann Harvey — Los Angeles, CA
Jim Hormel — San Francisco, CA
Paul Kuntzler — Washington, D.C.
Bettie Naylor — Austin, TX
Lois Galgay Reckett — South Portland, ME
Jerry Weller — Portland, OR

The War Conference was a success before it even started. The committee members represented a diversity of organizations, all willing to come together to mobilize gay America.

War Conference Organizing Committee

ROGER ANDERSON
Los Angeles

VIC BASILE
Executive Director
Human Rights Campaign Fund

PAUL BONNBERG
Mobilization Against AIDS

DAN BRADLEY
Miami

SHERRIE COHEN
Executive Director
Fund for Human Dignity

PAT CHRISTEN
Public Policy Director
San Francisco AIDS Foundation

DUKE COMEGYS
Co-Chair
Human Rights Campaign Fund

CRAIG DAVIDSON
Executive Director
Gay & Lesbian Alliance Against Defamation

JOE TOM EASLEY
Chair
Lambda Legal Defense and Education Fund and
HRCF Foundation Board Member

PAULA ETTELBRICK
Lambda Legal Defense and Education Fund

AVRUM FINKELSTEIN
Silence = Death

CHUCK FORESTER
Co-chair
Human Rights Campaign Fund
San Francisco

ANDY HUMM
Hetrick-Martin Institute

JOYCE HUNTER
National March on Washington
Steering Committee

HOWARD KATZ
HRCF Board Member
New York

JEFF LEVI
Executive Director
National Gay & Lesbian Task Force

MARIE MANION
East End Gay Organization

NICOLE MURRAY RAMIREZ
San Diego

HON. TOM NOLAN
Supervisor
San Mateo County, California

TORIE OSBORN
Los Angeles

JEAN O'LEARY
Executive Director
National Gay Rights Advocates

LOIS GALGAY RECKITT
Deputy Executive Director
Human Rights Campaign Fund

ERIC ROFES
Executive Director
Gay & Lesbian Community Services Center
of Los Angeles

MICHAEL ROSANO
City Council President's Office
New York City

BEN SHATZ
National Gay Rights Advocates

VIVIAN SHAPIRO
Co-chair
Human Rights Campaign Fund
New York

MICHAEL SHOWER
HRCF Board Member and
UNICEF

TOM STODDARD
Executive Director
Lambda Legal Defense and Education Fund

TIM SWEENEY
Deputy Executive Director for Policy
Gay Men's Health Crisis

ROBIN TYLER
Los Angeles/Provincetown

PAUL VAN SOUDER
Executive Director
People With AIDS Coalition (NY)

ROSE WALTON
State University of New York-Stoney Brooke

STEVEN WEBB
Silence = Death

TIM WOLFRED
Executive Director
San Francisco AIDS Foundation

INDEX

Abzug, Bella, 8, 21, 25, 202, 204
acquired immune deficiency syndrome. *See* AIDS
ACTION, 62, 65
Advocate, The, 8–9, 26, 35, 50, 53, 56
AFL-CIO, 63, 121, 133
AFSCME. *See* American Federation of State, County, and Municipal Employees
After Dark, 42
AIDS, 3, 4, 16, 32, 50. *See also* Human Rights Campaign Fund (HRCF)
   azidothymidine (AZT), 134, 159–163
   bathhouses, 53–54, 59
   Bush on, 78
   civil disobedience/demonstration/protests, 75–78
   Columbus, 166–167
   deaths, 52, 53, 55, 74, 76, 130, 190, 195
   discrimination against people with, 191
   Endean on, 55
   Falwell on, 53
   Goodstein on, 53
   government funding for, 45, 47, 72, 131
   government response to, 51–52, 73–74, 78, 139–140 (*see also* Clinton, Bill; Reagan, Ronald)
   HRCF's fundraising program, 71–72
   New York Native ad, 54–55
   New York Times story on, 51
   research and treatment, 147
AIDS Campaign Trust, 71, 131–132, 135, 186

AIDS Coalition to Unleash Power (ACT UP), 84, 128, 136, 155, 165, 186, 217
AIDS Research and Information Act (S1220), 85–86, 93, 176
Alfandre, Bob, 32, 37, 96–98
Allen, Leon, 104, 105
Altschul, Laura, 196
American Federation of State, County, and Municipal Employees (AFSCME), 34, 62, 63–64, 66, 135
American Foundation for AIDS Research (amfAR), 85, 92, 127, 133, 138
Americans with Disabilities Act, 191
Andelson, Sheldon, 107
Anderson, Wendell, 6
Anglin, Mike, 95–96
Ann, Mary, 61
Anti-Defamation League, 182
Apuzzo, Virginia, 76, 217
Aspin, Les, 199
AuCoin, Les, 23
azidothymidine (AZT), 134, 159–163

Baez, Joan, 25
Baker, James A., 40
Baron, Alan, 35–38, 39–43
Baron Report, The, 35, 39, 40, 42
bathhouses, 53–54, 59
Bauer, Gary, 83
Bayh, Birch, 31
Bean, Terry, 14, 17, 83, 208, 213
Bearse, Amanda, 207
Beatty, Warren, 41
Begala, Paul, 48
Bentsen, Lloyd, 141

Berg, Jerry, 26, 33, 86
Berkowitz, Richard, 92
Bernardo, Billy, 71
Birch, Elizabeth, 1, 100, 114–116, 187, 188, 204, 205–211, 218
black-tie dinners, 25, 30–34, 94–103, 107, 109, 118, 131, 184, 202, 215
Blount, Joe, 111
B'nai B'rith, 209
Bode, Ken, 41
Bond, Julian, 36–37
Boozer, Mel, 59
Bork, Robert, 122, 144–146
Bostock v Clayton County, 204
Bradley, Dan, 30, 33, 50, 66, 79–80, 161–162, 163
   addressing AIDS potesters, 76
   co-chair of HRCF board, 73
   HIV positive/AIDS, 73, 77
   Legal Services Corporation, 79–80
   personality, 74
   prediction, 118, 119, 120
   on Reagan's inaction on AIDS, 73–74
Braithwaite, Marilyn, 131
Breast and Cervical Cancer Mortality Prevention Act, 195
Broder, David, 40
Brown, Jay, 219
Brown, Jerry, 41, 199, 219
Bryant, Anita, 11–14, 16–17, 54, 59, 95
Bumpers, Dale, 40
Burton, Phillip, 130
Bush, George H.W., 78, 108, 113, 191, 192
Bush, Larry, 50, 56, 120
Bye, Larry, 14, 17, 18, 25–26, 86, 129

Callen, Michael, 92
Campbell, Jack, 9, 13, 17, 58–59, 83, 103
Cantor, Joe, 22–23, 32
Carter, Jimmy, 12, 15–16, 33, 79, 105
CBS Reports: The Homosexuals, 2
Celeste, Dagmar, 107
Centers for Disease Control (CDC), 51, 52, 130, 150–151, 190
   Task Force on Kaposi Sarcoma and Opportunistic Infections, 147
Chapman, Jim, 191, 192
Charles, Otis, 36
Cheney, Dick, 198
Cher, 207
Chernoff, Marty, 121
Church, Frank, 31
Civil Rights Act of 1964, 21, 204

Clendinen, Dudley, 43
Clinton, Bill, 1, 47, 48, 93, 100, 138, 188–189, 195, 196–198, 199, 201, 210–212, 215
Club Baths, 54, 58
Cochran, Thad, 193–194
Coelho, Tony, 143
Cofrin, Edie, 111–112, 208–209
Collins, Marvin, 108, 109, 110, 112–113
Columbus, Ohio, 108–109
Comegys, Duke, 74–75, 85, 107, 142
Concerned Americans for Individual Rights, 16
Congressional Action Alert system, 183
Constituent Lobby Day, 24
Cooper, Ted, 32
Coors, Dallas, 26, 28–29, 83
Corporate Equality Index (CEI), 207, 217–218
Cosper, Todd, 70
Costanza, Midge, 12, 76
COVID-19, 53, 100, 219
Cracker Barrel, 202
Crane, Phil, 16
Cranston, Alan, 31
Crinkley, Richmond, 133–134, 159–162
Curran, James, 146–147

Dade County Coalition for the Humanistic Rights of Gays (DCCHR), 58–59
Dannemeyer, William, 130, 142, 148–149, 152
DeGeneres, Betty, 1, 208
DeGeneres, Ellen, 1, 207–208
Democratic Farm Labor party, 8
Democrats, 117–120. *See also* Clinton, Bill
   election of 1980, 31
   dinners. *See* black-tie dinners
discrimination in hiring, 202
Dobson, James, 83
"Does Support for Gay Rights Spell Political Suicide?," 22–23
Dolan, Terry, 16, 31, 45
Donahue, 80
Donahue, Phil, 184
"Don't Ask, Don't Tell" policy, 198
Drake, Dwight, 196
Dronenburg, James L., 144
Dronenburg v. Zech, 144
Dufour, Philip, 70, 76, 100, 110, 184, 197

Easley, Joe Tom, 66, 168–170

final statement of War Conference, 170, 172–175
Eastern Airlines (EAL), 104–106
Eichberg, Rob, 169
Eisenhower, Dwight, 2
Eisenstodt, Joan, 100
EMILY's List, 71, 90, 101, 217
Employment Non-Discrimination Act (ENDA), 203–204
"Employment of Homosexuals and Other Sex Perverts," 2
Endean, Steve, 5–10, 14, 18–19, 24, 75, 83, 87, 132–133, 206. *See also* Gay Rights National Lobby (GRNL); Human Rights Campaign Fund (HRCF)
  accusations and criticism, 50, 56, 120
  Advocate, The on, 55
  AFL-CIO, 121
  Bean on, 213
  Bush on, 55
  death, 132, 213
  election (campaigns) of 1982, 50, 55, 56, 83
  Frank on, 213–214
  gay civil rights bill, 5–10
  McFeeley on, 213
  Mondale on, 215–216
  National Mailgram Campaign, 183
  pragmatic politics strategy, 19–20
  resignation from GRNL, 50, 56–57
  vision, 32
  Washingtonian on, 55
  Washington Post on, 55
Episcopal Church, 12
Equality Act, 204

Fairchild, Morgan, 101
Fairness Fund, 122–123, 127, 132, 153, 179, 181, 183, 190, 213, 214
Falwell, Jerry, 14–16, 31, 32, 80
Family Research Council, 83
Farrell, Mike, 33
Fauci, Anthony, 154–155, 160, 178
Federal Club, 109–112, 113, 114, 135, 155, 200
Federal Election Campaign Act of 1971, 25
Federal Elections Commission, 186
Feinstein, Dianne, 33, 86
Fisher, Mary, 193
Foglietta, Tom, 44
Forester, Chuck, 86–87
Foster, Jim, 9, 11, 32, 33, 53, 56, 86, 95

Frank, Barney, 41
  on Dannemeyer, 148–149
  Endean and, 45, 46, 213–214
  HRCF, 47
  Immigration Act of 1990, 195
  progressive causes, 46
  reelection campaign of 1982, 45
Fraser, Donald, 36
Furlong, Tim, 82, 129, 141, 142, 143, 145, 183

gay civil rights bill, 5–10, 31, 202–203
gay civil rights ordinances, 11–17, 18, 125, 135, 201
Gay Freedom Day parades, San Francisco, 6
Gay Men's Health Crisis, 149, 176
gay-related immunodeficiency (GRID), 52
Gay Rights Legislative Committee, 7
Gay Rights National Lobby (GRNL), 9, 18, 19–21, 24–26, 31, 45, 50, 55, 56, 57, 60, 61, 83, 109, 120–122, 127, 129, 130, 133
  advisory board, 25
  LCCR, 133
  merged with HRCF, 82, 88
  NGTF lobbying against, 20
  progressive organizations and, 182
  volunteer field associates, 24
Gelpi, Michael, 68, 110
Gerald, Gil, 117
Geto, Ethan, 34
Girls in Pearls, 192, 193, 194
Goodstein, David, 8–9, 18, 20, 26, 32, 33, 35, 50, 53, 55–56, 86, 120, 123, 169
Gore, Al, 100, 197
Gottlieb, Michael S., 127
Graupera, George, 186
Green, Bob, 13
Greer, Sue, 87
Griswold v. Connecticut, 144
GRNL. *See* Gay Rights National Lobby
Grossman, Mike, 109–110

Hannaford, Peter, 41
Harkin, Tom, 199
Harrington, Michael, 25
Hartman, Ray, 9, 18
Hatch, Orrin, 177–178, 180, 192
hate crime, 194–195
Hate Crime Statistics Act, 192, 195
Hatter, Terry J., Jr., 197–198

Heche, Anne, 1
Height, Dorothy, 1
Helms, Jesse, 16, 32, 130, 142, 148, 149–151, 152, 153, 162, 163, 176–177, 179–180, 192, 194, 215
Henderson, Wade, 1
Herman, Jerry, 184, 185
Hofstede, Albert J., 8
Hongisto, Richard, 33
Hormel, James, 1, 26, 83, 86, 197
"How to Have Sex in an Epidemic," 92
HRCF NET, 183
Hudson, Rock, 125–127
Human Rights Campaign Fund (HRCF), 1, 3–4, 19, 26, 27
   agenda, 181–182
   as an elitist organization, 215
   being bipartisan, 44
   black-tie dinners, 25, 30–34, 94–103, 107, 109, 118, 131, 184, 202, 215
   board/board members, 67–68
   building, 209–210
   celebrities/high-profile emissaries, 207–208
   computerized bulletin board, 183
   corporate repositioning, 206
   critical pillars, 120
   Federal Club, 109–114, 135, 155, 200
   Federal Elections Commission on, 186
   fundraising, 72, 83–84
   growth and influence, 3
   military's anti-gay ban, 197–201
   programs offered, 218–219
   sharing (activity), 67
   Western Union vs., 201–202
Human Rights Campaign (HRC), 1, 3–4
Human Rights Campaign National Dinner, 1, 100, 188, 210–211, 212, 215
Human Rights Ordinance of Boston, 191
Hunt, Alan, 41

"I Am What I Am," 185
Immigration Act of 1990, 195
Imperial Court of Nebraska, 88
Insiders Group. See Federal Club
International AIDS Conference, 75
International Imperial Court System (IICS), 88
International Lesbian and Gay Human Rights Commission, 93
"International Male," 42
Iskowitz, Michael, 178

Jackson, Jesse, 101, 118
Jarmin, Gary, 16
Johns Committee of Florida, 3
Johnson, Mary Lea, 126
Johnson, Winston, 102, 104–106

Kameny, Frank, 18, 76
Kaposi sarcoma lesions, 71
Kennedy, Anthony M., 145, 146
Kennedy, Edward, 31, 93, 144–145
Kennedy, John F., 40
Kennedy, John F., Jr., 39
Kennedy, Ted, 39, 41, 176, 177–178, 180, 192, 193
Kerrey, Bob, 199
killer amendment, 179–181
King, Coretta Scott, 102–103
King, Martin Luther, Jr., 62, 76, 103
Kinsolving, Lester, 51–52
Kirk, Paul, 118–119
Kirk, Ron, 115
Klose, Randy, 78, 81–82, 84–86, 92–93, 107, 123, 142, 196
Knutson, Donald, 93
Koop, C. Everett, 130, 154, 178
Koppel, Ted, 30–31, 163
Kramer, Larry, 76, 84, 136, 155, 186
Krim, Arthur, 137
Krim, Mathilde, 85, 127, 133–134, 137–138, 159, 193
Kuchling, Ray, 95, 96, 115
Kuntzler, Paul, 18

LaHaye, Tim, 16
Lawrence v. Texas, 145
LCCR (Leadership Conference on Civil Rights), 133, 203
Leadership Conference on Civil Rights (LCCR), 1, 25, 133, 135, 182, 203
Lear, Norman, 41
Lee, Carlton, 112, 143, 144, 183
Legal Services Corporation, 79–80
Legionnaires' Disease, 52, 53
Lesbian and Gay Civil Rights Bill, 184
Lewis, Ann, 117
Lewis, John, 62–63
LGBTQ Victory Fund, 215, 217
Lincoln, Abraham, 76
Lodge, Dick, 118
Lonergan, Dennis, 75
Los Angeles Times, 138
Lucy, Bill, 34, 63–65, 135

MacNeil-Lehrer News Hour, 39
mailgrams, 121–124, 153, 179, 181, 183, 200–202
Malcolm, Ellen, 71, 90
March on Washington (1963), 103
March on Washington (1979), 24
March on Washington (1987), 165, 169
March on Washington (1993), 213
Matlovich, Leonard, 76
McCleary, Don, 110–111, 114–116
McCloskey, Pete, 20
McFeeley, Tim, 187, 190–192, 195, 196, 197, 198, 200, 201, 202, 203, 204, 213
McGovern, George, 31, 33, 40
McPherson, Harry, 118
MedPac, 159
Meinhold, Keith, 197–198
Metropolitan Community Church (MCC), 12
Mikulski, Barbara, 27
military's ban on homosexuals, 20
Minnesota
  human rights law, 8
  law on oral and anal sex, 7
Mixner, David, 76, 199
Mondale, Joan, 216
Mondale, Walter, 30, 31, 33, 42, 94–95, 118, 215–216
Moral Majority, 15, 24, 31, 46, 50
Moscone, George, 33
Moynihan, Daniel, 31, 40
Moynihan, Patrick, 150
Mulley, Ken, 118
Municipal Elections Committee of Los Angeles (MECLA), 94
Muskie, Edmund S., 40

Nagourney, Adam, 43
National Academy of Sciences, 130
National Coming Out Day, 169, 210
National Congressional Club, 177
National Conservative Political Action Committee (NCPAC), 16, 24, 31
National Gay Rights Advocates, 76
National Gay Task Force (NGTF), 20, 120, 166, 179, 217
National Institutes of Health, 85, 93, 159–160, 181
National Journal, 39
National Lesbian and Gay Health Conference in Los Angeles, 74–75
National Mailgram Campaign, 183
National Organization for Women, 121

National Restaurant Association, 191
New York Avenue Presbyterian Church, 76
New York Native, 54–55
New York Times, The, 34, 138
Nightline, 30, 34, 49
"no promo homo" amendments, 177, 179
Norton, Eleanor Holmes, 101
Novak, Robert, 41
Nunn, Sam, 199

Ohio Education Association, 69
O'Leary, Jean, 9, 76, 169
"Operation Lift the Ban," 200
Out for Good (Clendinen and Nagourney), 43

Pease, Larry, 111
Perry, Troy, 9, 12, 58, 76, 179
political action committees (PAC), 3, 15, 25–27, 83
Powell, Colin, 198
Presbyterian Church, 12, 76
Profiles in Courage (Kennedy), 40
Proxmire, William, 162–163

Quinn, Patrick, 185

Randolph, Don, 88, 90, 91, 121
Rauh, Joseph, 25
Reagan, Ronald, 15, 16, 31, 40, 41, 44, 46, 52, 73–76, 78, 80, 81, 82, 90, 126, 130–131, 138, 140, 144, 145, 149, 155, 159, 165, 177, 181
religious right, 13, 14, 15, 19, 20, 23, 24, 32, 43, 50, 53, 120, 197
Republicans, 44. *See also* Reagan, Ronald
  election of 1980, 31, 46
  Legal Services, 80
Reynolds, Nancy Clark, 82
Richards, Ann, 101, 115
Richards, Marty, 126
Robb, Chuck, 198
Robison, James, 15
Romer v. Evans, 145
Rosen, Hilary, 82, 88, 129, 135, 136, 141, 143, 144, 161, 183
Rosenthal, Eric, 88, 89, 129, 131, 132, 182, 184
Russert, Tim, 40
Ryan, Phil, 168
Ryan White CARE Act, 192, 193

Sachse, Jeff, 209
Sass, Bob, 86
Save Our Children campaign, 13, 14, 59, 95
Schlafly, Phyllis, 16
Schneider, William, 41
Shapiro, Vivian, 34, 71, 74, 95, 101, 111, 134, 153, 156–158, 170, 215
Shellabarger, Steve, 67, 68–69, 87, 107, 109, 110, 166
Shepard, Matthew, 2
Shower, Michael, 165–167
Silvestri, Tony, 44, 66
Sledz, Carroll, 96, 99
Smith, Joe, 44
Smith, Steve, 70, 112, 143, 144, 183
Smoot Construction, 209
Sonnabend, Joseph, 92
Speakes, Larry, 51–52
Speak Out, 122–124, 153, 200, 201
Spear, Allan, 213
Spears, John, 41
Speron, Chris, 209–210
Spiegel, John, 36
Steinem, Gloria, 25, 37, 184
Stephenson, Adlai, 40
Stoddard, Tom, 199
Stonewall Inn, 3
Strub, Sean, 37–38, 42, 76
Studds, Gerry, 23, 101
Summerville, Cheryl, 202
Surgeon General's Report on Acquired Immune Deficiency Syndrome, The, 154
Swift, Killian, 131

Taylor, Elizabeth, 85, 127, 138
Terrell, Randolph, 111
Thomas, John, 68, 95–96
Thurman, Sandra, 192–194
Truman, Harry, 188
Tsongas, Paul, 31, 195–196
Tulsa, Oklahoma, 11–12, 14

Union of America Hebrew Congregations, 12
Unitarian Universalists, 12
United Church of Christ, 12
United States v. Windsor, 145
U.S. Catholic Conference, 133
U.S. Supreme Court, 21, 102
  Bostock v Clayton County, 204
  Griswold v. Connecticut, 144
  Lawrence v. Texas, 145
  Romer v. Evans, 145
  United States v. Windsor, 145

Vaid, Urvashi, 76
Valeska, Lucia, 20
Van Buren, Abigail, 184
Viguerie, Richard, 41
Voeller, Bruce, 9, 20

Wachs, Joel, 36
Wallace, George C., 119
Wallace, Mike, 2
Wall Street Journal, The, 39
War Conference, 164–175
  final statement, 170, 172–175
  initiatives, 169
  National Coming Out Day, 169
Washington Blade, The, 50, 56
Washington Post, The, 34, 39, 179, 194
Watanabe, Terry, 88–89, 90, 91, 121
Waxman, Henry, 130–131, 140, 141, 146–147, 148, 149, 159, 181, 184, 186
Weaver, Dick, 96
Weaver, Jim, 31–32, 36
Weicker, Claudia, 161–162, 163
Weicker, Lowell, 31, 44, 85, 93, 142–143, 148, 150, 161, 162–163, 180
Weiser, Tom, 19
Weiss, Ted, 55, 130, 140, 141, 148, 184, 186
Weller, Jerry, 9, 65
Western Union, 121, 201–202
Westheimer, Ruth, 184–186
Westmoreland, Tim, 146
Wexler, Anne, 82
Wexler Reynolds, 82–83, 143, 178–179
Weyrich, Paul, 16
Whitman-Walker Clinic, 98–99
Wiesel, Elie, 107
Williams, Bob, 191–192
Williams, Tennessee, 37–38, 42
Woodward, Kerry, 14, 17, 18, 24, 26, 33, 45, 212–213
WorkNet, 207

Printed in the USA
CPSIA information can be obtained
at www.ICGtesting.com
JSHW020737101023
49924JS00004B/13

9 798985 034165